THE EROTIC BIRD

THE EROTIC BIRD

PHENOMENOLOGY IN LITERATURE

Maurice Natanson

With a foreword by Judith Butler

PRINCETON UNIVERSITY PRESS   PRINCETON, NEW JERSEY

Copyright © 1998 by Princeton University Press
Published by Princeton University Press, 41 William Street,
Princeton, New Jersey 08540
In the United Kingdom: Princeton University Press, Chichester, West Sussex
All Rights Reserved

Library of Congress Cataloging-in-Publication Data

Natanson, Maurice Alexander, 1924–
The erotic bird : phenomenology in literature / Maurice Natanson ;
with a foreword by Judith Butler.
p.   cm.
Includes bibliographical references and index.
ISBN 0-691-01219-9 (cl : alk. paper)
1. Philosophy and literature. 2. Phenomenology in literature.
3. Phenomenology and literature. 4. Literature, Modern—History and
criticism. I. Title.
PN49.N35   1997   97-19372
809′.93384—dc21   CIP

This book has been composed in Galliard

Princeton University Press books are printed on acid-free paper and
meet the guidelines for permanence and durability of the Committee
on Production Guidelines for Book Longevity of the Council on
Library Resources

http://pup.princeton.edu

Printed in the United States of America

10 9 8 7 6 5 4 3 2 1

Kathy Victoria Natanson

Her miniature railroad
Standing in front of her;
Wearing an engineer's cap,
She holds up one hand—
The palm showing—
An adult woman,
Looking at you directly,
A greeting of acknowledgment
From a being unto death,
Calling for nothing,
But giving everything left
A smile can provide:
The right to farewell,
The right to recognition,
The right to wave back,
As trainmen always do.
In that moment of forgiveness,
The world shatters us
In the acceptance
Of what is transient:
The present as a hurtling
And an irremediable hurt.

Contents

Foreword

JUDITH BUTLER

THE USUAL TASK of a foreword is to give a context for the work that follows, to tie that work to what is familiar, and to provide a set of illustrative examples as points of entry into the work at hand. But I am struck by the impossibility of fulfilling such a task in relation to Maurice Natanson's *The Erotic Bird: Phenomenology in Literature*. Natanson's text does not presume that the reader has been engaged in the exegesis of phenomenology for several decades, but begins with examples, anecdotes, passages, and other fragments from the everyday. In that way, it would make no sense to add anecdote to anecdote in the effort to make this theory familiar. But more important, the familiar is precisely what is put into question by this text. Natanson's text refuses to offer the context for its own reading precisely because *The Erotic Bird* asks its reader to suspend belief in ordinary contexts. In order to understand what is written here the reader may well have to suspend beliefs about what literature is, what phenomenology is, and where the encounter between philosophy and literature takes place.

Phenomenology has been dismissed by some as a philosophy of "consciousness," where the presumption reigns that "consciousness" is a speculative and psychologistic notion, unnecessary or a diversion in relation to literary reading. Such arguments, however, presume that they know what they mean by consciousness: that it is an interior and ideal "stream" of perceptions, the property of a subjectivity cut off ontologically from a relationship to the world. Such notions, however, have little to do with the notion of consciousness offered here.

Following Husserl's theory of intentionality, Natanson argues that consciousness consists rather in a series of acts, repeated through time and temporalized in their very structure. Such acts posit objects within the horizons of the life-world, which is not to say that those objects or the life-world are produced by the mind as its sole effects. The world is irreversibly there, populated with objects for consciousness, but it is only "there" in the manner of being meant or intended. To be "intended" within phenomenological terms is not to be the object of a conscious wish: it is to be constituted, built up, through a series of acts. The thereness of objectness is made plain to a consciousness that intends or constitutes those objects, but it would be wrong to assume that consciousness manufactures those objects. It performs a paradoxical exercise, building up what is already there, at once layering what is disclosed, constituting the given. In this sense, the givenness of objects is made plain only for a consciousness that is structured as a corollary to the world itself. Intentionality thus characterizes a certain isomorphism between consciousness and its world, one that cannot be spatially grasped. This was the meaning of intentionality that entranced William James as well, and which he traces to the scholastic tradition. It is also the relationship that Merleau-Ponty once described as an "embrace of the world."

The notion that consciousness belongs solely to the domain of subjectivity thus misses the phenomenological point that subjectivity always belongs to the world: consciousness is always consciousness *of* its object, it is nothing without its preposition, and its preposition marks its kinship with the world that it interrogates. Consciousness is, thus, in its very structure, in an implicit relation to the world it seeks to know, and seeks to know that world precisely to the extent that it is "of" it in some way. What this means is that the terms of subjectivity that we often imagine to be residing in a psychic interiority, such as consciousness, memory, and imagination are to be found precisely in a constitutive and binding relation to the world, intentional relations that posit a world they do not make, that build up a world of objects whose thereness is disclosed as irrefutable.

If one is to look for this intentional structure of consciousness, one would have to consult the relations established by the preposition that follows it; in other words, one would have to ask, what is consciousness "of"? Thus, the turn to the object is the turn to consciousness, but not in any ordinary sense. The turn to the object is one that effectively sets the object into relief from its ordinary context, de-naturalizing the object, as it were, in order to gain access to its essential structure. Setting the object into relief, suspending one's everyday understanding of what the object is, becomes the route by which consciousness takes stock of itself as constituting the object at hand. What is constituted about the object only becomes clear on the condition of such a de-realization of its status, a suspension of the web of beliefs within which it is ordinarily held.

Here it seems important to note that this method is also what guides Natanson's approach to "phenomenology." We may think we know what phenomenology means and what it looks like, but it may be that phenomenology itself appears here in unfamiliar form. Indeed, it may be that phenomenology itself must be set into relief, cut off from what has become its naturalized status within ordinary intellectual contexts, for phenomenology to be known again or, equivalently, for the first time. Husserl's claim that a phenomenologist is a perpetual beginner finds confirmation in Natanson's work. One of the most established scholars of the phenomenological enterprise, Natanson here takes the risk of beginning again. What is phenomenology? Where is it to be found? What is its relation to irreality, and irreality to fiction?

The status of the phenomenologist as a perpetual beginner can be understood through recourse to Aristotle's view that philosophy begins in wonder. The epoché restores wonder to the object, and in a quite specific sense. It is not this or that quality, but rather the thatness of the thing—not what it is, its specific actuality in the world at this place and time, but that it is possible at all.

What is, then, the object that the phenomenologist seeks to know? It is not a list of its features or the variety of its forms, but what persists as an ideal unity in the course of imaginary variations, something which is called its "essence." Here again we ought not to rush too quickly to the conclusion that we know what an essence is, assuming that it hovers behind appearances, elusive and eternal. Consider Natanson's provisional definition: the intuition of an essence seeks the quiddity of an imagined object. "Essence" he writes "is the gnosis of perception." Eidetic intuition, the intuition of essence, is possible to the extent that such intuition is intentional—that is, correlated with the object it seeks to know prior to any possible act of knowledge.

The persistence of the object through various imaginary efforts to vary its form and features is not its actuality, but its ideality. Exceeding any given appearance of the object, ideality also makes that appearance possible: an excess in the object that establishes its irreducibility to any actuality.

Natanson does not offer in these pages, as he has elsewhere, a systematic exegesis of Husserl's views or the development of those views into a phenomenological theory of the social in the work of Alfred Schutz.[1] Instead, he proceeds by offering anecdotes from ordinary life, readings from literary texts, imaginary exercises that approximate what Husserl meant by "imaginary variation." He seizes on the brief passage as a way of exemplifying consciousness as it flashes up to illuminate its world. And the proliferation of such moments attests to the impossibility of a full or final exemplification of this process. The example that illuminates intentionality is necessarily oblique to the consciousness it seeks to show.

---

[1] For a comprehensive bibliography of Maurice Natanson's work, see the excellent bibliography compiled by David Royal in *The Prism of the Self: Philosophical Essays in Honor of Maurice Natanson* (Dordrecht: Kluwer Academic Publishers, 1995), pp. 335–44. For a full discussion of Husserl's work by Maurice Natanson, see *Edmund Husserl: Philosopher of Infinite Tasks* (Evanston: Northwestern University Press, 1973). For his writings on the work of Alfred Schutz, see *Anonymity: A Study in the Philosophy of Alfred Schutz* (Bloomington: Indiana University Press, 1986) as well as his edited volume, *Phenomenology and Social Reality: Essays in Honor of Alfred Schutz* (The Hague: Martinus Nijhoff, 1970).

Natanson sets out to interrogate the convergence of the intentionality of consciousness and the fictive dimension of literary works. What Natanson writes here is not a phenomenology *of* literature, but an evocation of the phenomenological in literature. He does not ask how best to apply phenomenological doctrine to the reading of the literary text, but whether the "art of fiction may tell us the truth about the fictions natural to the mind." Such a formulation is immediatly misleading, for what is "natural" to the mind is precisely what makes any analysis of the mind irreducible to naturalism. The positing action of the mind intends or means an ideality in the object, an ideality that from the point of view of ordinary life can appear only as irreal. Thus, in Natanson's work, the power of the example is precisely the illumination of the irreal within the ordinary; the visual equivalent would surely be the opaque doorways and obscured tunnels in Edward Hopper's paintings. [Consciousness haunts its objects as their own proper irreality.] Thus, Natanson can refer to the fictive universe of intentional consciousness, an ideality of the object that can only appear within the real as the irreal.

Husserl made clear that it was only through an imaginary experimentation that the essence of the object might be known. Such an experiment of imaginary variation not only takes time, enumerating the variety of perspectives by which an object might be constituted and known, but it also lays out the temporality of the object itself, the sedimentation of its features, the specific time of its unfolding. The object known through imaginary variation is never the same as the actual object, and yet that actual object is revealed as a possible permutation or adumbration of the object in the course of its imaginary travels. Thus, the point of such a phenomenological thought-experiment is not to fix the actuality of the object, but to render its actuality into a possibility: to show the contingency of *this* appearance within the temporal horizon of the object as a unity of its own possibilities. Rendering the actual possible is in many ways the reverse of deductive empiricism, the method that seeks to filter out the possibilities to know what is, finally, the actuality. Phenomenology seeks to tease the possible from the actual object, to display its ideality, not as an invisible perfection that lurks behind the phenomenal object, but precisely as the irreality of its givenness, the strangeness of quiddity, that it is rather than not. This insight into what makes the object possible means that one must turn to the horizon in which it appears; this is no easy task because a horizon is not the same as the objects that it makes possible. And yet, there are moments in which insight into the horizon are enabled. Max Scheler, a phenomenologist whose works focused on ethics and aesthetics, identifies the tragic as such a moment, for the recognition of the tragic, he argues, is not that such an event has happened but that one lives in a world in which such an event can happen—where it is possible at all. That oblique relation between the event and the world that makes it possible is precisely the preoccupation of eiditic intuition. Thus, Natanson reminds us that essences are common-place: "just as immediately as one can hear a sound, so one can intuit an 'essence.'"

From the claim that intentional consciousness posits an ideality of the object emerges the central relation between phenomenology and the fic-tive domain. The irreality of the object appears only to a consciousness that can suspend what it ordinarily knows about that object in order to begin to ask, with Scheler, what is the world in which such an object can emerge as a possible object? If the object is possible, if there is an ideal condition for its emergence and existence, how is it that we come to understand the object itself as possibility? Importantly, the bracketing of the familiar world does not involve a loss of that world; it remains per-ceptually before the phenomenologist, but in a mode of irreality. Thus, the route to the ideal is precisely through the familiar, through the anec-dotes and examples it delivers that cast doubt on the foundational status of actuality: this is the everyday operation of the epoché. The imaginary is thus a domain that includes the fictive and constitutes the *domain of possibility* as the essence of the actual. This domain is intended, which means that it is neither a feature of the object nor of consciousness, but precisely of that moment when consciousness discovers itself as what haunts the familiar boundaries of the world.

For Natanson, the literature that converges with phenomenology is precisely that which enters the familiar only to illuminate its constitutive reality. Literary works that compel us to suspend our belief in the famil-iar through examples drawn from familiarity enact an epoché, that phe-nomenological drama which exposes consciousness at the heart of its object. Natanson himself makes this clear in his own quasi-fictive tales drawn from everyday life—the sphere of the natural attitude, as phenomenologists claim—in which the past and future inhere in the moment of present experience, revealing the present moment as an ad-umbration or possible permutation of time, fragmented from the con-tinuum that is also condensed within itself. The future and the past are precisely not "given" as phenomenal features of experience, but they form the horizon within which what is given appears.

It is no easy matter to attend to qualities that are not given, but which make the given possible, lace its emergence, hover at its boundaries. At such moments, language appears to be forced into figuration to come to grips with this non-given quality of things. Natanson himself turns to metaphors to describe this temporality that makes the given possible: "the pulse of the mundane" and the "current of existence." In the work of Thomas Mann, Natanson traces the fugitive time of the leitmotif, the recurrent and variant emergence of form, not as a static or unyielding notion but as the essence of change.

No simple inspection of a literary work can illuminate this form that is the essence of change. The form cannot be excised from the time in which it occurs; indeed, it can be grasped only in time, by a consciousness whose apprehension is structured by an internal time-consciousness. The peculiar temporality of Mann's work, for instance, is not the same as chronology, nor is it otherworldly; it articulates the temporality within which ordinary time is experienced, a temporality that is its condition and its essential strangeness.

Natanson offers a view of existential phenomenology as a further elaboration of phenomenology in its transcendental and social forms. His view is not opposed to these other kinds of phenomenology, but its focus is perhaps different. When the object that phenomenology seeks to know is human reality, when the question, as it were, turns upon the questioner as its matter, then phenomenology also turns to finitude, understood not merely as what ends human time but as that which makes it possible and pulses throughout its everydayness. The literary works that Natanson chooses are ones that seek to approximate this pulse of finitude in the everyday.

Although Natanson considers in these pages a novel, a short story, and a play, it is perhaps the philosophic poetry of Wallace Stevens that stages the encounter between philosophy and the fictive to which Natanson seeks to bear witness. Stevens writes in his poem, "The Motive for Metaphor," of "the obscure moon lighting an obscure world / Of things that would never be quite expressed."[2] In this poem, as in so many others, Stevens gestures toward this obscure yet fundamental horizon of finitude that is also the focus of Natanson's work. "The obscure moon lighting an obscure world" could be a formulation for intentionality itself: obscure because never quite expressed, and yet the occasion for expression all the same. What is grasped of phenomenology in literature is the essence of the finite world in the course of change. Stevens writes further that in the obscure world

you were never quite yourself
And did not want nor have to be

Desiring the exhilarations of changes:
The motive for metaphor, shrinking from
The weight of primary noon
The ABC of being,

No simple exegesis in this domain, no "ABC" that might lead the way. In the place of any such linear expressions are the exhilarations of

[2] Wallace Stevens. "The Motive for Metaphor," in *The Palm at the End of the Mind: Selected Poems and a Play,* edited by Holly Stevens (New York: Vintage, 1972), p. 240.

changes, a poetic notion that comes close to understanding the mobile form, the essence of temporality, that the existential phenomenologist seeks to illuminate, with whatever obscure light is at hand.

Natanson shows how the zone of the fictive emerges through the common experience of the word as a site of *possible* meaning. Indeed, metaphors enact the displacement of the familiar, and inaugurate the variations of possibility that begin to render the familiar irreal. Natanson puts the matter this way: "Metaphors are condensations of language in which words *become*, in which words escape their bounds and reverse our perception of what is real. 'To be strong in metaphors' . . . means . . . to track the normal for the sake of misleading it, discomforting it, and . . . to alienate it."

The suspension or disorientation of the familiar happens in Mann, Kafka, and Beckett in different ways, but with similar effects. *Waiting for Godot* effectively brackets the principles that govern everyday existence, forfeiting the world of reality for a perspective on what composes the world in surreptitious ways. Similarly, in Mann's *The Magic Mountain*, we see how what is remembered and anticipated converge at the present moment, a particularly dense event of immediacy. Thus, the "leitmotiv" in Mann functions as the temporal horizon in Husserl, the quality of what is not given, but which constitutes the given essentially. In Kafka, the irrealizing effects of the fictive are offered perhaps most dramatically when the workday is disrupted by a fatal transformation. And yet, the cockroach is not pure fancy, but a fleeting insight into the essence of the workday, a defamiliarization that nevertheless reveals the "underside" of what makes such a day possible.

Natanson believes not only that the intuition of essences takes place in sudden starts, in the immediacy of the moment, but that in presenting the world consciousness enacts the very intentionality it seeks to know. The reader of literature seizes upon such moments as they emerge in the course of a reading, and this means that the time of reading is invariably interrupted by the time of life. That constant interruption emerges in Natanson's work as the very presentative rhythm of consciousness as it finds itself in the landscape of its fictive universe. Bringing forth the past and charting the associations that reading unleashes, Natanson enacts the temporal horizon of the reader's consciousness, one who not only reads the world in literature but rediscovers the fictive as the essence of the world. This kind of traveling is not always linear or exegetical, but it returns, faithfully, to that moment of immediacy, dense with time past and future, in which the ordinary suddenly becomes strange, and that strangeness is exposed as the condition of possibility of the ordinary. Importantly, the fictive domain irrealizes the world, but it does not deny its reality; neither does it escape the world. Literary works perform this irrealization of the world, and this is their peculiar intentionality: they provide the suspended occasion for considering any given configuration of the ordinary as something yielded by the world as one of its possibilities. Although no example can quite capture the strange and wondrous occasion of its own possibility, the moment in which the example nevertheless illuminates what it cannot capture is the moment of phenomenological insight.

Natanson's text abounds in such moments, insights culled from the everyday that consistently disorient us with respect to what we take for granted. The literary texts recall a life-world that exceeds them, and yet the life-world is rediscovered in the literary text inflected as irreal. Thus, Mann's words about his own work might well apply to Natanson's as well: "The book itself is the substance of that which it relates . . . its aim is always and consistently to *be* that of which it speaks."

Acknowledgments _____

To Dimitri Constant, friend of philosophy, who has been this book's comrade and who has improved its text substantially. His help was providential.
To Dimitri, my Alyosha!

To David Royal, the unremitting intelligencer of these pages, which have benefited from his rigor, and whose continuing loyalty has helped to sustain me.
To David, Kierkegaardian and lawyer!

And above all to Lois Natanson, the first audience this work had and its most telling critic, who kept my fragile craft from overturning in the Kafka rapids and whose persistent honesty helped me avoid still worse literary misfortunes.
To Lois, my inwardness!

Maurice Natanson

THE EROTIC BIRD

One _____

Phenomenology in Literature I

Plato, the reddened flower, the erotic bird
  (Wallace Stevens)

IN AN ENTERPRISING and provocative essay entitled "Philosophy as/ and/of Literature,"[1] Arthur C. Danto explores a number of questions concerning the relationship between philosophy and literature. Among other matters, he is interested in the attempt to turn philosophy into a text, to "read" philosophical works as though they were, indeed, literary texts. The result of Jacques Derrida's deconstructive ferment, as I would put it, is to activate from the text an unlimited number of readings, to announce the impossibility of restraining the signification of a poem or a story or a philosophical meditation. To place Derrida among his texts in America, one might declare that it is always July 4th being celebrated with the total inventory of all fireworks as well as with unending night. Danto has his critical comment to make about deconstruction but he also has larger themes to examine. Is philosophy part of the family of literature? Or is there a distinctive responsibility to truth which the philosopher must recognize as his privileged shackle? If so, how is "truth" to be taken here? For Danto, truth leads to the reality of the reader of, say, a literary work; truth proves ultimately to be a metaphor of consciousness: the metaphor of the "I" of the consciousness of the reader. Perhaps we are delivered from representationalism to the ontology of the metaphor, denoting a sovereign consciousness. Hegel is invoked as the genius of the occasion. However, we are given not idealism but metaphoric autonomy as the locus of truth. Thus literature is liberated from the captivity of philosophy at the same time that philosophy is returned to the bosom of its history in the embrace of the reader, the metaphoric "I."

In the course of his essay, Danto provides a clue to a rather different aspect of the philosophy/literature debate, a clue which he leaves hanging. Danto writes:

Responding to a review of *The Realm of Truth* by his amanuensis, Santayana wrote: "It is as well that now you can take a holiday; which doesn't exclude the possibility of some day returning to them [the pages of the book] with

freshness of judgment and apperception. Perhaps then you might not depre-
cate my purple passages, and might see, (what is the historical fact) that they
are not applied ornaments but natural growths and *realizations* of the
thought previously moving, in a limbo of verbal abstractions."[2]

Santayana is suggesting that rather than style or rhetoric being a dis-
pensable addition to philosophical discourse, the kind of language in
which argument is embedded serves a function different from that of
linguistic adornment—the verbal foam of tossing seas. Santayana's
"style" clarifies fugitive abstraction, makes evident the encirclements
(the "fringes" of meaning, as William James called them) of reference
and possibility which otherwise would be lost to consciousness. We
come to one of those little words which Danto does not include in his
title: philosophy *in* literature. Consider a passage from Santayana's *The
Realm of Truth*:

> A faith founded on logic is an acrobatic and insane faith. It was not logical
> necessity, but hard practical evidence, that first suggested mathematical ideas
> to the mind and afterwards confirmed and imposed them. Animal faith
> honours mathematical science—a fantastic construction in itself—for measur-
> ing reliably the footsteps of that stealthy material power that pervades the
> world. If mathematics measures these footsteps perfectly, mathematics is per-
> fectly true. The reality of psychologists—subjective presence, whether sensu-
> ous or conceptual—belongs to a different moral or aesthetic sphere, not me-
> diated by animal faith and not itself conveying knowledge of truth, true as the
> account of such experience may be which is conveyed later by memory or
> sympathetic fancy: for often the art of fiction may tell us the truth about the
> fictions natural to the mind.[3]

"An acrobatic and insane faith": a faith founded on logic makes not
only deductions but demands. A Being which is Perfection *must* exist if
to lack existence is to mean anything less than Perfection. An attribute
must know how to tumble if gymnastics demands tumbling and if theology demands the attribute. But an acrobatic faith is a different affair.
The logic of faith has its requirements, but the acrobatics of faith point
to the ceremony which the believer enacts rather than describes or portrays. If the Ontological Argument for the existence of God is an example of a faith founded on logic, then the acrobat is a performer who
makes of necessity reality, and therein, for Santayana, lies the insanity of
such a faith. It may well be that some individuals have come to believe
in a supreme Being as a result of the invincibility of the Ontological Argument. I cannot imagine a more tedious faith. But whether tedious or
not, such a road to God must be taken most seriously by those in search

of faith or by those who proclaim that faith is grounded in logic. The last claim underlies Santayana's notion of an "insane faith." Not implausible, not less than convincing, not irresponsible, but insane. We are reminded of the "holy fool." But insanity is quite another matter. Simple faith, naive faith, childlike faith—these are all modes of sane faith; they are in the manner of faith, not its substance. Insane faith, however, signifies the leap of the acrobat, his ultimate tumble, from the concept of necessity to the ontological splendor of a divine Being.

The point of this brief Anselmnian adventure is that the language which Santayana uses—the language of "an acrobatic and insane faith"—is not a patch of purple prose but a way of making evident, of exposing, the way in which philosophy is *in* literature, *in* the text of a philosopher whose magnificence of "style" is sometimes derided as poetry (or at least poetic), not philosophy. What do we have then, an accident on the information highway? If much of Santayana's writing is to be taken as literature, then the philosophy in it is not to be understood as royal language but as an elucidation of certain states of affairs, as a close viewing of the inwardness of language. We are driven, indeed, to an inspection of how philosophy is to be understood when it is in the precincts of literature. Before that, however, a word is owing to the Ontological Argument. I spoke of a tedious faith. Coming to faith by way of the Ontological Argument may or may not be tedious, but the Argument itself is far from dull. In fact, I think it is the most exciting of the traditional rational arguments for the existence of God. It is the most elegant and the most sophisticated of the traditional arguments. Still, it is my limitation that I cannot imagine a bedazzled believer in God, newly come from the Ontological Argument. I see the Argument, rather, as providing a scaffolding through which the meaning of Divinity may be grasped. Perhaps, once the edifice is erected, the scaffolding may be removed so that the believer may behold the object of his faith. For my part, it is the scaffolding which illuminates the object and reveals its splendor. The genius of the Ontological Argument lies in its heuristic power.

How, once more, is philosophy to be understood with regard to literature? The first step toward appreciating that question requires some satisfaction in attending to a related question: Are there concepts in philosophy which may be said to be poetic, intrinsically poetic? Wallace Stevens wrote "A Collect of Philosophy"[4] in response to that intriguing unsettler. Stevens says:

> the idea of the infinity of the world, which is the same thing as a sense of the universe of space, is an idea that we are willing to accept as inherently poetic

even at moments when it means nothing at all, just as we are willing to assume that the rising and the setting of the sun are inherently poetic, even at moments when we are indifferent to them. The idea of the infinity of the world is a poetic idea because it gives the imagination sudden life.[5]

It might be thought that at least some philosophers have poetic ideas. Leibniz comes to mind.[6] Stevens was not secure enough in his grasp of philosophy to rely completely on his own discoveries. He wrote to a number of personal friends or acquaintances who might provide him with instances of poetic ideas; he heard from Jean Wahl, Paul Weiss, Jean Paulhan. But mostly, they did not aid Stevens greatly because they did not fully grasp what he had in mind for his "Collect." In fact, Stevens was not at ease with his project, as is indicated in the volume of his *Letters*.[7] I do not think that Stevens regarded the "Collect" as a successful fulfillment of his plan; nor do I think that it "works." Still, it includes some extremely insightful passages. It is a pity that Stevens did not trust his own instincts, for the results are often valuable. Jean Wahl, both a poet and a philosopher wrote to Stevens:

> I am just now reading the *Méditations Cartesiennes* by Husserl. Very dry. But he affirms that there is an enormous (*ungeheueres*) a priori in our minds, an inexhaustible infinity of a priori. He speaks of the approach to the unapproachable.[8]

Neither Wahl nor Stevens mentions as qualifying poetic ideas in philosophy Husserl's "phenomenological reduction" or his concept of the "transcendental ego." As with Santayana, we will see later what was missed. The language Wahl uses resonates oddly in my memory: "an enormous (*ungeheueres*) a priori in our minds" recalls to me the opening line in Kafka's *The Metamorphosis* ("Als Gregor Samsa eines Morgens aus unruhigen Träumen erwachte, fand er sich in seinem Bett zu einem ungeheueren Ungeziefer verwandelt.")[9] We have a rendezvous with Gregor.

It should be clear that the issue for Stevens in "A Collect" was not style, nor was it philosophers noted for their style: say, Nietzsche or Bergson. Rather, Stevens is concerned with two supremacies, that of philosophy and that of poetry. He writes:

> The most significant deduction possible relates to the question of supremacy as between philosophy and poetry. If we say that philosophy is supreme, this means that the reason is supreme over the imagination. But is it? Does not philosophy carry us to a point at which there is nothing left except the imagination? If we rely on the imagination (or, say, intuition), to carry us beyond that point (as in respect to the idea of God, if we conceive of the idea of God as this world's capital idea), then the imagination is supreme, because its

powers have shown themselves to be greater than the powers of the reason. Philosophers, however, are not limited to the reason and, as the concepts, to which I have referred, show, their ideas are often triumphs of the imagination.[10]

For Stevens, ultimately, philosophy and poetry acting together in the integration of reason and imagination constitute the supreme creation. It is worth noting that, for Stevens, "intuition" may be substituted for "reason," or at least that reason is not blind to the possibility of intuition. We are back, in fact, to the vocabulary of Santayana as well as that of Husserl. What is meant by intuition in both thinkers is the unmediated apprehension—the seizure—of the given in experience. "Experience" in the sense of *Erlebnis*, not *Erfahrung*. We mean a given caught up in the stream of lived experience rather than being part of the spectacle of public awareness. Erlebnis includes affection between human beings; Erfahrung includes SMOKING FORBIDDEN ANYWHERE IN THIS BUILDING. That which intuition apprehends in immediacy is what is denoted by essence. Intuition is the agency of essence, the agency which makes it possible for the quality of redness, say, of this particular red gown to be distinguished from the red of the cloth from which it had been cut. It would make sense to say that the patch of that cloth was red in the same way the gown was red; it would not make sense to say that the quality of redness of that patch was red in the same way that the gown was red. The quality has a fictive being; the patch has a substantial being. A patch of the quality of redness would be a contradiction in philosophical terms. The fictive and the substantial lead separate ontological lives.

We have come to the end of our detour. In quest of "philosophy," we have considered, through Wallace Stevens, the significance of a "poetic idea." Style led us to take that detour. But it must be said that humility did not serve Stevens well in his "Collect." He might have realized that he was the originator of a classic poetic idea: "The poem is the cry of its occasion." There was no need to write to Jean Wahl; nor, indeed, did Wahl serve him well in the case of Husserl. "Dry" the *Cartesian Meditations* might be, so dry in fact that not much is needed to set them crackling into flame. Wahl was a careful and knowledgeable reader of Husserl; he might have encouraged Stevens to read him. At the time of their correspondence, the *Cartesian Meditations* was available only in a (very good) French translation (the original German would not arrive on the scene until years later). Meanwhile, Stevens read French with ease; he should have had an opportunity to discover phenomenology. As it was, he hovered at its edges, as his *Letters* shows. I believe that the poetry of Wallace Stevens is surely philosophical; it should be suggested, however, that it is philosophical—without self-consciousness or deliberation—in a phenomenological way. In fact, the search here is not for philosophy but for what I take to be its poetic essence: phenomenology. Philosophy in literature will prove to be, at least in my interpretation, phenomenology in literature. Thus, our task is not to define philosophy once more but to clarify the particular manner in which phenomenology may be said to be "in" literature. And this clarification must avoid the repetition of being still another introduction to phenomenology.

Husserl's phenomenology implies a "philosophy," a methodology, a descriptive enterprise, a vast logic, an incursion into the realm of every-day life, into what the founder of phenomenology called the *Lebenswelt*. That life-world embraces, let alone "contains" the most trivial gesture no less than the grandest conceptual scheme. No wonder Jean-Paul Sartre was captivated by the first serious mention of phenomenology he had heard, which came from Raymond Aron. We are given the account by Simone de Beauvoir:

> Sartre was greatly attracted by what he heard of German phenomenology. Raymond Aron . . . in preparing a thesis on history was studying Husserl. When he came to Paris [in 1932], we spent an evening together at the *Bec de gaz*, rue Parnasse; we ordered the specialty of the house: apricot cocktails. Aron pointed at his glass: "You see, my little comrade, if you are a phenom-enologist, you can talk about this cocktail, and that is philosophy." Sartre grew pale with excitement, or nearly so. This was precisely what he had wished for years: to talk of the things as he touched them and that this was philosophy.[11]

Fortunate as we are in not having to define philosophy, still more fortunate are we in not having to go around the mulberry bush of phenomenology. There is a plentiful supply of introductions to Husserlian phenomenology available. But it is not merely the convenience of such a richness of rehearsals of the terms and tenets of phenomenology which absolves us from having to add another account to the archive; the point is that our interest in phenomenology, for the moment, lies in quite a different direction. If it is phenomenology *in* literature which concerns us, then we can bypass definitions of phenomenology with a clear conscience because the phenomenology which is in literature is not the same creature as the phenomenology which is properly understood in work on phenomenology *of* literature, a paradigmatic example of which is Roman Ingarden's *The Literary Work of Art*. I am not in competition with Ingarden. Rather, my interest lies in the manner in which a literary work, in *some* instances, may reveal a phenomenological structure which has been formed or shaped by the literary work in which it has been confined or in which it has lain immanent. The revealing of the phenomenological character of the literary work does not bring into being a new phenomenology, to be distinguished from Husserl's version. Quite to the contrary, phenomenology in literature presents a different perspective or profile (Husserl's term was "Abschattung") of classical phenomenology. There are not two different phenomenologies here, nor are there two different versions of phenomenology. What I have called phenomenology in literature is isomorphic with the phenomenology created by Edmund Husserl. What *is* different requires a longer explanation.

My own approach to and utilization of phenomenology might be called "existential phenomenology." In a field of philosophical thickets, "existential phenomenology" proves to be an especially spiky thorn. In a way, as soon as one has to go into explanations, distinctions, adjustments, the case is already lost. Let me say what "existential phenomenology" is *not*. I am not interested in a marriage between "existentialism" and phenomenology. They would prove to be disagreeable partners. Before the honeymoon was over, there would be threats of divorce and separation heard from both sides. Nor would group therapy help. There is some justification to the charge that "existential phenomenology" is a contradiction in terms. There is a simple way out of these troubles (though it is not the path I will choose to take): to understand by "existential phenomenology" the application of traditional Husserlian method to such thematic subjects as "anguish," "obsession," and "dread." After all, the psychiatrist, if not the phenomenologist, is confronted with such phenomena as "disgust" and "filth." Or, we should say more cautiously, the psychiatrist is confronted with his patient's report of disgust, for example, "finding a dead mouse in a tub of butter."[12] We are all, as members of the life-world, faced with occasions when shame, the odor of vomit, the smell of death assails us. There are phenomena of dirt and decay in our daily lives. How could the phenomenologist ignore what every person living his life cannot help but notice? Yes, a phenomenology of clinical obsession, as Erwin Straus has shown,[13] is not only possible but necessary as a propaedeutic to a comprehensive understanding of our own being-in-the-world. But if we choose not to understand "existential phenomenology" as the application of Husserlian method to what are usually called "existential categories" or to the noxious or the disgusting, then what do we mean by our language?

By "existential phenomenology" I understand a way of attending to the "things themselves," as Husserl calls them, which emphasizes their emotive coloration and "boundary" character (a phenomenological counterpart to what William James calls the "fringes" of meaning). And by "emotive coloration" I mean the felt aspect of an experience which otherwise can only be named by a generic class: the emotions. Rather than a "subjective" coloration of the real as "magical," there is the presentation of the world as "magical." In Tennessee Williams' *A Streetcar Named Desire*, Blanche says, "I don't want reality, I want magic." But the irruption of magic may come from the world, not the self which chooses.[14]

The distinguishing marks of "existential phenomenology" rather than phenomenology *tout court* are the attention paid to relations between assertions made (reminiscent of James' radical empiricism), the contextual aura which surrounds the presentation of phenomena to consciousness, and the quality of that which is *not* given—the moorings, one might say, of the context itself. In conduct, as Alfred Schutz has shown convincingly, that which is not done, that which is abstained from, that which remains an unchosen option for action (the surgeon's decision not to operate, the stockbroker's decision not to sell at a certain price at a certain time, the general's decision not to attack)—all these modes of conduct are also modes of action, albeit more subtle and non-behavioral forms of intercession in the experience of humankind. Existential phenomenology is not an alternative to Husserl's version of phenomenology nor is it in competition with traditional phenomenology. The difference between existential phenomenology and its more sanctioned form lies both in the objects it selects for examination and in the attention it provides in describing and analyzing what may be called "borderline" experience, that is, phenomena which are intersubjectively recognized as fugitive to cognition but naggingly persistent in our daily lives: the lack of decisive mood or emotive temper or the yawn between immediacy and expectation when neither is self-consciously considered but still ap-presented to consciousness.

Existential phenomenology is a matter of emphasis and of focus, certainly not a new discipline. In fact, what I have been describing in writing about existential phenomenology is merely my own way of doing phenomenological work. Dorion Cairns has remarked that by "phenomenology" Husserl meant whatever he was doing at the time. So, in a sense, I am confessing that what I am doing, though it is often removed from the strict procedures of Husserl, is still phenomenology, at least phenomenology as I practice it. I have not taken out new citizenship outside of the country of phenomenology; I am a wayward but loyal subject, someone who has suffered for traditional phenomenology precisely because I have given it an "existential" turn. If I am guilty of philosophical obliquity, then I must confess that I have established no divisiveness in phenomenology; it is just that some may regard me as having a "poetic" fancy. To that deception I would plead guilty if only

I were certain that those who use the language of poetry used it authentically. We are back to Wallace Stevens.

Many years ago, I spoke at a phenomenology conference which was also attended by the late Aron Gurwitsch, an authoritative phenomenologist for whom I had absolute respect. I was never in his classroom but he taught me profound lessons. At the meeting, I had, among other things, maintained that phenomenologists had an obligation to examine the phenomena of the demimonde. Gurwitsch scolded me for reducing the status of phenomenology, for turning away its proper business to scandalous attractions, for (perhaps) debasing the phenomenologist's role. We had always differed on the work of Jean-Paul Sartre. Gurwitsch approved of the early Sartre but balked at *Being and Nothingness*. He seemed especially vexed with what he took to be exhibitionist rigmaroles such as Sartre's definition of consciousness (the for-itself) as being that which it is not and not being that which it is. Such wordplay was for the audience, it was café talk, not serious philosophy. I argued that if Gurwitsch was right, Sartre had chosen a vast and impenetrable mausoleum in which to bury his crowd-pleasing antics. Gurwitsch wanted nothing to do with "demimondanity," and Sartre was contaminated. After each of us had spoken, the audience applauded. But philosophy is not to be judged by applause meters; they are irrelevant. Nevertheless, I felt tinged with the charge of trafficking illicitly with the "enemy." Later, I struck out on my own in choosing bizarre if not radical stylistic devices in which to tell my phenomenological tales. By then, my teacher in phenomenology, Alfred Schutz, as well as my informal mentor, Aron Gurwitsch, had died. They would not have given wholehearted approval to what I had written, and I knew that. But I also knew the Hasidic story of the rabbi who succeeded his revered father in a synagogue in the old country. The son did things somewhat differently from the way of his father. Finally, a delegation of elders asked for an audience with the son. They confessed the gravamen of their complaint. The rabbi was surprised. "Why, what do you mean?" he said, "I do *precisely* as my father did: he didn't imitate and I don't imitate."

With all the distinctions between Husserl's phenomenology and my own version, it should be understood that both traditional phenomenology and existential phenomenology are confronted with common complaints by more nearly analytic critics. First, there is the matter of what might be called "density." Philosophers are fond of contrasting "hardness" and "softness." Nor is this distinction restricted to phenomenology. "Hard" philosophy yields (or it is said to yield) definitive results. Such results may be tested; they are subject to the inspection of other observers, ideally in the way that natural scientific results may be

confirmed or disconfirmed. Philosophic work in logic and in foundations of mathematics are examples of "hard" endeavor. Gottlob Frege is
a hard nut. Ludwig Wittgenstein is like one of those candies which is
hard on the surface but which contains a liquid center: mysticism, perhaps. Bertrand Russell, apart from the work he did early in his career
with Alfred North Whitehead and other logical efforts (and setting aside
his social and political books), was empirically oriented. He advanced
different versions of empiricism, but he followed an old tradition in British philosophy; Hume would have approved of him. Yet, his mysticism
notwithstanding, Wittgenstein exceeded Russell in hardness. Perhaps an
analogy might help: Russell was to Sherlock what Wittgenstein was to
Mycroft. The search for hardness was endemic to such schools of philosophy as logical positivism. Softness in philosophy is typified best, perhaps, by Henri Bergson. The bitter implication of such allusions is that
softness means mush. Apart from his early works such as *Logical Investigations*, the start of traditional phenomenology, Husserl—so the complaint goes—largely failed the test of hardness.

The second complaint against the phenomenologies to which I have
alluded is that their proponents are proclaimers of large programs that
are vociferously voiced but rarely enacted. They spend much time talking about what they mean to do instead of doing it. Husserl, it is true,
wrote several books concerned with the beginning of his discipline; he
seemed extraordinarily involved in map making rather than in traveling.
That, at least, is the impression seized upon by many of his critics. I
think the impression is false. It may be that Husserl lent some superficial
credence to the charge of his critics. He was like Moses, destined to
point to the phenomenologically promised land without going there.
But that too is a screen. A careful reading of the "middle" and "late"
Husserl shows convincingly enough that in addition to mapping he examined the phenomenological structure of subjectivity, intentional consciousness in both its "subject" and "object" polarities (its noetic and
noematic aspects), the logic of immediate experience, the roots of negation, the formative character of fictive reality, the foundations of psychology, the aporias and crises of the Spirit, and the paradoxes of history. This list is far from exhaustive; it inadequately summarizes bits and
pieces of a vast domain, viewed both systemically and methodologically.
In fact, it is at this point that some of the problems of phenomenology
begin—problems of understanding on the part of the reader of Husserl's
books, or, more generally, the student of the project of phenomenology. It is possible to identify strictly methodological issues in phenomenology but it is not possible to comprehend them without the philosophic perspective which phenomenology provides. The phenomena
which phenomenology describes must be seen phenomenologically in

order to be comprehensible. To understand phenomenology one must become a phenomenologist. It is at this point that droves of well-wishers, let alone the merely curious, part company with Husserl and his crew. The demand is insulting! The demand is overbearing! The demand is philosophically outrageous! In any event, the invitation to phenomenology is circular: a hysteron proteron.

It would appear that to say that one must be a phenomenologist in order to understand phenomenology is analogous to asserting that religious truth can be grasped only by the faithful. But how narrow a claim is actually being made here? Is it being suggested that only those gifted with perfect pitch can appreciate music? Must you already be a member of the club in order to seek admission? We can avoid both circularity and absurdity by recognizing certain elements of entrapment. When it comes to analyzing the world of everyday life, it does not matter that we are already members of society. We can take a step back and look at, scrutinize, what we have hitherto taken for granted. The question is whether we can see everything relevant to our concerns from "a step back" or whether the character of any item in our field of vision can be scrupulously characterized from "a step back." Can we discern the nature of the backward step we have taken or is there a blind side to "a step back"? Is "stepping" itself excluded from analysis, so that a philosophical maneuver proves to be somehow impossible or else illusory? Are we caught in one of Zeno's paradoxes? I think that the apparent entanglement can be resolved if we choose to put into relief the landscape of our lives and the pageant of our beliefs. That putting into relief—that abstention from immanent affirmation—is known in phenomenology as the first moment of "reduction," Husserl's term for entering into phenomenological work. It must be our business, in time, to present the considerable complexity of that entrance. Meanwhile, we must take stock of where we are in this discussion.

What has been recommended, if not established, is that style in philosophy is much more than a matter of writing well; that philosophy and poetry have shares in the realm of the imagination; that "hard" and "soft" are misguided terms for describing philosophical work; that philosophy may be understood as phenomenology, in both Husserl's sense and in the domain of existential phenomenology; that the considerable specific accomplishment in descriptive as well as analytic phenomenology can no longer be brushed aside with labels such as "programmatic." Rather than being paralyzed in the vise of "in and about," the observer of mundane reality is capable of being "in" what he observes as well as a spectator of his own scene by invoking the phenomenological "reduction," the abstention from complicity with the reality perceived. We are led, then, to a paradox of explanation: how can we utilize the phenomenological reduction without first being phenomenologists? The paradox is a reminder of what has already been said about having to be a phenomenologist before being able to accomplish phenomenological work. Is there any way of avoiding an exposition of phenomenology, of repeating what has been said dozens of times?

A way of proceeding recommends itself in the example of everyday experience. Instead of expounding a phenomenology *of* the mundane, I will examine the phenomenology to be found *in* the mundane. That, at least, is my immediate mission: to show forth instead of talking about.

In "The Death of Ivan Ilych," Tolstoy's protagonist cannot grasp the truth of his dying.

> He could not understand it, and tried to drive this false, incorrect, morbid thought away and to replace it by other proper and healthy thoughts. But that thought, and not the thought only but the reality itself, seemed to come and confront him.
>
> And to replace that thought he called up a succession of others, hoping to find in them some support. He tried to get back into the former current of thoughts that had once screened the thought of death from him. But strange to say, all that had formerly shut off, hidden, and destroyed, his consciousness of death, no longer had that effect. Ivan Ilych now spent most of his time in attempting to re-establish that old current.[15]

It is in the notion of the "current" of existence that Tolstoy has hit the phenomenological note. The "current" of existence is that pulse of mundane, day-to-day life which throbs in the body of each human being but which is not noticed or remarked on until one's "pulse" is taken in an examination of some kind. Of course, the current may be understood in terms of routine, and within routines of various kinds, the current is felt without being explicitly noticed. The current is immanent to life; the individual is, in phenomenological language, "pre-predicatively" aware of the current of his being. We shall have cause to consider the relationship between the current and the significance of death, as that reality appears in Tolstoy's story. For the present, it is the current itself which calls for closer attention.

A distinctive part of the difficulty in providing a clear characterization of the current of existence is simply that in ordinary daily life that current is hidden from consciousness. The question, How then do we know it is there? is shallow. We are not playing games with refrigerator lights. The first point to be considered regarding the current of existence is that what is hidden here is concealed in a still larger realm of fugitiveness: daily life itself—what we have referred to as mundane existence—may be reverted to linguistically but is rarely comprehended in its ongoing being, in the transient sense of its character. In fine, daily life *happens* to each of us but is taken for granted in its occurrence. It is hardly satisfying to suggest that if the current of existence is secret, there is a still larger secrecy having to do with everydayness. Yet this unappealing path must be pursued. If we can grasp the manner in which daily life is taken for granted, we can perhaps understand the way in which the current of existence flows through our lives. Fortunately, there is a point of access to the taken-for-grantedness of everyday existence; it resides in what we take to be typical in our experience.

Typically, in ordinary life, I am at the center of my perceptual universe. That is to say that my body is at the "still point" of the flux of comings and goings which take place in my field of perception. I am where my body is. From that central focus I look out at the world around me. What is and what is not within reach depends on my bodily presence. At once, however, a complication introduces itself: my body is, strange to say, a "tensed" reality. Alfred Schutz has shown this clearly:

> We may say that the world within my actual reach belongs essentially to the present tense. The world within my potential reach, however, shows a more complicated time structure. At least two zones of potentiality have to be distinguished. To the first, which refers to the past, belongs what was formerly within my actual reach and what, so I assume, can be brought back into my actual reach again. . . . The assumption involved is based upon the idealizations, governing all conduct in the natural sphere, namely, that I may continue to act as I have acted so far and that I may again and again recommence the same action under the same conditions.[16]

This "again and again" aspect of typification in everyday life is crucial to the performance of all mundane action. The most evident feature of everyday life is the possibility of repeating the simplest action: to cut from the steak before me this piece and that piece and still another piece in the taken-for-granted activity of adult eating. Along with this a priori of repetition which is axial to everyday reality there is what Husserl would call a "horizon" of continuity which underlies all understanding of human action. As an example of "continuity" let us think of the typification of an expert, sharp, industrious lawyer, one whose professional curiosity is fully matched by his natural insatiability for learning as much as he can about everything he can which is even remotely related to let alone relevant to his "case." Now he is representing a client in litigation about a question of ownership—legal ownership—of a pet cat whose destiny is part of a viciously contested divorce case. The lawyer knows a great deal not only about his client and about his client's soon-to-be divorced wife but also about the person who gave the cat to the couple as a wedding present. And he knows who represented that friend when his car went off the road in a drunken driving case fifteen years earlier as well as what happened to *that* lawyer's eldest son when, in his senior year at a very fancy private school, he took the blame for a friend's cheating and would have been dismissed from school had it not been for the intervention of an Episcopal bishop who wormed the real story out of the cheater and, behind the scenes, redeemed the almost outcast young man, much to the satisfaction of the principal of the school, whose desire to avoid scandal was second only to his fear of being exposed in a tax-fraud case which had fortunately just been settled out of court. And our lawyer also knew the exact amount of the settlement.

Using more nearly phenomenological language, Schutz discusses "continuity" in terms of what he calls the "stock of knowledge" which the individual has: "this stock of knowledge actually at hand contains zones of manifold degrees of clarity and distinctness. It carries along infinite open horizons of the unknown but potentially knowable. It shows relevance structures of various types, all of them founded upon the attentional modifications originating in our practical, theoretical, or axiological interest."[17] In our example, the sire and dam of the pet cat are irrelevant to the divorce case and therefore of no interest to our lawyer. However, if the animal is a prize winner and worth a great amount of money, the lawyer would certainly look into the pedigree of the cat. As it stands, the pet has only sentimental or emotional value to its owners; the lawyer need not study its pedigree. Where does the horizon of continuity end? In our example, when the professional and personal curiosity of the lawyer is fully satisfied and the possible utility of his information for the future is assured. The lawyer's files contain a mountain of material which has not been used in his case and will, in all likelihood, never be thought of again. Continuity ("und so weiter" in the language of Edmund Husserl) remains the a priori of the world of daily life, and this helps us to understand the experiential remoteness of mundanity itself: it takes an extraordinary impulse to say to ourselves, in effect, "How strange! There *is* a world; there *is* daily life."

Husserl introduced the coinage "epoché" into the vocabulary of phenomenology, and by it he meant the act of willed abstention on the part of the phenomenologist from believing in the world. Epoché does not imply disbelief; rather, it means a purposeful intention not to take for granted what common sense ordinarily does take for granted: the very reality of the world of our everyday affairs. By invoking epoché, the phenomenologist "neutralizes" and undercuts a crucial philosophical commitment which helps to establish the current of existence—the commitment to an unexpressed, unacknowledged affirmation of what may be called the "truth" of mundane life, that what we behold in our perceptual field is, on the whole, the case ontologically. Our perception of the world can be relied on, acted upon, insisted on if necessary. Things, in this view, are realities and not appearances of some "in-itself" nature. What we are given in the perceptual reality of everyday life is unconcealed legitimacy. The deep believing in the givenness of our world as true (at least until counter-evidence offers itself) is the unshakable foundation of our lives in social reality. Schutz makes this point in especially original terms:

> Phenomenology has taught us the concept of phenomenological *epoché*, the suspension of our belief in the reality of the world as a device to overcome the natural attitude by radicalizing the Cartesian method of philosophical doubt. The suggestion may be ventured that man within the natural attitude also uses a specific *epoché*, of course quite another one than the phenomenologist. He does not suspend belief in the outer world and its objects, but on the contrary, he suspends doubt in its existence. What he puts in brackets is the doubt that the world and its objects might be otherwise than it appears to him. We propose to call this *epoché* the *epoché of the natural attitude.*[18]

There has been some misunderstanding of Schutz's "epoché of the natural attitude," as though he were revoking or replacing Husserl's notion of epoché with another version. Nothing of the kind is the case, of course, as a straightforward reading of the statement by Schutz quickly reveals. Still, it might appear as if an additional kind of epoché were being added to Husserl's canon. To avoid any misunderstanding, let us say that the "epoché of the natural attitude" is an elegant way of comprehending the profound believing-in-the-world which characterizes daily life—the "natural attitude" in the language of Husserl. Unlike the epoché of Husserl's phenomenology, Schutz's passing suggestion of an epoché of the natural attitude is not a self-conscious, willed conceptual act. The epoché of the natural attitude does not put the fear of a methodological God into the individual taking his ease in the life-world. What Schutz is touching on is the epistemologically haphazard manner of ordinary "believing-in." Santayana, we will recall, termed such belief "animal faith": the whale sounding in its vast ultimacy. The phenomenological claim is that there is philosophical complicity in the activity of the natural attitude, a naive realism which taints both belief and believer.

If it makes sense to speak of a naive realism, is there also a philosophical vantage point which might be called "naive idealism"—the conceptually uninformed view that reality is essentially a product of the mind? It would seem not, for idealism is an achievement of analysis rather than a view remote from artifice or reflection. We might say that a naive idealism which was capable of a reflective turn upon itself would be some version of solipsism. If phenomenology is taken as a form of idealism—something which Husserl explicitly rejected—then it might be asked whether its logical end is not a solipsism of the passing moment. In a discussion following one of his papers, I heard Professor Leo Strauss maintain that a phenomenology of history was impossible because there is no historical phenomenon. Although I would have thought that Husserl's position in *The Crisis* would be enough intrinsically to refute Strauss' contention, it is certainly a view shared by a number of informed readers of Husserl that the immediacy of the moment (and nothing more) reveals the phenomenon. Moreover, there are those who deny the essential line of argument in *The Crisis*. Eric Voegelin presents an illustrious example of an intellectual repudiation of the phenomenological view of history. The root of that repudiation lies in the attitude taken toward the view that there is an "Archimedian point" of consciousness sufficient in placement as well as power to generate a philosophy of consciousness. Voegelin writes:

> there is no absolute starting point for a philosophy of consciousness. All philosophizing about consciousness is an event in the consciousness of philosophizing and presupposes this consciousness itself with its structures. Inasmuch as the consciousness of philosophizing is no "pure" consciousness but rather the consciousness of a human being, all philosophizing is an event in the philosopher's life history—further an event in the history of the community with its symbolic language; further an event in the history of mankind, and further in the history of the cosmos.[19]

The "worldliness" of philosophizing, in this critique of Husserl, cannot be cleansed; the fabric of consciousness might be shredded but it cannot be made immaculate. Much as Husserl abjures solipsism, some of his critics insist on his philosophical imprisonment in its unsparing dungeon. But solipsism has a methodological as well as a metaphysical face. "Methodology" may not be a stylish term today; it seems to be one of those activities which turns inward upon itself, threshing what has already been winnowed. By methodological solipsism in phenomenology is meant, at least as I am using the phrase, a procedure which attempts to utilize only those aspects of consciousness which are born of consciousness, that is, those features of intention and reflection which are not borrowed from or indebted to psychological activities, to brain processes which are understood as part of "actual" events in nature, events which "occur" in the human body. Not the actual but the fictive is at issue in phenomenology. To speak of a methodological solipsism is to say, without obtuseness or pride, "I am the world." The meaning of that claim will deepen greatly as we proceed.

If it is methodologically correct, in phenomenological terms, to speak of "the world," it is also possible, and correct, in metaphysical terms to speak of "our world." Again, informed critics of Husserl's work are at odds concerning the status of "The Other" in phenomenology. Sartre has cut through phenomenological issues by claiming that the Other is the one who *looks* at me. I find myself at the end of the Other's "Look." For those who do not accept Sartre's ontology, the Other (as presented, for example, in Husserl's *Cartesian Meditations*) is severely problematic in phenomenological terms. Schutz himself did not think that Husserl had resolved the problem of the Other. If that be true, then the grounding of the social world—of *our* world—is left hanging. An Aristotelian mind, or a mind at work in Aristotelian fashion, finds that if the bottom step is faulty, the staircase cannot be built. I disagree. This is not the place to work through Husserl's arguments regarding intersubjectivity. I will merely say that what holds for a phenomenology of the natural attitude (for an examination of the life-world) also holds for a phenomenology of the a priori structure underlying the natural attitude. The Other, given in fleshly presence in mundane life, is a figure within the landscape of the life-world, but the comprehension of that figure in essential terms, as a possibility of the natural attitude, remains a phenomenologically legitimate problem in a phenomenologically legitimate realm. Husserl calls that realm transcendental subjectivity. Regarded from the standpoint of transcendental subjectivity, the Other is "constituted" in intentional consciousness.

To the cry "what I want is living flesh, not logical constructs!" the phenomenologist's reply (and this certainly includes the voice of the existential phenomenologist) is that "reduction" (including transcendental reduction) is not an act of substitution of the living for the logical but a way of comprehending the living in terms of fictive possibility. In a way, a translation of this sentiment is that literature is an entrance to reality. If the possible may be actualized—and it may—then phenomenology is understandable as *in* literature, not only in terms of potentiality but as a shaping force. The question of how phenomenology can be in literature comes to clarity when it is recognized that "in" refers both to literature and to phenomenology. The imagery of insertion must be abandoned. At the same time, the notion of something "uncovered" (like ancient coins discovered deep in the earth) is a misleading idea. In phenomenological reduction, what is *meant* or *intended* gives the object its signification, gives the event its coherence or chaos. The "current" of existence, viewed from a reduced (or transcendental) perspective is intrinsically intersubjective in its nature. That is to say, the "current" of which we have spoken is a feature we take to be true of the Other no less than something found in ourselves. What we take to be true of the Other, in this instance, is a temporal flow which must be true of the Other because the reality of inner time makes itself evident by the presence of the Other. In the current of existence, what Ivan Ilych seeks to return to is a world free of the disasters which contaminate his present; but to regain the current of the past is to be present in a *world*. The difference between what is living and what is constituted wanes in the reality of loss.

The central thesis of this essay is that the "current of existence" is the phenomenological clue to the essence of literature. I have purposely posed my thesis in risky terms. In what sense is it justifiable to say that there is an "essence of literature?" It must surely stiffen critical resistance when the handful of literary works which are studied in the following chapters are, in effect at least, taken to represent "literature." It will be evident in the following discussion that I am concerned with a very few literary works of the twentieth century—a far cry from what world literature represents. If I speak of the "current" of literary work, I am not introducing a signal which will run the track of every novel ever written. With enough qualifications, however, all that will come out of a philosopher's throat is phlegm. Despite everything, "essence" remains the worst offender. Perhaps it is too late to rescue the term from its despoilers. In phenomenological language, "essence" refers to a method, called "eidetic intuition," which seeks the quiddity of an imagined object, a constant unity of characteristics which hold throughout a series of imaginative variations. Essence is neither hidden nor secret; it is not the gnosis of perception. Essence, in these terms, is the unmediated apprehension of what presents itself to consciousness—consciousness no longer in the world but within what Husserl calls the "irreality" of the world: the fictive universe of intentional consciousness, the world as *meant*.

So far, I have referred to Edmund Husserl, to some of the terms of his phenomenology, and to his fundamental point of departure; but I have refrained from quoting him directly. Instead, I have relied largely on Alfred Schutz. The reason that I have not cited Husserl himself is simply that his style and language are rather clotted; he is not his own best friend when it comes to explaining phenomenology. Moreover, when it comes to presenting the phenomenological doctrine of essence, the more mature Husserl (let us say from 1913 onward) is, ironically, more difficult to understand than the earlier Husserl. However, style or language taken together do not present an insurmountable obstacle in understanding a difficult philosopher. And so I turn now to some of Husserl's formulations regarding the phenomenological significance of essence. A comparatively clear formulation is given in "Philosophy as Rigorous Science" (1910–1911). Husserl writes:

> Intuiting essences conceals no more difficulties or "mystical" secrets than does perception. When we bring "color" to full intuitive clarity, to givenness for ourselves, then the datum is an "essence"; and when we likewise in pure

intuition—looking, say, at one perception after another—bring to givenness for ourselves what "perception" is, perception in itself (this identical character of any number of flowing singular perceptions), then we have intuitively grasped the essence of perception.[20]

And he continues a little later, writing that everything

depends on one's seeing and making entirely one's own the truth that just as immediately as one can hear a sound, so one can intuit an "essence"—the essence "sound," the essence "appearance of thing," the essence "apparition," the essence "pictorial representation," the essence "judgment" or "will," etc.—and in the intuition one can make an essential judgment.[21]

In this view, essence is commonplace and the intuition of essence is commonplace. What disturbs the lucidity of the scene is what Husserl calls the "naturalizing" of consciousness: the introduction of facticity— the facticity of nature—where it does not belong. That "naturalizing" Husserl calls "psychologism": the decisive blurring of the difference between essence and event, intuition and actuality. Thus, the "current" we have been trying to illuminate may be approached in at least two different ways. The first way looks to consciousness as a by-product of neural activity. The idea of neural fibers firing in the brain—discharging—is held to account for any sense of "current." The second way regards the "current" in intentional terms, that is, as the "object" (in a more nearly grammatical sense of the word) of certain acts of remembering, certain acts of a temporal character, certain acts of anticipation as well as retention. Intentionality has nothing to do with planning or "meaning to" in the sense of "I intend to vacation in Hawaii next year." To the contrary, intentionality as a phenomenological concept—a most central part of the very meaning of Husserl's thought—refers to the activity of consciousness. All thinking is thinking-of something, all remembering is remembering-of something, all anticipation is anticipation-of something. In fine, all consciousness is consciousness-of something. Here is a vast noetic web which forms the subject matter of phenomenology. If, for Husserl, it might be said that his methodological solipsism generates the claim: "I am the world," so his "metaphysical" enterprise—the activity of intentionality—gives rise to the judgment: consciousness is the hammer of phenomenology.

Two

Phenomenology in Literature II

IT IS POSSIBLE now to enter into fictive reality—not by way of an imaginative construct or through the silver of a mirror but as the "irreality" intended by noetic acts which constitute a purely *meant* modality of being, the "object" as correlate, the "object" as noema.

We have just presented so crystalline a formulation of the nature of "fictive reality" that any elucidation may endanger its fragile clarity. Still, the risk must be taken. A reformulation must be attempted if the life-world is not to be dashed to linguistic bits. *Someone* must take responsibility for the English language. Whatever presents itself in perceptual awareness is a candidate for phenomenological scrutiny. But, in what we earlier spoke of as "reduction," when the presentation is seized in its unmediated givenness, in its untampered-with freshness, it is possible to locate the pure phenomenon, the "thing" as *meant*. It is usually useful to try an illustration. At this very moment—honestly—the image of my Uncle Drummond (he was always known as "Drummond") has come to mind. Specifically, Drummond giving me a quarter as he was about to leave our home after a visit. "This is to spend on girls, kid," my uncle said as he put the coin in my palm. He winked. There used to be a lot of winking before Lit-Crit entered the scene. I was told that Drummond was quite a "card." Well, that very same Drummond came to mind a moment ago: red bow tie with white polka dots, starched white shirt, maroon blazer, deep gray trousers, cordovan loafers. All that in a moment? Yes, but the moment needs perceptual disentanglement. Uncle Drummond is the "scene" before me, memorially. I cannot now say that I noticed his tie as my hand closed over the quarter or that I became aware sometime during his visit that he was wearing loafers. What is before me vividly in the remembered instant is Drummond, Drummond himself but also Drummond clad in a blazer, Drummond, it would seem, in technicolor.

Still further about Drummond: I don't remember the season of year during which the visit occurred, and so I can't say what should have been present. Did Drummond have a hat, a coat? Anyway, if I noticed the loafers, what about his socks? I have a very dim recollection of argyle hose—but that may have had to do with some other visit. The hose do not *present* themselves in the moment I remember, when Drummond winked at me. And most certainly, there is no flash of garter present. In the simplest, summary terms, my memory of Drummond on that occasion points to his tie, shirt, blazer, trousers, and shoes. But these items forcefully present themselves as a unified polarity of consciousness toward which the acts of tie-perception, shirt-perception, blazer-perception and so on all point. These presentations are not inductive generalizations of what bow ties with white polka dots look like; the bow tie itself presents its perceptual credentials. The tie is itself given, given *in person*, Husserl would say. What I have as my memorial portrait is "the thing itself," not an image or a conception of what somebody very likely looked like—not something to do with the style of the age but instead something given in perceptual immediacy, by way of memorial consciousness, something *meant*. The adequacy of the remembered moment raises still other phenomenological questions. Is each of the meant aspects of "the remembered" equally vivid as well as equally complete? Did Drummond wear his bow tie at an angle—a jaunty Maurice Chevalier? I do not recall. Were Drummond's shoes burnished to a high shine, a gleaming cordovan? I cannot say for sure. But I know full well that if someone were to ask me, "Couldn't those loafers have been colored burgundy?" my response would be, "No; they were cordovan." "So sure after all these years?" "Yes." "Anybody could make a mistake." "Quite so, but I remember what I remember. I was there."

With the experiencing of a perceptual object or state of affairs as being given with certitude as *this* object or *this* state of affairs, we come to the phenomenological concept of *evidence*. Husserl writes:

> Evidence is, in an *extremely broad sense*, an "*experiencing*" of something that is, and is thus; it is precisely a mental seeing of something itself. Conflict with what evidence shows, with what "experience" shows, yields the negative of evidence (or negative evidence)—put in the form of a judgment: positive evidence of the affair's non-being. In other words, negative evidence has as its content evident falsity. Evidence, which in fact includes all experiencing in the usual and narrower sense, can be more or less perfect. *Perfect evidence* and its correlate, *pure and genuine truth*, are given as ideas lodged in the striving for knowledge, for fulfillment of one's meaning intention.[22]

We shall say, then, that the memorial intention of Drummond is given evidentially. You see, the language is not as bad as it could be.

Husserl's German word is "Evidenz." It would be difficult to avoid translating "Evidenz" into "evidence." (David Carr, translator of Husserl's *Crisis*, suggests that "self-evidence" be considered in some contexts.) In philosophical terms, we must be cautious. Evidence refers to what counts as support for a conclusion. We have evidence that he bought the revolver two weeks before the murder; that his hatred for the victim never diminished over the years; that he stood to profit immensely from such a sudden and final dissolution of the partnership. The evidence is inescapable; it weighs heavily against the accused. And there is still more . . . forensics, ballistics, witnesses. They say that the defense is scrambling over a new theory that secondary smoke can cause temporary insanity. Let us hope that justice will be done. Meanwhile, we are trying to understand Husserl's concept of Evidenz. And the first thing about it is that evidence is nonderivative; it presents itself directly to intentional consciousness: it is the blue tone of that revolver as *meant*, that is, as perceived, insofar as it was perceived, and no more and no less. In this way, we come to the absolutivity of evidence, the "itself-given" quality of evidence. Husserl writes:

> Any evidence is a grasping of something itself that is, or is thus, a grasping in the mode "it itself," with full certainty of its being, a certainty that accordingly excludes every doubt. But it does not follow that full certainty excludes the conceivability that what is evident could subsequently become doubtful, or the conceivability that being could prove to be illusion—indeed, sensuous experience furnishes us with cases where that happens. Moreover, this open possibility of becoming doubtful, or of non-being, *in spite of evidence*, can always be recognized in advance by critical reflection on what the evidence in question does. An *apodictic* evidence, however, is not merely certainty of the affairs or affair-complexes (states-of-affairs) evident in it; rather it discloses itself, to a critical reflection, as having the signal peculiarity of being *at the same time the unimaginableness* (inconceivability) of their *non-being*, and thus excluding in advance every doubt as "objectless," empty. Furthermore the evidence of that critical reflection likewise has the dignity of being apodictic, as does therefore the evidence of the unimaginableness of what is presented with ⟨apodictically⟩ evident certainty.[23]

The second thing about Evidenz is that no ontological claim attends the recognition of apodictic evidence—"apodictic" meaning not a psychological sense of certitude but rather an absolutivity which presents itself in person to consciousness. In plane Euclidean geometry, there are three kinds of triangles: equilateral triangles, isoceles triangles, and scalene triangles. It is apodictically evident that there are these three possibilities. It is not a logical proof which provides conviction to this evidence, nor is it some order of psychological determinacy which does the trick. "In person" givenness signifies the apodicticity of an intuition of certitude which rests on neither logical proof nor psychological inevitability. What is *meant* in this case is the "state of affairs": precisely three kinds of triangles are possible, every other specimen being either a repetition of one of the three or not a plane triangle at all.

I have asserted that evidential claims carry no ontological weight. That allegation should be redeemed. I have not said either explicitly or implicitly that Drummond's tie is real, that the material of which it is made is real silk. Nor is that Beretta made of steel and capable of firing real bullets—that claim has not been made in connection with Evidenz. The reality, the real being of the object or state of affairs is not posited, is not at issue in the matter of phenomenological evidence. That is "real" which presents itself *in person* to perceptual consciousness as real, is intended or meant as real. To the question, "Is it really real?" no reply is offered because we are not concerned with ontological matters. The Magician made the real elephant disappear before your eyes. Was it done with mirrors? Was there a huge, complex, trap door in the floor of the stage? Houdini hid keys in his mouth: Mulholland was stupefying. What's a poor phenomenologist to think? No problem. The elephant on display is intended as real, his swaying trunk is intended as swaying. Whether artifice has rendered the "apparently" real elephant "seemingly" real, what is intended as real cannot (apart from verbal exchanges) be undone evidentially. If I am the world and if that world is hell, then I am scorched apodictically. We are not in the sweet by-and-by but in the wretched now: the incandescent present. Did the elephant vanish, disintegrate before the audience into nothingness? What is given in Evidenz to the beholder of this magical scene is the perceptually intended elephant. Perhaps for an audience of children, the Magician has arranged to have a few of the older children go on stage and to let one of them feed the elephant an apple. Did a tinge of delicious reassurance course through the child's body as the behemoth delicately spirited the proffered apple away and into its maw? That tinge was "itself-given" in apodictic evidence.

We are now prepared to discuss the double aspect of intentional consciousness: the noetic (or subject polarity) and the noematic (or object aspect). The relationship between the noetic and the noematic polarities of consciousness is deeper than even the word "intimate" can imply. We are concerned here with amazements of intentionality which point to the unheard-of extent of subjectivity and the infinitude of "objectivity." To play with implications of the terms for a moment: the noema is the *morphé* of the noesis; the noesis is the sense of the *morphé*. Intentionality is a flow, a river in which consciousness is immersed, making it unnecessary to say that one can "step" into the river; one *is* the river. Appeals to Husserl's writing may be at best dubious aids to clarity, but we may as well fire the gun:

> The concept of intentionality, apprehended in its undetermined range, as we have apprehended it, is a wholly indispensable fundamental concept which is the starting point at the beginning of phenomenology. The universality which it designates may be ever so vague prior to more precise investigation; it may enter into an ever so great plurality of essentially different formations; it may

be ever so difficult to set forth in rigorous and clear analyses what makes up the pure essence of intentionality, which components of the concrete formations genuinely contain it in themselves and to which components it is intrinsically alien—in any case, mental processes are observed from a determined and highly important point of view when we cognize them as intentive and say of them that they are consciousness of something.[24]

Phenomenology, then, is a discipline of correlates. The noetic intends the noematic. In the life-world, the correlates are taken for granted; they form a movement of pre-reflective awareness in which the "intentiveness" of consciousness is hidden from the ordinary activity of perception. Such hiddenness is not an ontological state of affairs. There is nothing to "look inside," as it were. Or "looking inside," there is nothing to find. Correlations of meaning do not occupy space; if anything, such correlations as we are speaking of are temporal in character. It is *temporality*, however, which is at issue here, not time in the sense of chronology. Husserl speaks of "inner-time consciousness": the flow of the intentional sense of the temporal toward its noematic correlate. It is necessary to remember that the meaning with which we are here concerned is noetic-noematic correlation. The "object" of concern is the irreal, not the "thing" that parlormaids polish or the reeds that basket weavers bend. And even in the relationships that permeate the life-world, it is not contracts, however informal, which bind one person to another but the "sense" of the contractual which underlies agreement. Not fact but essence is the gateway to phenomenology. To understand intentionality as the axis of phenomenology is to recognize that it is essential and not factic aspects of reality which are at issue. In his book *Ideas*, Husserl makes it quite clear that getting to essence, not to fact, is the clue to pure or transcendental consciousness:

> *pure or transcendental phenomenology will* become established, *not as a science of matters of fact, but as a science of essences* . . . it will become established as a science which exclusively seeks to ascertain "cognitions of essences" and *no "matters of fact" whatever . . . the phenomena of transcendental phenomenology will become characterized as irreal.* . . . Other reductions, the specifically transcendental ones, "purify" psychological phenomena from what confers on them reality and, with that, their place in the real "world." Our phenomenology is to be an eidetic doctrine, not of phenomena that are real, but of phenomena that are transcendentally reduced.[25]

We shall set aside for present purposes the question of the order of the "reductions" in phenomenology and turn instead to the nature of the distinction between "real" and "irreal." "Irreal" does not mean "unreal"; "irreal" signifies a turn away from the given fact or event in a situation of any kind to, instead, the possibility of that fact or event. But the point goes further. In the "fact-world" of daily life, the "reality" of a sign in the window of a restaurant, announcing "LUNCH BEING SERVED," is irrealized if it be noted that the restaurant is closed—closed for good. The sign hangs on as a haunted signifier, a semantic leftover of the life-world. No doubt, it might, it could be true that lunch is now being served in some restaurant; but not this one. The sign continues to retain its factic legitimacy (if the restaurant reopens it might be used authentically); it has lost its factic decency. To believe in it still is to have lost all sense. To line up for lunch here is dementia. "We are in line, waiting for lunch which will not be served," is a statement of the absurd. In terms of the noetic-noematic relationship, it may be said that waiting in this phantom line is, for those acquainted with the situation, anticipating a negative result. As the logicians teach us, from a false proposition, everything follows—which means that nothing follows. If "this is sugar and it is sweet" is false, then "this is alum and it is sweet" as well as "this is alum and it is not sweet" both follow. The sweetness and bitterness of logic presuppose no poet.

Where the noetic intends a fictive reality, we may imagine a poet concealed in the iambics. Once that poet has been exposed, the fiction crumbles. As Wallace Stevens writes: "there is a kind of secrecy between the poet and his poem which, once violated, affects the integrity of the poet."[26] Thus not only the poem but the poet crumbles. It would appear that intending the noema is a fragile act. This is not the case. The acts of intentionality are rays of sensibility, not strands of steel with which bridges are built. Stevens' poet is exposed when the public violates its province and comes between the poet and his poem. In phenomenological terms, the unity of intention is fractured when the noetic and noematic are sundered. The relationship between the two is internal. The noetic intends the noematic. It is not the "object-thing" which is intended—that may be thought of—but the *meant* "thing," the "object" as meant in the acts of seeing, perceiving, recalling, imagining, and so on.

What is *meant*, in this way, is not "in" the world, has no "being" in the realm of daily life, does not "live" in history. Yet the noetic and the noematic components of intentionality accompany, in a priori form, all acts that are possible in "actuality." Husserl maintains:

Phenomenology . . . actually encompasses the whole natural world and all of the ideal worlds which it excludes: phenomenology encompasses them as the "world sense" by virtue of the sets of eidetic laws connecting any object-sense and noema whatever with the closed system of noeses, and specifically by virtue of the eidetic concatenations of rational positing the correlate of

which is the "actual object" which, thus, on its side, always exhibits the index
for the whole determined system of teleologically unifying fashionings of
consciousness.[27]

The "sense" of the life-world, understood in this manner, constitutes
the irrealized meaning of human relationships in the "real world." Is
fiction, then, twice removed from reality? If this were so, the entire phenomenological enterprise would be misunderstood at its root. Irrealization is not a "removal" from reality but rather an abstention from claiming the ordinary as real, an abstention which is under the control of a
methodologically willed procedure. The real thing does not disappear or
go on a philosopher's holiday; it is *bracketed*, in the same way, fundamentally, that the mathematician may place an expression of *his* language in brackets; it no more disappears than mathematics "appears."
The sense in which mathematics, or logic for that matter, is "there" is
more Pickwickian but less or other than quixotic.

It is possible now to recognize that all talk of either methodological
or metaphysical solipsism must be transcended by Husserlian phenomenology. "I am the world" is true as a preliminary step toward transcending any form of solipsism which is associated with philosophical idealism of any kind. Phenomenology, as Husserl has stressed in *Ideas* quite
explicitly, has nothing to do with any form of idealism (or realism, for
that matter). It is not a version of Schelling's transcendental idealism,
let alone Hegelianism of any order. What makes phenomenology
unique is that it retains full respect for psychology, while repudiating
psychologism, without yielding to a version of descriptive psychology
and without giving up the possibility of a genuine phenomenological
psychology—one whose foundations reside in transcendental subjectivity. Phenomenology maintains the need for a pure absolute of consciousness, a discipline of the a priori, whose expression is that intentionality of which we have already spoken. Short of a discussion of the
various levels of reduction and the meaning of what Husserl calls tran-
scendental-phenomenological reduction, we *are* moving toward a
clarification of the nature of the "fictive." Why not take on transcendental reduction? Because the philosophical vocabulary for talking its
language, let alone the syntax, is still (and will remain) fugitive to us. "I
am the world" remains true; it also remains true that what is comprehensible about that statement is the visible portion of the phenomenological iceberg.

It would appear, tip of the iceberg or not, that the doctrine which
holds that "I am the world" is inevitably an expression of solipsism and
therefore in conflict not only with philosophical realism but with the
mundane cry of the life-world itself. This criticism is a partial and

twisted critique of phenomenological "solipsism." In truth, Husserl repudiated both traditional forms of idealism and realism, as I have tried
to make clear. It follows that he is not putting forth a new conception
of "solipsism." It is only by taking a partial view of the meaning of "I
am the world," an incomplete understanding of what underlies solipsism, that a skewed interpretation of phenomenology results. Husserl
writes:

> Our phenomenological idealism does not deny the positive existence of the
> real . . . world of Nature—in the first place as though it held it to be an illu-
> sion. Its sole task and service is to clarify the meaning of this world, the precise
> sense in which everyone accepts it, and with undeniable right, as really exist-
> ing. . . . *That* it exists—given as it is as a universe out there . . . in an experi-
> ence that is continuous, and held persistently together through a thread of
> widespread unanimity—that is quite indubitable.[28]

The large claim which emerges from this discussion of phenomenological idealism (and its transcendental conditions) is at first glance quite
strange, and more cautiously viewed even stranger. The claim is that
with or without the world as ordinary people know it, as everyday life
reveals it, the underlying logical structure of the world would still hold,
that is, to reduce matters to seeming simplicities, that two times two
would still be four. Furthermore, the underlying structure which is said
to hold true, whether or not there are any human beings to remark its
truth, is the generative force which makes the world possible as an intersubjective reality. Supporting the "I" of "I am the world" is a transcendental "I," a transcendental ego which, for Husserl, is the ultimate
ground, the absolute, for the individual in the life-world, his fellow-
men, and the social reality all of us share as human beings. Everything
"in" the world is relative in some manner to everything else; the transcendental ego alone is nonrelative. It is in this context that Husserl
writes: "only transcendental subjectivity has ontologically the meaning
of Absolute Being, that it only is non-relative, that is relative only to
itself; whereas the real world indeed exists, but in respect of essence is
relative to transcendental subjectivity, and in such a way that it can have
its meaning as existing . . . reality only as the intentional meaning-prod-
uct of transcendental subjectivity."[29]

We are in danger of losing ourselves in transcendental marshes when
our objective lies in a phenomenological clarification of the "fictive."
Although nothing is ever lost in concerning oneself with the transcendental ego, it sometimes happens that one attends a performance of a
string quartet where the instruments are all the rage: Stradivarius and
Guarnerius while the music fades. Let us return to the fictive and confront it staunchly.

Somewhat like a schematism, the fictive lies between the "real" of common sense and the "imaginary" of poetry. Perhaps a summary formulation will be of some use. First, we, as ordinary human beings in the taken-for-granted world of everyday life think of ourselves, regard ourselves at least, as real (certainly not as imaginary) beings. Second, the self (the "I" or individual) is aware of things and other persons in the everyday world. So the real includes self and Other. In the same breath, there are time dimensions which are relevant here: the present in which I perceive a large lump of plasticine; the past which includes my memories of modeling materials being used; the future in which I may perceive a finished piece of work, a work of art, perhaps. The real is, if not perdurable, at the very least reliable as *there* in its perceptual givenness. We shall leave aside illusions of various kinds and recognize emphatically that the real demands our obeisance. What is real may be counted on, relied on, and recognized (in principle) by the Other as there in much the same way as the rest of us encounter it and interpret its character. A load of coal may be viewed by different people as potential fuel, a commodity, or something blocking our path, but coal it is and coal it remains. And if we are what Alfred Schutz calls "wide-awake adults" in the world, we do not, under ordinary circumstances, seek to arrange to haul it to Newcastle.

Arguments about "relativism" are out of place here. As it has been remarked about the possible causes of the First World War, whatever differences of opinion exist between historians and theorists on the subject, at least one thing is not in dispute: that Belgium invaded Germany. So the real is taken for granted not only as real but as real without appeal, real without recourse to further consideration. Now, the "irrealization" of the real brings us to the fictive. Husserl presents some distinctions which are useful at this point. In discussing what he calls "the *neutrality-modification of the normal perception*," Husserl says:

> let us suppose we are observing Dürer's engraving, "The Knight, Death, and the Devil."
>
> We distinguish here in the first place the normal perception of which the correlate is the "*engraved print*" as a *thing*, this print in the portfolio.
>
> We distinguish in the second place the perceptive consciousness within which in the black lines of the picture appear to us the small colourless figures, "knight on horseback," "death," and "devil." In aesthetic observation we do not consider these as the objects . . . ; we have our attention fixed on what is portrayed "in the picture," more precisely, on the "depicted" realities, the knight of flesh and blood, and so forth. That which makes the depicting possible and mediates it, namely the consciousness of the "picture," . . . is now an example for the neutrality-modification of the perception. This *depicting pic-*

ture-object stands before us *neither as being nor as non-being*, nor in any *other positional modality*, or rather, we are aware of it as having its being, though only quasi-being, in the neutrality-modification of Being.[30]

If we shift the province of the imaginary to poetry instead of pictorial art, then we may envision the role of metaphor in the fictive, which both literature and painting, say, share. Dürer's engraving presents a knight who is "real" within the "reality" of the engraving. What is depicted is the human-real conflict of someone—a hero of the ontological—caught between finitude and temptation. The metaphorical reality is no less "real" than the tidal pull of the Lebenswelt, the suction of Being that makes us part of the social world. To common sense, it may well be that nothing will ever convince anyone—"in his right mind," as the saying goes—that something imaginary is the same as something real. Suppose we grant that. What is left is the considerable problem of understanding the meaning of "being in one's right mind." Is the conflict I suspect Dürer's knight is having—his "in-betweenness"—qualitatively different from the conflict I experience when I choose between equally damned paths? Criminals were once buried at crossroads; is that so far from crucifixion? In Luke we learn that one thief was saved and the other damned. Is "believing" the account of Saint Luke so far removed from believing in Dürer's print? If it be protested that we do not "believe" in that print at all, let it be said that even some of those who refuse to believe in the destiny of the two thieves may still believe in Christ. Is it forbidden to merge the "hero of the ontological" with the "hero of the Absurd"?

What is permitted—and necessary for our discussion—is that "belief" in fictive reality signifies an acceptance of the intentional correlation of the noetic-noematic relationship which is the "material" of Beckett's Vladimir and of Estragon's conflicted love for his companion. "There are times," Estragon says coldly to Vladimir, "when I wonder if it wouldn't be better for us to part." And later, Estragon says: "I sometimes wonder if we wouldn't have been better off alone, each one for himself. We weren't made for the same road."[31] I believe in the sadness of Estragon's statements. That he is a fictive being in Beckett's play does not diminish the sadness which I feel. If it be said that this sadness is the result of the stagecraft and acting power of a "good" Estragon or, if I am restricted to the text of *Waiting for Godot*, my imagination of the kind of performance a first-rate actor who is playing Estragon might give, then I repudiate so psychologistic an explanation by distinguishing between the finality of the meaning-structure of the play and some psychological response to the play, seen or imagined. I would just as quickly, as a phenomenologist, reject any claim that the "sadness" I experience in

Estragon is due, as has been recently said, to activity in the right hemi-
sphere of my brain. The anatomical "seat" of the emotions and the
meaning-structure of noetic-noematic correlates are independent of
each other, even if it be granted (which I do not grant) that emotions
are reducible to brain activity. The sadness at issue here cannot be quan-
tified whatever the state of the human body may be. If sadness is correlated to a tremor of the brain (it used to be the heart), that is no indica-
tion that the tremor discriminates between sadness and grief, sadness
and mourning, sadness and melancholy. Grief, mourning, and melancholy are modalities of the spirit. Causation and meaning are the great
divide in phenomenology.

There may be worse epistemic errors than conflating causation and
correlation, but Husserl's central point concerning psychologism is that,
beyond conflation, there is a philosophical naturalism which cancels the
meaning of the distinction between event as signification and event as a
happening in nature. He writes:

> psychology is concerned with "empirical consciousness," with consciousness
> from the empirical point of view, as an empirical being in the ensemble of
> nature, whereas phenomenology is concerned with "pure" consciousness,
> i.e., consciousness from the phenomenological point of view.
>
> If this is correct, the result would then be—without taking away from the
> truth that psychology is not nor can be any more philosophy than the physical
> science of nature can—that for essential reasons psychology must be more
> closely related to philosophy (i.e., through the medium of phenomenology)
> and must in its destiny remain most intimately bound up with philosophy.
> Finally, it would be possible to foresee that any psychologistic theory of
> knowledge must owe its existence to the fact that, missing the proper sense of
> the epistemological problematic, it is a victim of a presumably facile confusion
> between pure and empirical consciousness. To put the same in another way:
> it "naturalizes" pure consciousness.[32]

It is now evident, I think, that attributing the feeling of "sadness" to
a region of the human brain ignores the entire point of the irrealization
of experience in the constitution of the fictive. If I am saddened by the
death of Father Zossima in *The Brothers Karamazov*, that sadness cannot
be distinguished from the sadness I feel at the death of my grandfather,
if the causal locus of "sadness" is in the human brain. But the sadness in
the two cases is quite different. If the feeling, whatever it be, of religious
belief can be precisely duplicated by taking a pill, then genuine belief
and pill-belief are brain-identical. What the belief is *of* matters not at all
in this example of causal belief. The Hollywood actor, Pat O'Brien,
played Catholic priests so often in movies that, on occasion, he was told
by a highway patrolman, "Now, Father, I'd take it a bit more slowly;

twenty miles along the road there's a Protestant on patrol." Can an actor give Communion? What the sadness "is of" may be psychologized in acting on the stage in real theater; what the sadness "is of" is constituted as a noematic unity of meaning in the case of a death of someone in my family whom I love. Kaddish is said for the character Morris Bober in Bernard Malamud's novella *The Assistant*. Would it be appropriate for a Jewish reader of that work to go through a period of ritual mourning for the protagonist?

If the irrealization of experience yields the fictive, it may be asked whether the technique or manner of the irrealization affects the quality of the fictive. Is irrealization a device of some more or less mechanical phenomenological procedure, or is there an art to reduction, to put the matter generically. In mathematics, the art of the mathematician does not lie in calculation; that can be done by a machine. "Elegance" demands the artful human being. We have returned, in a way, to the subject of style. I have suggested that style and content are integral in philosophical work, that they find their apogee in phenomenology. I remain mindful, if unconvinced, of Harold Laski's summation of Bergson in a letter to Justice Holmes: "a stylist but he isn't a thinker; and metaphors aren't metaphysics." In any event, I rule out of literary as well as philosophical court anyone such as Laski who can say of Henry James' *The Ambassadors*: "a second-class mind dealing with fundamentally third-class material."[33] Lest I be accused of not casting the first stone, I must affirm (not admit) that the "literature" in this book's subtitle is confined, as far as illustration and application go, to a severely restricted assortment of works. It is as though I were accused of having not merely pockets of ignorance but entire wardrobes. And as far as their presence in this book, the charge, properly understood, is legitimate. Whole literatures have simply been left out of consideration. From all world writing, I have selected a pittance (however brilliant) of authors. I plead guilty but have reasons. First, I am not concerned here with making universal claims about phenomenological method (although I believe that method is not parochial). Second, I readily agree that I am no René Wellek, no Erich Auerbach, no Leo Spitzer; neither am I Aristotle, Descartes, or Leibniz. Without cowering, I am unashamed to remind the reader that I am Maurice Natanson.

Now I wish to show the conjoint relationship between irrealization, the fictive, and what we have referred to as the current of existence. In the course of everyday life, in the midst of the life-world, the individual—I, for instance—observe "people" as I walk along a crowded thoroughfare. "People" are Others, other human beings, like myself. When I see them, or occasionally come into contact with them, it is never the total being of the Other which I perceive but only some aspect—some adumbration, as Husserl says—that I come to be acquainted with. There is a certain slouch of a shoulder, the carriage of a torso, the bewildered face—each part of the Other, anxious or at ease, seemingly terrorized or abrupt in its presentation of itself in the world. To be sure, the part or aspect is *of* the individual; but I may not notice the person I pass in any studied way. It is the aspect which "substitutes" for the whole, the integral Other. The "aspect" intends the entirety, intends the interiority, intends the fierce quiddity and unforgiving ultimacy of any one of us. I have, in the most casual of ways, grasped the "style" of the person. Once again, no ontological claims are asserted or implied. That shrug of finality may, "in reality," be the first move on the part of the bargainer. That smile may be a smirk. That appearance of hopelessness may indeed be hopelessness. Down and out may be down and out. In the traffic of the Lebenswelt, adumbrations are the powers of expression: I observe, therefore I am.

The irrealization of the particular is the assertion of the universal. Typicality replaces individuation. The fictive has become, or can be understood as becoming, the turn from "reality" to the possibilities of the "real." That means, among other things, that what is "given" as reality is "preinterpreted" as simple, or hidden, diminished or angular or ribbed or porcine. What is "given" to us in mundane life is what Schutz calls "the world as taken for granted." He writes:

> all knowledge taken for granted has a highly socialized structure, that is, it is assumed to be taken for granted not only by *me* but by *us*, by "*everyone*" (meaning "every one who belongs to us"). This socialized structure gives this kind of knowledge an objective and anonymous character: it is conceived as being independent of my personal biographical circumstances. The typicalness and the objective character of our unquestioned experiences and beliefs also inheres in those dealing with relations of causality and finality, of means and ends, and therefore, with the practicability of human actions (ours and those of our fellow-men), within the domain of things taken for granted. For this very reason there is an objective chance taken for granted that future actions typically similar to those which have been proved as practicable in the past will also be practicable in the future.[34]

Here, then, is the life-world: it is a realm of anonymity. The pulse of that world we have called the "current" of existence. The term "current" is borrowed from Tolstoy but the meaning of the term is the property of phenomenology. In the course of daily life, everyday existence, we not only take for granted the routines of our lives as well as the typified acts of Others but we encounter the central images of our own landscapes, those interior realities which we cherish and secretly cultivate. Fifty years have not dimmed my love for a series of glorious French film actresses or a chanteuse: I still adore Arletty; I dream passionately of Patachou, with her French raincoat and high heels. And Louis Jouvet is still a reality to me, as is Raimu, Harry Bauer, Michel Simon. What shall I do? I cannot abandon—I do not wish to abandon—the memories which still thrive in my life-world. Laugh as I may to myself about myself, those memories are indelible. They are the noematic ghosts of my youth, no less real for being fancies. They are the stump of history.

The "taken for granted" includes not only memories but perceptual experience which is ongoing in a thick and living present. As Schutz has pointed out, I take it for granted, "until further notice"—a phrase we shall encounter still again—that everyday life in the future will be pretty much what it has been in the past and that everyday life in the present is pretty much what it was like in the past. Obviously there are interruptions and basic changes: wars, catastrophes, plagues, and other devastations alter the "taken for granted." But we know that; what is not as obvious is that a certain "taken-for-grantedness" arises in the midst of disaster; "life" continues to be "daily life" for survivors, even if that life is "unlivable." In the "ongoing" flow of perceptual experience in the everyday world there is a rhythm to be discovered: the current of our lives. At the same time that the current is felt, it is also the case that extremity permits love. At the core of plague, there is the knowledge of exile.[35]

The limit of the current is exile; at that point, the sufferer locates his loss in love and either enters into the "cross current" of endurance and faith or persists in "common decency." Or the sufferer dies. The rhythm to be discovered in utter adversity, in the clutch of plague, is the compassion which Camus' Dr. Rieux calls "common decency." Being altogether outside the current of mundanity is death. It is useless to speak of coma, brain death, Pick's disease or other forms of absolute senility; our interest is in charting the life-world, not the death-world. The current of everyday life cannot be traced by delicate ink on a slowly turning drum. We are in the incandescence of everydayness; later we shall turn to final night.

Once again, it was Alfred Schutz who spoke of our "taking daily life for granted" and then introduced the caution: until further notice. What that means is simply that the rhythm of everydayness can be interrupted by emergencies, broken into, as it were. Earlier, and from a different standpoint, John Dewey said as much. Stopping the flow of the current for a time, breaking its rhythm, is not like turning off the gas or the electricity. We are not considering a purely mechanical model. Rather, the appropriate metaphor is more likely to be found in medicine: Angina pectoris—Coronary ischemia. Pressure or pain. Estopped not by a decree of law but by an organic ineptitude of the body itself, Counsel was about to object but slumped in his chair suddenly. Estopped; caught in the cross hairs of law and medicine and almost fired on by the Huntsman on High. Reprieve: six weeks of rest in the country, a reduced work load in the office, lectures about some pills, irresolution about bed. *Touch of angina, was it? Muscle affected, was it? Mother's side of the tree? Return, could it? Doctor an indiscreet questioner, was he? Embarrassing, was it? Wanted to throttle him, did you? Son of a bitch!* Whatever the level, no matter how high or trivial the import of the event, something is hindered from happening as it usually does, is thrown off its ordinary course, announces "further notice." But such intervention is part of the taken-for-granted world. There are routines for emergencies, typified courses of action for initiating emergency formulas. What the ambulance cannot take along with the patient is the mundane world in which both remain rooted. Everyday life—the life-world—remains the unchangeable matrix of all change.

What we have referred to as the conjoint relationship between irrealization, the fictive, and the current of existence shares one central element: temporality. As we have mentioned, Husserl speaks of temporality as "inner-time consciousness." It is not difficult to establish the credentials of temporality as a phenomenological "conjoiner." The "stuff" or "texture" of what has been irrealized is not a "something" but a "somewhat." Irrealization has moved the particular from its setting as a "thing" in the natural or social world to an essential "somewhat" in a nonchronological domain. From chronology as life-world time (newspaper, stock market, railroad deadlines) we move to temporality as the inwardness of movement along the inner horizon, as Husserl put it, of becoming. It should be said that we are not expositing Husserl's theory of inner time or of inner horizon, nor, for that matter, Husserl's phenomenology in general. To be clear and to be fair, I am formulating my own views throughout these pages, from the perspective of what I have called an existential phenomenology, that I profess, which is greatly indebted to Husserl and to Schutz, but for which I alone am ultimately responsible. To counter, "But Husserl (or Schutz) did not say that about temporality or sociality" is to miss the point of the perspective from which I write. Of course, it is easy to say of that perspective that it yields responsibility along historical lines at the same time that it propounds views which historical figures have not embraced or have only partially embraced or have suggested for purposes other than mine; I have chosen to be an existential phenomenologist and to accept the conceptual as well as historical difficulties which attend such a choice. My final appeal is to the reader: Do you find what I have to say convincing and, at least here or there, illuminating? If the answer is unequivocally "No!" then back to Husserl or Schutz is all I can rejoin. At least, I have made an effort to clarify what belongs to me and what belongs to others. Again, the reader will have to determine whether that effort is consequential.

If irrealization has become somewhat clearer, we may go on to the fictive. If "actual" (or "real") is the antonym of "fictive," then presumably the fictive has no biography: it is not, it never was, it never will be. It is "made up," imagined, a piece of artificiality. As writers warn the reader in a note preceding the novel: if any individual alive or dead resembles any character portrayed in the story, it is an unintentional coincidence. The fictive soars above actuality, an imperious eagle. At the same time, it must be said that the fabric of the fictive has its distinctive quality. No "imaginer" is required by the fictive; no intensity of concentration is demanded; the fictive is neutral—any reader may have access to the character in the story. It should be clear that prose, not poetry is being considered. Prose gives trouble enough; poetry "machinates." In prose fiction, then, the fictive quality has an anonymous source. The author, even (and perhaps especially) the narrator cannot be trusted. The fictive takes on life within the fiction; we should congratulate the "fictor" instead of Dickens. We compliment the author because the "fictor" is out of reach. To be sure, the novel did not write itself, but the fiction becomes independent of its writer. The intentional fallacy spreads like a relentless stain over the entire production. The reader shoves the writer aside, while the author stands by, dead or helpless. If inner time is the "stuff" of the fictive, then fiction can "date" only chronologically, not temporally. Hans Castorp will always be arriving at the Berghof; he will always be met by his cousin, Joachim; he will forever get lost in his adventure in the chapter of *The Magic Mountain* entitled "Snow." Prose fiction is set like fixed sculpture, at least in respect to the "caught" quality of fiction. We know that Henry James made some changes (often for the worse, in my opinion) in the "New York Edition" of his works. Such matters do not impinge on our business here. The notion that the author is in control of his creation must be intelligently repudiated. As Aharon Appelfeld says: "My real world was far beyond the power of imagination, and my task as an artist was not to develop my imagination but to restrain it, and even then it seemed impossible to me, because everything was so unbelievable that one seemed oneself to be fictional."[36]

The current of existence remains to be discussed. Freed from its psychological moorings for purposes of phenomenological scrutiny, the current is intermittently recognized. Its signal might be described as unconscious if that language were permitted us; it is not. The signal of the current is sometimes seen or heard or felt in inappropriate moments. I am thinking of Tolstoy's "The Death of Ivan Ilych": "Once when

mounting a step-ladder to show the upholsterer, who did not understand, how he wanted the hangings draped, he made a false step and
slipped, but being a strong and agile man he clung on and only knocked
his side against the knob of the window frame. The bruised place was
painful but the pain soon passed, and he felt particularly bright and well
just then."[37]

The "signal" here is not the stab of pain felt by Ivan Ilych but rather
the ground of well-being against which the pain announces itself and, at
the same time, announces the current of well-being. Pain and brightness
combine to permit Ivan to feel the current, which all along coursed
through his life unheeded and, as the phenomenologists say, "unthema-
tized." When the current remains itself, unsounded, unexamined, "un-
thematized," one just lives. For the philosopher to declare that "the unexamined life is not worth living," is to speak outside of the immanence
of the mundane. Within life, as it were, the current is not felt but
"lived." "J'existe mon corps," wrote Jean-Paul Sartre in L'Être et le
néant: I live my body, we might translate. But that "living" is pre-reflective, in Sartrean terms. These are also phenomenological terms. With
the reflective gaze of philosophy, the current is made thematic, put into
relief, rendered the object of inquiry. It might appear from this description that philosophy resides outside of life and, with deliberate effort,
fixes upon and seizes it. If a defense of ordinary unreflective existence is
possible in superior terms, it is made by that grand observer of the scene
of a peasant family at table, who said: "They are in the truth."

There is a different way of regarding the relationship of "inside" and
"outside" in this context. It might be said to advantage that the seizure
of philosophy is implosive, that philosophy in this aspect bears some resemblance to the "falling disease"—epilepsy. The epileptic "aura" becomes translated into wonder, the disease is what Erwin Straus used to
call "dis-ease." But let us leave this conceit for more secure ground. My
idea is that philosophy is implicit in ordinary experience, that is, in everyday life. Being implicit, philosophy's station is that of a secret activity,
one which is denied when the common phrase "philosophy of life" is
used. If the notion of a current of existence has any real utility, its use
lies in the circumstance that the inwardness of philosophy argues against
any kind of imposition. Ideology may be imposed; philosophy is chosen.
Why, then, is there secrecy involved in what I have remarked on? The
answer is that the choice of philosophy, in my terms, is the release of
secrecy, so that the current is thematized. The finest imagery for my
view is to be found in Plato's Meno. It is in remembering that we come
to know. Whether or not we depend on Plato, it may be suggested that
philosophers of indirection up to Kierkegaard (whom Husserl admired
as a scintillating thinker) are convinced that the imposition of philoso-

phy upon the individual is a conceptual failure if only for the reason that imposition presupposes the meaning of the individual, whereas philosophy seeks to uncover that meaning.

Irrealization, the fictive, and the current of existence, taken together, are "moments" in the course of intentionality. We have considered temporality to be the "stuff" of intentionality. I take that to be phenomenologically true and essential to our entire discussion of phenomenology in literature. The character of temporality, then, is not only the negation of chronology but inherently similar to the result of irrealization: the creation of a "correlate" of consciousness which is fictive and which corresponds to the current of existence. What Husserl calls phenomenological reduction is, apart from an abstention from the predication of reality or being regarding the object of perception, a conceptual movement away from psychological awareness to the establishment of correlates of intentional acts. In phenomenology we are not talking of the ordinary thing observed or of the psychological activity involved in observing it, but instead we are concerned with a "reduced" field: the essential structure of the act of intending and the essential structure of the correlate of that act. The latter is what Husserl calls the "noema" and the former the "noesis." From different perspectives, we have arrived at the same unities of meaning which are to be found in the stream of intentional consciousness. Phenomenology, in these terms, is the "science" of correlation and of correlates. It is just as well to unquote the phenomenological meaning of "science." The traditional meaning or conception of science (natural science) must first be made clear, if only briefly. Husserl's view of science in the traditional sense is closely linked to the psychophysical dimension of natural science. He writes:

> All natural science is naive in regard to its point of departure. The nature that it will investigate is for it simply there. Of course, things there are, as things at rest, in motion, changing in unlimited space, and temporal things in unlimited time. We perceive them, we describe them by means of simple empirical judgments. It is the aim of natural science to know these unquestioned data in an objectively valid, strictly scientific manner. The same is true in regard to nature in the broader, psycho-physical sense, or in regard to the sciences that investigate it—in particular, therefore, in regard to psychology. The psychical does not constitute a world for itself; it is given as an ego or as the experience of an ego . . . and this sort of thing reveals itself empirically as bound to certain physical things called bodies. This, too, is a self-evident pre-datum.[38]

The central philosophical fact of natural science, according to Husserl, is that the starting point of the natural scientist takes for granted the being of nature and of the natural scientist himself. This philosophical naiveté, this fundamental presupposition regarding the world and the self, is a naturalistically oriented realism which affects not only the specific judgments of the scientist but orients the inquirer a priori in such a way that what is located as problematic as well as the methodological approach to the problematic is predetermined. Without self-conscious examination or analysis, the philosophical viewpoint of the scientist is taken for granted as correct and as necessary. In effect, as Husserl sees it, a crucial philosophical decision has been made unconsciously by the natural scientist, as though it were utterly inconceivable that the question of starting point or the question of the nature of the being of the inquirer were legitimate, let alone necessary issues for science and the scientist. Realism is one of many philosophical perspectives, not a God-decreed epistemic or metaphysical necessity. It is common sense, of course, which is closest to philosophical realism. The phenomenological standpoint stresses the recognition that what Husserl calls the "General Thesis," "according to which the real world about me is at all times known,"[39] is not a single act but a continuing believing-in, whereby the world is accepted as an ultimately reliable ground.

Phenomenological science is based on that egology we have already described: the in-person presentation of Evidenz. At the same time, it is crucial to trace the evidential given to its origin in the becoming of intentional consciousness. What has been termed "genetic phenomenology" must remain a separate and unwritten chapter in this discussion. What we are examining under the rubric of "origin" is a different matter and must be discussed. The philosophical concern with origin is perhaps the most basic aspect of phenomenology. We are not interested here in the ordinary meaning of history; neither are we concerned with some psychological retreat of consciousness to its biological sources. Instead, the turn to origin in phenomenology refers to the interior history of inwardness in the building up, the constitution, of intentionality. The ground for this constitution is that of transcendental subjectivity and, ultimately, the transcendental ego. The stream of intentionality has direction and structure; our experience of the world is rooted in the constitutive activity of the transcendental ego, which is the source of our being. But that assertion is jargon-burdened and difficult to reduce to more accessible terms—difficult to translate. Nevertheless, an effort must be made. Though it is perilous, phenomenologically, to give an "example," some attempt is necessary to translate the genuinely deep language of phenomenology into a more lucid way of seeing the foundation of our world. What is needed is a way of tracing the "our" back to the "I," the "we" back to the ego. Our descriptive-explanatory effort must now reverse itself, so that the transcendental ground of "origin" may be understood as the entrance to the very life-world from which we began. In our Lebenswelt is our beginning.

Three

Phenomenology in Literature III

IN HIS ESSAY "Some Leading Concepts of Phenomenology"—a paper designed to be an introduction to phenomenology—Alfred Schutz, after an exposition of Husserl's theories of "rigorous science," "intentionality," "reduction," "constitution," and "eidos," says:

> And now I am afraid I have to disappoint the reader. A trained phenomenologist would not regard the foregoing as an account of phenomenological *philosophy*. He would perhaps admit that one or two questions of what Husserl called phenomenological *psychology* have been touched on. Phenomenological philosophy deals with the activities of the transcendental ego, with the constitution of space and time, with the constitution of intersubjectivity, with the problems of life and death, with the problems of monads; indeed, it is an approach to the questions hitherto called metaphysical.[40]

In similar fashion, I must offer my regrets. I have written about some central concepts in phenomenology, including transcendental subjectivity, but have not either described or analyzed the problems of phenomenological philosophy. In order to do so, I would have to invoke, *employ*, the method of phenomenological-transcendental reduction. And this I have not done. If I have employed anything, it is various dodges to avoid that level of reduction. But in my case, as distinguished by what Schutz did in his essay, the situation is worse, for I have introduced the notion of an "existential phenomenology." My impieties are many. A hostile critic would accuse me of taradiddle.

There must be accountability. I have already taken responsibility for the nomenclature as well as notion of "existential phenomenology." Now it is necessary to be still more explicit. The sense in which I have employed the language of "existential phenomenology" involves several distinctions. First, some negative warnings. There is not something called "existential phenomenology" in the writings of Edmund Husserl. We are not dealing with a "type" of phenomenology (an equivalent in language-use of "Marburg Neo-Kantianism"). We are not concerned with an identifiable "school" of philosophy. To be sure, there have been important existential thinkers who have been influenced by Husserl (in varying degrees: Heidegger, Sartre, and Merleau-Ponty, for example). We are not asserting that Heidegger was an "existentialist," only that it is not wildly misleading to recognize a strong existential strain in his thinking, even if his philosophical commitment is elsewhere. Sartre, perhaps, comes closer to the appellation. In truth, the most nearly pure existential thinker could not have been influenced by Husserl—Kierkegaard. Second, some affirmations. In additon to phenomenologically oriented (or influenced) thinkers who have established themselves—however differently—in the stream of existential thought, there is the matter of conceptual convergence between existentialism and phenomenology. On this point there is no doubt in my mind that Husserl's phenomenology would have to be considered the more fundamental philosophical as well as methodological force. In "existential phenomenology," the word "existential" is a modifier of "phenomenology," not an indicator of a kind of phenomenology, let alone a competitor to Husserl's version. We are involved in necessary distinctions and discriminations. Were our chapters to have titles, this one would have to be called "reservations." But these are reservations in the service of clarity; nothing to be apologetic about. My third consideration follows.

What the meaning of "existential phenomenology" comes to, basically, is a self-description of my philosophical procedure. I am not trying to combine disciplines; neither am I attempting to found a new subject in the spectrum of philosophy. Rather, I am trying to be as clear as I can manage about how I view and endeavor to "live" phenomenology. And as I have already indicated, I do not expect plaudits for my efforts. To the contrary, "existential phenomenology" is born with enemies, hounded from opposite sides, but enriched by the ambiguities it generates. Far from repeating, "Here I stand; I can do no other," I am peeking out of my hiding place and inquiring, "Have they stopped throwing stones?" This is not where I wish to be; it is where I find myself. Even as I write these words, I seem to hear voices saying: "Wipe your nose," "Act your age," "Your father is looking for you," "Are you going to get it!" The sounds of childhood are closing in. Since phenomenology is also a science of beginnings, it should not be a surprise that early memories return. Now, standing alone, as an adult, I can say with some assurance: I trust that it is clear that the way in which I interpret phenomenology is considered and deliberate, whether or not it meets with approval. I have never believed in Husserl's contention that rigorous science implied generations of phenomenologists working on the edifice of a *mathesis universalis*. I would rather translate Husserl's vision of rigorous science into the image of philosophy itself: a shattering of assumptions, a devastation of the taken for granted, a perpetual reconnoitering of the life-world in search of the self.

It is ourselves and others who comprise the life-world; the Lebenswelt is a peopled world. At the same time, it should be recognized that
"society" is not a synonym for the world we are investigating. "Social
reality" comes closer to representing our topic, but it is the interpretation as well as the perception of being-in-the-world that is involved cen-
trally in forming what is meant by the life-world. And it must be further
understood that the world as perceived is hardly the whole of the philosophical scene. My perceptual reality is built out of what I see and sense
as well as what others have seen and sensed, as I think of or, more
broadly, intend what they have perceived. Included in those perceptions
of others is the idea (and sometimes the record) of what others who died
before I was born (what Schutz terms "predecessors") have seen and
sensed. The present is a condensation not only of the past but, in human
terms, the future—what our "successors" (as Schutz calls them) will experience and how they will act; at least our expectations, our ideas, our
notions of their conduct. Of course, we are speaking of those who will
be born after we die. The mode of attitude must necessarily be predic-
tive but we can also influence by our present actions what our successors
will be likely to confront as a "world." In its major focus, phenomenologically, the life-world must be seen as the common-sense reality of human beings in their daily lives, understood in terms of their—the human
beings'—interpretation and understanding of that common-sense reality. Speaking of the life-world, Aron Gurwitsch says:

> What is meant is the world as encountered in everyday life and given in direct
> and immediate experience, especially perceptual experience and its derivatives
> like memory, expectation, and the like, independently of and prior to scien-
> tific interpretation. At every moment of our life, we find ourselves in the
> world of common everyday experience; with this world we have a certain fa-
> miliarity not derived from what science might teach us; within that world we
> pursue all our goals and carry on all our activities, including scientific ones. As
> the universal scene of our life, the soil, so to speak, upon which all human
> activities, productions, and creations take place, the world of common experi-
> ence proves the foundation of the latter as well as of whatever might result
> from them.[41]

Gurwitsch emphasizes an important point that I have left implicit in
the discussion of the Lebenswelt thus far: the experience of common-
sense life is not derived from scientific theories or results. In life-world
terms, my fear of getting cancer has nothing to do with the scientific
theories or results. In life-world terms, my fear of getting cancer has
nothing to do with the scientific understanding of that malignancy.
Even if the layman is unusually well informed about cancer, being well

informed is far from synonymous with scientific understanding. Obviously there are considerable ranges of being informed or uninformed about disease. It is quite possible that I am afraid of getting cancer because I was born in the month of June and have powerful, if eccentric, interests in the zodiac. Were someone to ask me, "Are you afraid of getting carcinoma?" I might reply, "Don't be ignorant!" The phenomenological concern with the life-world is neither unscientific or anti-scientific; it is, epistemologically speaking, pre-scientific. Husserl maintains that the constructs of the natural sciences are grounded in what Gurwitsch calls the "soil" of the Lebenswelt. In his book, *The Crisis of European Sciences and Transcendental Phenomenology* (which we have earlier referred to simply as *The Crisis*), Husserl also utilizes the imagery of "soil." "The concrete life-world," he writes, "is the grounding soil [der gründende Boden] of the 'scientifically true' world."[42] There are two axial features of the life-world to be considered: first, its "pre-givenness" and second, its "pre-predicative" aspect. We take them up in turn.

Husserl summarizes neatly what he has said in *The Crisis* about the "pre-givenness" of the Lebenswelt:

> the life-world, for us who wakingly live in it, is always already there, existing in advance for us, the "ground" of all praxis whether theoretical or extratheoretical. The world is pregiven to us, the waking, always somehow practically interested subjects, not occasionally but always and necessarily as the universal field of all actual and possible praxis, as horizon. To live is always to live-in-certainty-of-the-world.[43]

In short, the social world within whose confines our lives are lived is a pre-interpreted reality. Not only pre-interpreted by my predecessors but pre-interpreted by my contemporaries. Both the physical objects and the social events of daily life are, first of all, understood (broadly speaking) by each of us as usually having a kind of history: those events have been observed and interpreted by our forebears; second of all, the living individual interprets interpretations handed down to him. This family has always been Methodist, Republican, pacifist; that family has always been anti-church, decisively anarchist, and its sons have volunteered in every war in the history of the nation; the other family is Jewish, will not remove to Israel until the Temple has been rebuilt, and awaits the coming of the Messiah. The interpretive world in which all of these families live is rich with historical signification which transcends genealogical considerations. "We have always been . . ." is more than a matter of tracing back the affiliations or attitudes of predecessors; there is a hermeneutic at work here which reflects the epistemic claim that knowledge is knowledge-of, and that the "of" is itself a knower, an interpreter of its own time as well as a rememberer of still earlier times. At the same time, "We have always been . . ." suggests matters of loyalty, opposition, ultimate commitment, as well as unconcern in some things. To understand the stance of a member of one of these families at a particular time is to understand a fundamental feature of pre-givenness: the concept of "situation." Jean-Paul Sartre writes: "What men have in common is not a 'nature' but a condition, that is, an ensemble of limits and restrictions: the inevitability of death, the necessity of working for a living, of living in a world already inhabited by other men. Fundamentally this condition is nothing more than the basic human situation, or, if you prefer, the ensemble of abstract characteristics common to all situations."[44] Having a past then, having a present, demands interpretation within a situation; and the "same" situation may be understood in violently contradictory ways. As Sartre reminds us: for the Romans, Carthage was conquered; but for the Carthaginians, Carthage was enslaved. The primordial situation of every individual includes the pre-givenness of a pre-interpreted world. Thus far, it might appear, the phrase "existential phenomenology" has been used in a rather defensive way, as if the "existential" part were the more easily intimidated member of the pair. In the cause of clarity, the "existential" might appear to have received an apologetic tone. Nothing could be more wrong. Sartre's notion of "situation" has an intensely voluntaristic dimension. "Situation" is *chosen* by both Romans and Carthaginians. But the choice arises in the inevitable context of pre-givenness. Had the Romans not invaded Carthage, its inhabitants could not have "chosen" to consider themselves enslaved. I am not free to undo the Second World War; my freedom is chosen within the confines of what Sartre calls "facticity." I may, in pathology, deny the war; I may refuse to accept the death of my son in that conflict; but I am not free to erase the past. Despite all the nihilation in his ontology, Sartre is bound, as he not only admits but affirms, by the facticity of history.

Pre-predicative experience is more nearly an epistemic consideration. At the same time, it is vital to Husserlian phenomenology and, in a modified way, to Sartrean thought. Something of its range will be indicated here. Schutz writes:

Phenomenological analysis shows . . . that there is a pre-predicative stratum of our experience, within which the intentional objects and their qualities are not at all well circumscribed; that we do not have original experiences of isolated things and qualities, but that there is rather a field of our experiences within which certain elements are selected by our mental activities as standing out against the background of their spatial and temporal surroundings; that within the through and through connectedness of our stream of consciousness all these selected elements keep their halos, their fringes, their horizons;

that an analysis of the mechanism of predicative judgment is warranted only
by recourse to the mental processes in which and by which pre-predicative
experience has been constituted.[45]

According to Schutz, the typologies formed for the realms of
predecessors, contemporaries, consociates (those contemporaries with
whom we share space and time—our families, friends, co-workers), and
successors have different pre-predicative structures, depending on such
factors as intimacy and anonymity. Just as important is the distinction
which Schutz draws between the Other and the Thou, the former involving anonymous constructs whereas the latter involves fellow human
beings—Selves. For Schutz, "The Thou-orientation is a pre-predicative
experience of a fellow being." The experience of the Other is quite different. Schutz writes: "The Other who is a mere contemporary is not
given to me *directly* as a unique particular Self. I do not apprehend his
Selfhood in straightforward pre-predicative experience."[46]

In Sartrean language, the pre-predicative realm of experience is translated into the terminology of the "pre-reflective." The difference between the two is considerable when it comes to understanding levels of
consciousness. For Sartre, all consciousness has a pre-reflective dimension. There is a pre-reflective *cogito* which is the ultimate source of the
activities of conscious life. The pre-reflective cogito is not a level of consciousness or to be understood in such a way that an elevator of reflection moves up and down the townhouse of awareness, making epistemic
stops. Rather, the pre-reflective cogito is seen *through* the cogito, in
what Sartre would call a lucid glance. And although consciousness is
intentional for both Husserl and Sartre, the latter conceives of intentionality as a centrifugal force: consciousness is "out there," in-the-
world, at the end of one's glance. "I is an other," Rimbaud said, and
Sartre takes his point of departure from that utterance, as a deliverance
from subjectivity. Seeking to understand Husserl better than Husserl
understood himself, Sartre writes:

> Husserl has restored to things their horror and their charm. He has restored
> to us the world of artists and prophets: frightening, hostile, dangerous, with
> its havens of mercy and love . . . everything is finally outside, everything, even
> ourselves. Outside, in the world, among others. It is not in some hiding-place
> that we will discover ourselves; it is on the road, in the town, in the midst of
> the crowd, a thing among things, a man among men.[47]

Apart from the question of whether this goes beyond Husserl, it is
unquestionably an existential reading of phenomenology. The "of" in
intentionality has been carried to its finality; more importantly, it is the
Sartrean doctrine of the ego which gives meaning to that finality, for it

is the ego which is thrown out and finds itself "in-the-world." For Sartre, there is no "subjective" core of consciousness remaining. It is in this sense that we are "delivered from Proust."[48] In place of subjectivity there is, for Sartre, nothingness—depending on the facet or placement of the term, that means freedom, temporality, choice, and a host of related concepts. But it is not only Husserlian intentionality which Sartre has transformed; the phenomenological status and meaning of what Husserl calls the "transcendental ego" are shattered by Sartre's attack on subjectivity. Sartre writes: "the phenomenological conception of consciousness renders the unifying and individualizing role of the *I* totally useless. It is consciousness, on the contrary, which makes possible the unity and the personality of my *I*. The transcendental *I*, therefore, has no raison d'être." And Sartre drives home his attack with the charge: "Consciousness is loaded down; consciousness has lost that character which rendered it the absolute existent *by virtue of non-existence*. It is heavy and *ponderable*. All the results of phenomenology begin to crumble if the *I* is not, by the same title as the world, a relative existent: that is to say, an object *for* consciousness."[49]

Something paradoxical has arisen. Earlier I said that I do not accept Husserl's idea that phenomenology requires (as he envisions it) generations of phenomenologists working to build the structure of a universal formalism. Now Sartre, the existential philosopher, asserts that there is no need for a transcendental *I*, the transcendental ego. My "existential phenomenology" would seem to be invaded from both the phenomenological and the existential side. What a mess! My survival as a credible philosopher seems to depend on some magic of extrication. But philosophers are not without resources: whenever our nouns are threatened, we try to seek cover in our adjectives; if that does not work, we look for distinctions. The last is what I must do now. The way out lies in a double negation. Neither do I hold with Husserl on universal formalism nor do I associate myself with Sartre on the repudiation of the transcendental ego. I urge everyone to use Occam's razor with utmost care. Indeed, as though two hundred years of lemmings had found their sad way to the sea, even the names (let alone the thought) of so many philosophers of the past two centuries are virtually unknown to graduate students of philosophy in today's academy. It is time to move slowly. There is no need to repudiate Husserl because of his vision of ultimate achievement: the total edifice of phenomenology completed, constructed solidly on the foundation of Evidenz, constructed once and for all. Neither is it commanded that Sartre's ontological demands be granted. In fine, a *mathesis universalis* is not the only way of understanding phenomenology's future, nor is the transcendental ego in the way of pure intentionality.

In Sartre's "non-egological" conception of consciousness, as it has been called, a certain solemnity of intentionality has been replaced by the sprightliness of nihilation. Lucidity has replaced *gravitas*. What remains dubious, from a Husserlian perspective, is the question of how the constitutive activity of consciousness is to be treated. It has been assumed in the discussion so far that the source of constitution is the transcendental ego. If meaning in the phenomenological universe of discourse is not to be disclosed in its formative agency in the region of transcendental subjectivity, then it would appear that either the idea of such primal formation is to be given up or the entire nature of transcendental consciousness is in need of review. Sartre has opted for a spontaneity of intentionality in which constitution simply happens. He writes: "It is consciousness which unifies itself, concretely, by a play of 'transversal' intentionalities which are concrete and real retentions of past consciousnesses. Thus consciousness refers perpetually to itself."[50] Some fiddle seems to be going on in this fast-moving game of *chemin de fer*. Where do the "transversal" intentionalities come from and where do they go? How does the phenomenologist determine that "consciousness refers perpetually to itself"? In his haste to throw out the bath water of an inhabitant of consciousness, Sartre has thrown out the resident infant. It is necessary to inquire whether a phenomenological hoax has been committed. Or it may be that the existential setting of Sartre's approach to intentionality is responsible for the mischief suspected.

Aron Gurwitsch has pointed out with great clarity what I think is an analogous case of an existential refusal of the transcendental reduction and its consequences. He writes: "No transcendental question is raised by Merleau-Ponty as to the constitution of the pre-objective world. On the contrary, he accepts it in its absolute factuality. If Merleau-Ponty has not developed a phenomenology of perception in the full transcendental sense, it is because the existentialist setting of his investigations prevents him from performing the phenomenological reduction in a radical manner."[51] What the implications of this discussion of Sartre and reference to Gurwitsch are for "existential phenomenology" and our future examination of literature must be left in abeyance for the time being—and perhaps still longer. These matters, existential and phenomenological, as well as their relation to radical reduction, appear in the horizon of a larger set of problems: the aggravations of the Lebenswelt. To that moaning patient we must return our full attention.

Within the life-world, any reflective turn of consciousness upon some aspect of the life-world proves to be indistinguishable from regarding a particular of the life-world. That is to say, one may focus upon an aspect or scene or problem of the life-world but not touch upon the framework within which that concrete aspect appears. The particular seized upon does not carry a label declaring it to be part of its framework. The home does not carry a sign within it designating it as a home. Some homes of historical importance may have special signs, indicating the original owner's or occupant's study or something of the kind. But the ordinary life-world home is bereft of such indicators. It is simply home. It is easy to imagine "fun homes" in which signs have been placed: "This is where the Jenners cook," "this is where the Jenners entertain," and other winners. The home is hardly subdued which lacks such attractions. There are subtleties: the mirror in the Dutch painting which reflects the scene of the living room. But no mirror reveals the life-world. That the living room scene reflected in the mirror *is* a scene gives us a powerful reminder that life within the Lebenswelt goes on. Beyond that, the mirror reflects the everydayness of that occurrence. Auden's ship moves on past the amazement of "a boy falling out of the sky."

Is there no reflection of the life-world as life-world because of the enormity involved—so much life-world? Surely, the answer lies in a different direction. The life-world is not a container but a term for the unlimited essentiality (or typicality) of everydayness. Essentiality—essence—is challenging but has the on-and-off quality of being misleading. "Essence" is a word inherently suggestive of a small, gemlike something—the tiniest pea within a Russian-doll-like series of containers. Everything superfluous gotten rid of, the core is a magnificent simple. The word "essence" has done considerable harm to phenomenology. Instead of denoting quintessence, Husserlian essence refers to an epistemically uncontaminated quale. I prefer to say that instead of diminution, essence implies dispersion—as when a drop of ink spreads upon touching a blotter. The essence of a fragrance cannot be sought in something contained; uncontainment is the clue to the perfumer's vocation as well as the wine-taster's calling. However different these examples are from the phenomenologist's art, they are suggestive of a democracy of presentation instead of what is often taken to be a mystical and hidden act: the intuition of essence. "Intuition" is simply unmediated apprehension, direct seeing. It need not be denied that Husserl's favored sense is vision. At the same time, intuition is not limited to the visual. There does seem to be a delicate range in the phenomenological senses: vision, hearing, touching, tasting, and that fugitive from eidetic justice—olfaction. But the ancient physicians, swirling samples of urine in pans, smelled as much as they looked. Among the moderns, Hermann von Helmholtz and Erwin Straus have concerned themselves with the sensation of odor. In another sphere, the same art in different refinements is practiced by the vintner and the auscultator. Essence cannot properly be conceived of as a presence amidst the unity and diversity of the senses; that it can be intuited is the grace of corporeality, the gift of incarnation.

If the life-world is the unstated given of our daily existence, then our being-with-Others may be taken as an a priori of the Lebenswelt. Again, it is the typicality of the world of everyday life which is being stressed. The world, then, may be "given" in two ways: as a factic reality in which "the elevator is crowded" or as the crowded elevator irrealized in favor of its possibility. Is the last less crowded? No, but "its being crowded" is caught in a finer net than unease can weave. "Being crowded" is at once too many bodies in a highly confined area for comfort and the meant intentional correlate of the small acts which taken together "mean" discomfort. The a priori at issue is not the ghost of perception but the condition of there being perception. But to assert, as I have, that the world may be "given" in two ways is the same as saying that the world may be "taken" in two ways. The point is not some version of Wittgenstein's "duck-rabbit," but rather the recognition that "the elevator is crowded" as a self-conscious awareness is not the same as the pre-reflective grasp of the otherwise "same" phenomenon. The first is a cognitive act, the second is a pre-reflective act. Let us change the image slightly. We are waiting for the elevator on the fifth floor of a very tall building, hoping to descend to the first floor. I push the button for "down"; in time the elevator stops and opens its doors: a sardine tin; we smile and the front row of sardines smile—hopeless. Pre-predicatively, we wait for the next elevator in the same pre-predicative spirit in which we had just smiled. Getting tense? Impatient? Late for the next appointment? Here too we are tinged with the pre-predicative. All we can do is to give a pre-predicative shrug.

It would be a serious error in phenomenological terms to think of the life-world as given or taken as a kind of "horizontal" reality. Even though we have considered the pre-given character of experience and stressed the pre-interpreted world of predecessors, it might well appear that what is pre-given is all on an epistemic par or that it is only special events or circumstances in the pre-given realm which stand out as important to the individual in his experience in the life-world. It is of vital importance to understand that, for Husserl, there is what might be called a "vertical" history of the pre-predicative realm. Husserl refers to the "sedimentation" of meaning—the building up of past experience to constitute the present. In the return to the past history of the "meaning-world," there is a logic of the pre-predicative realm, a way of tracing back present complexes of meaning (noetic-noematic unities) to their constitutive elements or layers of meaning. The pursuit of the sedimentation of the past is, in its ultimate force, the phenomenological return to origin. We are not speaking of psychological beginnings but of transcendental sources of consciousness, of transcendental subjectivity.

In effect, a double regression is at issue in the phenomenological conception of pre-predicative experience. First, there is a movement back to the life-world to determine the evidential sources of constructs at work in both the social and the natural sciences. It might be said that constructs are to Husserl what "mediation" (in Hegel's sense) was to Kierkegaard. A red light of warning goes on when either of these terms is used for these philosophers. Not artificially constituted constructs but the uncovering of noematic complexes of meaning is the object of phenomenological work. But there is a second level of interpretation to be ascribed to the sedimentation of meaning in the search for origin. This last we have already mentioned. Husserl conceives of the steps involved in this transcendental regression as an uncovering of hidden elements in the formation of experience. The life-world, then, is grounded in the intentional activities of transcendental subjectivity. Husserl summarizes the matter in this way:

> the retrogression to this transcendental subjectivity constituting the pregiven world takes place in two stages:
>
> 1. *In the retrogression from the pregiven world* with all of its sedimentations of sense, with its science and scientific determination, *to the original life-world*.
>
> 2. *In the regressive inquiry which goes from the life-world to the subjective operations from which it itself arises.* For the life-world indeed is nothing simply pregiven. It also is a structure which we can question regarding the modes of its constitution.[52]

Although illustrations are extraordinarily difficult to offer for the second step in Husserl's statement, let us at least try. Take the notion of "familiarity" as it is ordinarily understood—its dictionary definition, for a start: "close acquaintance with or knowledge of something." Obviously, we are speaking of one of the meanings of "familiarity," but already some difficulties arise. The "something" of which there is said to be close acquaintance or knowledge may be a thing, an event, a situation, a text, or a person. The kind of familiarity involved in each instance may be different. Let us select the simplest example. I am familiar with my home. That may signify: I know where the kitchen is, where the medicine chest is to be found, how many rooms there are; the ordinary sort of thing. To the San Francisco question, Do you have a view? I may answer: I live in a basement apartment; I catch sight of the occasional ankle. But I know a lot about my quarters: start with three steps down, a steel-backed oak door (inherited from a previous tenant who is said to have tried in vain to sever connections with his social club, had moved a great deal, was described as being depressed, and was not last heard from), a small foyer which is furnished with a genuine elephant's foot

cane and umbrella stand, and a rather spare room which has been vari-
ously described as the living room, the drawing room, and the reception
area. The walls are festively decorated with bullfight posters. Is it necessary to go on? We call it home. Lived here for eight years. Know the
neighbors. Have the papers delivered every day. What more need be
said? Familiar. Any distinction needed between familiarity and familiar?
Forget it.

Now a bunch of remembers: Remember when the landlord first
showed you the flat? Remember that sclerotic face of his? Remember
how to every question he answered: "Whatya mean?" Is there plenty of
hot water? Whatya mean? Will you repaint? Whatya mean? What's the
rent? Plenty! All right, it's a done deal. Whatya mean? And there's that
declivity in the bedroom floor. Impossible to explain. Anybody asks, I
tell them that I lift weights. An accident. Something to do with joists.
There's some things, they can't be explained. When I first asked the
landlord, he said, "Whatya mean?" The place is small, cozy, familiar.
You know what I mean?

Now a bunch of first-night phenomena: When I was trying out the
mattress, someone in the apartment above me started to hit some
metal—a pipe probably—with what sounded like a hammer. You never
heard such banging—a real uproar. Or should it be called a downroar?
Then heavy rain commenced, something fearful. I checked the bathroom ceiling; it had lupus. I called in the landlord to inspect it. "Looks
like lupus," he said. The falling plaster missed me by inches. I decided
to ignore the landlord. Leaks had started up everywhere. First night
blues, I thought. Wait until my phone is connected; there will be a flash
fire.

Now some provisioning: The next day it had cleared. My first visit was
to the corner grocery. "I'd like a dozen eggs," I said to the woman behind the counter. "Whatya mean?" she replied. "Are you married to the
landlord?" I asked. "Don't get familiar," she said.

Yes, I am familiar with my home, but everything that has been said
about it in our illustration is a function of the first stage of retrogression
which Husserl mentions. We have not entered the transcendental
sphere, but we are on our way. The vestibule of subjectivity, so to speak,
consists in the sometimes dramatic awareness that my home *is* home,
that such an entity exists at all. We are surprised or amazed by a secret
door but take it for granted that there is the rest of the room. It is by
making the "rest of the room" an amazement that we can secure its singular secrecy. The familiarity of home is most often explained—if it is
explained at all—by psychological concepts of repetition, memory, and
association. My neighborhood is familiar because I have seen its stores,
apartments, and buildings hundreds upon hundreds of times. If a particular place undergoes some fundamental change, *that* registers as some-

thing new amidst the familiarity of the old. In time, "something new" will become absorbed into the scene. "There may once have been a dry-cleaning establishment there," says an old man, "I'm no longer sure; it was there when I was a boy." We are not surprised by such statements. There is a familiarity to familiarity. There may also be a familiarity about states of affairs which seem to be reasonable but, strictly speaking, do not follow: if two and two are five, then three and three are seven. "Your face looks familiar, didn't we go to the same high school? You were on the swimming team, weren't you?" "No, I went in for gymnastics, the rings." "Yeah, that's right; I thought you looked familiar; I remember you now." All of this may be so. Familiarity transcends error. The transcendental source of familiarity is identity, often comprehended in a muted aura of memory. That which does not belong to the noematic nucleus of identity is set off against the strange. Thus, when Schutz writes of familiarity he contrasts not with the unfamiliar but instead the strange.

The setting off of the strange is accomplished in pre-reflective spontaneity, in what Husserl calls the "passive syntheses" of transcendental consciousness. At this moment we are self-consciously inquiring into such doings. There may well be a psychological history of the strange, as the individual has experienced it. It might be necessary to return to the banal nursery light. But how did the banal come to be considered banal? Increments of repetition do not account for original threats caught in the critical mass of apperception. Is there a something "originarily" strange? Familiarity, understood at the transcendental level, emerges in consciousness as a victor over the strange. Pursuing this line of inquiry, I believe that the strange is a hiddenness uncovered by the familiar. Not "set off against," then, but hidden within. Acquaintance-ship is certainly an odd phenomenon, in any case. I remember taking the Southern Railroad during the time of the Second World War for a trip from Knoxville, Tennessee, to my home in New York City. It proved to be a milk train, stopping about every forty miles or so. I got off at this train's terminus: Washington, D.C., where I had to change to the Pennsylvania Railroad. While on the Southern, I found myself seated next to an old woman from Tennessee. She explained in her garrulity that she had lived all of her life in a small town nearly forty miles from Knoxville, that she had been visiting her daughter. She was interested in my destination. "New York City," I said. "Oh," she replied, "I know some people who live in New York. Why, there's Thomas Wilson; do you know him? And there is Grady Tuley; do you know him? Amanda Phillips; do you know her?" When I said that I did not know any of these people, the old lady looked at me with a hint of sadness, I thought, and ended our conversation by remarking: "Well, you don't seem to be very well acquainted."

A very different kind of acquaintanceship is to be found in quite other realms. One has only to think of Robert Frost's poem "Acquainted with the Night" and its opening and closing line: "I have been one acquainted with the night," to recognize the sense of passage beyond the frontier of familiarity. The movement from the familiar as reassuring, to the strange as deeply threatening is nowhere more evident than in Freud's essay on "The 'Uncanny.'" Among a number of other considerations of the signification of the "uncanny," Freud turns to E. T. A. Hoffmann's story about "The Sand-Man." In modern or at least recent times, the Sand-Man is usually regarded as a genial, mythic, or folkloric figure who is mentioned when little children rub their eyes around bed time and are asked, "Sand-Man in your eyes?" It's going to bed time, going to sleep time. Brewer's *Dictionary of Phrase and Fable* tells us: "'The Sand-Man is about.' It is bedtime, for the children rub their eyes, as if dust or sand was in them."[53] Hoffmann transforms the Sand-Man into an antihero of the Uncanny: "He is a wicked man who comes when children won't go to bed, and throws handfuls of sand in their eyes so that they jump out of their heads all bleeding. Then he puts the eyes in a sack and carries them off to the moon to feed his children. They sit up there in their nest, and their beaks are hooked like owl's beaks, and they use them to peck up naughty boys' and girls' eyes with."[54] In Freud's discussion of the uncanny, the strangest aspect of the strange, I would say, is its *unheimlich* character, its "lost to home" aspect, its "un-homeness," its "other side of the mirror" quality. What is uncanny about "un-homeness" is that the very quality of assurance which is locked in familiarity is unlocked in *Unheimlichkeit* and transformed into a threatening vagueness, a hovering instead of a fixity. In disease there may or may not be an uncanny factor experienced by the observer. Freud writes:

> The uncanny effect of epilepsy and of madness has the same origin. The ordinary person sees in them the workings of forces hitherto unsuspected in his fellow-man but which at the same time he is dimly aware of in a remote corner of his own being. The Middle Ages quite consistently ascribed all such maladies to daemonic influences, and in this their psychology was not so far out. Indeed, I should not be surprised to hear that psycho-analysis, which is concerned with laying bare these hidden forces, has itself become uncanny to many people for that very reason.[55]

The stilted, lunging movements of the spastic do not ordinarily occasion a sense of the uncanny in the observer; but the epileptic fit is in a different category. I do not believe it is usual in medical circles to speak of a "spastic personality," whereas it is not uncommon to hear of "an epileptic personality." What is called in medical terminology an "intellectual aura" is described as "a dreamy state which may precede an epileptic attack."[56] To speak of an "epileptic personality" is to oversimplify a highly complex and variable matter, but the epileptic aura appears to be fairly constant. Its description is interesting. Sensations rising from the region of the stomach or abdomen toward the throat

> are frequently accompanied by an emotion of dread which may, however, be independent or accompany other abnormal mental phenomena. Also very distinctive are the *déjà vu* and the *déjà vécu* experiences; these are often coupled with other falsifications of memory or imposed recollections e.g., of the first epileptic fit, or the panoramic memory of the patient's whole life appearing in a flash. . . . Other experiences closely linked with these are the uncanny feelings of change in the outer world or in the self, derealization, *depersonalization* and disturbances of the body image. If these mental experiences are very vivid, they may take on the character of an illusion; visual illusions are the commonest, and may consist in seeing people as distorted, flattened, or elongated or as only half figures. *Forced ideas* experienced like passivity phenomena in eternity or infinity may suddenly present itself to the patient, or a storm of indescribable thoughts may race through his mind. An *affective aura* is common and the description given of this aura by Dostoievsky suggests commencement of excitation in a temporal lobe focus: ". . . a feeling of happiness which I never experience in my normal state and of which I cannot give the idea . . . complete harmony with myself and with the whole world." Sudden feelings of despair, guilt, anxiety and terror may form the content of the aura in other cases. Premonitions of death, of the end of the world, basic religious or philosophical doubts, suicidal and aggressive urges also have been described.[57]

Earlier, we stepped back from the idea that in certain respects philosophy resembles epilepsy. No doubt that was a circumspect retreat. But there is a suggestiveness in the statements we have found in psychoanalysis and psychiatry. When Freud remarks that psychoanalysis itself may invoke the uncanny to some, we might remember Hans Castorp's reaction when Joachim tells him, soon after they have met on the Mountain, that Dr. Krokowski "psycho-analyses" the patients.

> "He what? Psycho-analyses—how disgusting!" cried Hans Castorp; and now his hilarity altogether got the better of him. He could not stop. The psycho-analysis had been the finishing touch. He laughed so hard that the tears ran down his cheeks; he put up his hands to his face and rocked with laughter.[58]

Death and eroticism have been uncannily joined, for a moment before the statement about Dr. Krokowski, Joachim has informed his cousin that the highest of the sanatoriums have to send their bodies down on bobsleds in the winter, when the roads are blocked. And Hans bursts into laughter. It is then that Dr. Krokowski's activities are mentioned and received with uncontrollable laughter. All of this occurs upon Hans Castorp's very arrival, but what is a highly inappropriate response to death—whatever one might say of psychoanalysis—is a prescient shudder of resonance with Krokowski's central thesis: "all disease is only love transformed."[59] Regarded in this way, the range of love parallels the range of experiences associated with disease: wonder is the transcendental clue to both philosophy and death.

If what started as a discussion of the "strange" has ended as a recognition of "wonder," it is not remarkable that existential philosophy should strike some as an abnormal interpretation of the life-world. Not epilepsy—too close to neurology for the unimaginative observer—but "disease" is sometimes the reaction to existential philosophy on the part of the uninformed. A matter of radical difference of philosophical opinion is not at issue in this case. What we have here is closer to a retching of the mind at that aspect of the surmised uncanny which challenges the unexamined substance of the familiar. Disease as love transformed is shocking to a sensibility which has ingrained in it the denial of any legitimate nexus between eroticism and death. Such a relationship would be considered decadent and profoundly repulsive. Indeed, there is in disease an aptitude for the repulsive; there is also an affinity for education—a peculiar word to be found in these regions—education as the formative quality of human being, the victory over matter. In his long conversation about life with Hans, Hofrat Behrens, in the respect he gives to death, comes down on the side of form:

> ". . . living consists in dying, no use mincing the matter—*une destruction organique*, as some Frenchman with his native levity has called it. It smells like that, too. If we don't think so, our judgment is corrupted."
>
> "And if one is interested in life, one must be particularly interested in death, mustn't one?"
>
> "Oh, well, after all, there is some sort of difference. Life is life which keeps the form through change of substance."
>
> "Why should the form remain?" said Hans Castorp.
>
> "Why? Young man, what you are saying now sounds far from humanistic."
>
> "Form is folderol."
>
> "Well, you are certainly in great form to-day—you're regularly kicking over the traces . . ."[60]

In fact, Hans is caught in the essential paradox of humanism: dying and death cannot be alien to him; but the ascent of his transformation cannot be denied.

Viewed from the standpoint of transcendental phenomenology, the strange is the familiar in denial. The life-world, far from being a map of the familiar, is more nearly a hive of typified activity. A "swarming" of the familiar as though never seen before. And, indeed, the "freshness" of the seeing is an aspect of wonder—wonder hitherto concealed under the guise of the ordinary, the everyday, the familiar. Within daily life, the natural attitude gives "everyman" things and events and people as they *are*, that is, in the reality of the naive—as they "be," if we could speak that way. Transcendental consciousness sees what the natural attitude presents but also sees "through" its sedimented history, its constitutive "upbuilding." Our effort at illustration—the exploration of the familiar—cannot be entirely successful because there is a stubbornness seen in Evidenz and what is exemplified—the "moral" of the seen. Between actuality and explanation there is an inherent dividedness which thwarts completely satisfying description. We cannot be *being*. That means that the natural quality, the relaxed state of doing this or that is only partially truly understood in terms of spontaneity. Cleaning the window pane with a clean rag and some commercial preparation which smells of ammonia—cleaning in spontaneous swirls, which at once attacks dirty places on the pane and recognizes the result of the cleaning movement—is seized as a double movement before reflective inspection intercedes. Is this "seizure" something that happens or something which may occur? The question is psychological. In transcendental terms, the noetic-noematic activity consists of a doubling of purely intentional acts. Is everything always lucid to consciousness? A different sort of example comes to mind.

When I was about six or seven years of age, what now appears to me as a rather odd practice occasionally took place in elementary school. The memory is somewhat obscure. Something like this: the teacher announced that she was going to pick out of the thirty or thirty-five children in the class one pupil for some—I suppose—exalted, rewarding purpose. We children sat at our desks with our hands uniformly clasped together and with a conscientious, earnest, *good*, and intense expression on our faces. As the teacher studied all of us, each of us (I at least) strained silently to be the best. After an unbearable two or three minutes, the teacher would call out the name of the winner. Looking back at it now, so many years later, what I recall seems eerie. What was going on? What pedagogic device was being put to use? I do not remember ever being chosen but I might have been. In any event, nothing further comes back to me. If I was not chosen, there must have been *some* disappointment; if I *was* chosen, it would seem reasonable that the reward or what accompanied the honor would have stuck in my memory. Neither disappointment nor exhilaration nor their long-ago traces remain; what remains, apart from the event itself, is the sense of muscular strain, straight back, arms tensely outstretched, concentration. Did some of the children look at the teacher so that their pleading expression might register? Did some of us stare straight ahead? Were some of us really relaxed? What *was* all of that? All that comes to mind in response is what was never there in childhood: Kierkegaard's title, *Purity of Heart Is to Will One Thing*. What are we to do with this utterly opaque illustration, this memory of a straggly childhood? Fortunately, what I remember coincided, I learned years later, with an inquiry into the mental health of public school teachers. The initial data received by the researchers were so alarming that the entire investigation was terminated. Have we gone far from epilepsy to madness?

Far from madness, we are concerned with a kind of deliberate focus which memory provides. The "how" of recall is subordinate to the "what" of memory. Let us call this monkey business of childhood classrooms, the "exercise." Very well, then, the what of the exercise is the noema: stiffly-attentive-toward-teacher. It is possible to flesh out the noema, to circumscribe it in more exacting terms. To add or subtract. In the transcendental attitude, however, it is irrelevant whether the noema includes some attention paid the folded hands. Nor is the object of my gaze a necessary part of the unity of the perceptual retention: the face of the teacher is simply missing. Was I staring into nothingness? It makes no noematic difference. What does matter is the exercise. Transcendentally, I look through the mechanics of the "how" in seizing the "what" of intentional experience. And so I come to understand, in this way of looking *through* the natural attitude to the recognition of the noema, the sense of the intentional object as being *meant*. The exercise returns to me not as a memory or a perceptual ghost but rather as a part of the essential world of the intended past. It is a bit like watching a building being constructed and retaining its "inside" while regarding its manifest surface. In Husserl's terms, the once-seen "inside" is appresented to my gaze as some aspect of the completed edifice. Am I appresented to myself in recalling the exercise? Not for Husserl, but I am, memorially speaking, aware of an essential feature of consciousness: what is *not* remembered, what is *not* given to recall is as critically present as what *is* remembered. The noema presents itself memorially in a horizon of loss.

Perhaps we have paid insufficient attention in our meditations to the temporality of the past as well as the present. But it is quite evident that the future has not even been approached. What a gloomy prospect! Anticipation, expectation, imagination—each treacherous, each a phenomenological tangle. Without explanation or justification—no pompous holding forth—we shall choose to consider imagination. Later, Sartre will argue that in imagination lies our freedom. For the moment we must keep from shaking. As we have persuaded ourselves, perhaps the best way is to start with an example. Join me! In ten days my orals come; or, more precisely, I must go to my orals. The committee is already set. In my opinion, three of the five appointed examiners are incompetent. As soon as I receive my degree, I will join my colleagues in saying that they are guilty of errors not even a graduate student would make. Before I can do that, the orals must be passed. Does anyone fail? At that late date in the career of graduate study, *fail*? Alas, failure may come from other reasons than the disapproval by a majority of the committee. I am told that some candidates, from the time they enter the examination chamber, fall into a state of shock—their eyes glaze over; a trauma. Some clutch a rosary; some ask if they can go to the bathroom and do not return; some feel nauseated. One especially solicitous examiner cried out to his student ten minutes before the examination was scheduled to end: "Hang in there Porter, it's almost over"—and then threw the contents of a glass of water in the candidate's face. Things can get hectic on such occasions; things can get out of hand. I am not suggesting that this sort of behavior is the norm, but you can understand why I face my orals with some temerity. Nothing is definite: a page in one of the copies of the dissertation may turn up missing; I once saw a roach emerge from buckram. What else is there to be but daring?

In anticipating my orals I imagine the scene: I am seated, as is usual for such occasions, at the end of the seminar table, in easy sight of the examining five (it sounds like the Rochester five or the Newark five—a civil rights case), and I am in the middle of the usual ten-minute summary statement of what my dissertation is all about, when I find myself saying: "I never should have entered this field; I knew it was a mistake when I did my writtens; there are no jobs to be had; Trotsky was right about permanent revolution . . ." and my advisor interrupts: "Yes, thank you. Hollins, would you begin the questioning, please?" Professor Hollins turns toward me and says: "Let us begin in *medias res*. You emphasize—as so many do, I might add—the independence Hans Castorp demonstrates in the face of his several mentors, but I do not find any reference to, let alone discussion of, his deeper relationship to Krokowski. Is there evidence that Castorp is being psychoanalyzed?" I remember the scene: secretive Hans (observed by but not noticing his cousin) enters "Dr. Krokowski's analytic lair." Now we are going to step back from that moment and enter the "reduced sphere," where the oral defense is bracketed from attention, where Castorp's visit to Krokowski is recognized as a fiction at the same time that it is irrealized and rendered

a correlate of the intentional acts which intend it. Transcendentally regarded, Castorp and Krokowski are possibilities of the imagination. To
be sure, there is a text; Hans is not a butcher and Krokowski is not a
dairyman. Yet Hans, an ordinary fellow at bottom, comes to have a mystical experience, and Krokowski, a physician who gives lectures on psychoanalysis, proves to be a magician of the uncanny. What is irrealized
in transcendental reduction is already a fiction, but now it becomes clear
that the fiction at issue—characters in a novel in this instance—is a set of
possibilities waiting, as it were, to realize themselves as Hans and
Joachim and Krokowski. What are they while waiting? We arrive at a
bracketed domain of inquiry: the ontological status of essence.

In the realm of essence, possibility is king. But having said that, it
becomes unsatisfactory to proceed to the royal residence. It might be
ventured that we are in the ontological vicinity of Plato's Ideas. That, in
turn, leads us to think of the meaning (as we have reflected before) of
the "existence" of numbers.[61] I pass on to the consideration of the possible as "imaginary." The imaginary is not synonymous with the imagined. Sartre, in the early part of his career, wrote two books having to do
with "imagination": *L'Imagination* and *L'Imaginaire*; the former, although it includes a chapter on "The Phenomenology of Husserl," is a
survey—in a phenomenological spirit—of the problem of "the image":
the latter (published in English as *The Psychology of Imagination*) is also
concerned with the image but is more broadly interested in what might
be termed "The Imaginary Life" (the title, in fact, of one of the chapters).[62] It is in *The Psychology of Imagination* that Sartre begins to develop, in phenomenological terms, his theory of "nihilation." In short,
the imaginary is the home of possibility. "Imagination," Sartre, writes,
"is not an empirical and superadded power of consciousness, it is the
whole of consciousness as it realizes its freedom; every concrete and real
situation of consciousness in the world is big with imagination in as
much as it always presents itself as a withdrawing from the real."[63] In
Sartrean analysis, negation becomes the condition of a nihilating reality.
Nihilation is the meaning of the freedom of consciousness. Irrealization
in its movement from Husserl to Sartre undergoes some radical changes,
but the phenomenological treatment of negation as a presence rather
than a psychological or logical dismissal of the phenomenon of absence
brings the two philosophers closer than might appear upon casual inspection. It is not too much to say that possibility in phenomenology is
grounded in the Nihil.

It might seem as if we are trying to bolster our point of view regarding
existential phenomenology by entering a bit into the territory of Sartre
as an existential phenomenologist. That appearance is misleading, for

what we have been doing, perhaps illicitly, is presenting some of the views of Sartre as a phenomenological ontologist. Since ontology has fallen under the epoché of transcendental reduction, ontology has been bracketed and is not part of the game; it is, in a way, *hors de combat*. Nevertheless, the brackets are gracefully rigid, they breathe, some oblique osmosis happens, ain't none of us perfect. After all, we have not been altogether scrupulous. "We" has been invoked in these pages as frequently as "I." No doubt, we are loose practitioners. *Tant pis*. But this is a sentimental mode of evaluation. We are faced not with a problem of leakage but with a far more fundamental question of genuine philosophical methodology: How is it possible to show, to "show forth" the results of phenomenological inquiry? Let us grant that there is Evidenz and let us open wide the gates of reception for the admission of the results of phenomenological investigation. Still, how can our treasures be publically displayed? In a way, we are driven back, it would appear, to first-person assessment, to happenings which for all their intentional noematic status are the self-contained fireworks of the metaphysical solipsist. If there is an end, in the end each of us must appraise the surge of experience which roars toward him, filter out its components, make sense of the elements of the life-world.

If there is noematic security, there is also noetic uncertainty. Husserl's phenomenology is sometimes apprehended as a monolith: a giant of certitude. It would be more historically prudent to recognize the reality of Husserl as an almost perennial beginner—by his own affirmation. Phenomenology, led by Husserl, trails behind it a huge sack into which errors, distortions, failures, unripe assertions, and a host of other mistakes are thrown. The image is the reverse of what seems to be a nineteenth-century Santa, short clay pipe alight, a merry, purposeful face, carrying a sack of goodies to the boys and girls who breathlessly await his visit. No reindeer for the moment, no chimneys, just Santa the lugger, en route. Today it is Christmas time again; bring out the plastic tree. Hang on it the baubles of failure: reach deep into the bag of phenomenological disasters; never mind the goodies. Today's children are no longer waiting for Santa; they are wise to rarified pharmaceuticals. Let drivers beware of whom they pick up; these are knowledgeable kids. Little phenomenologists every one of them. And as they trip merrily through the life-world, let not only juniors but seniors marvel at what God hath wrought. We are led to wonder whether there is a primordial life-world, an *Ur-Lebenswelt* which contains the molds for chaos and death. The large department stores which used to hire Santas whose job it was to sit children on their laps and listen to requests are now in Chapter Eleven bankruptcy status; the Salvation Army has modernized. In fine, the world has caught up with phenomenology. It is time to make arrangements for final reckonings. I telephone the mortuary of my choice and am astonished by hearing a recorded message. By the time I recover my wits, I hear:

> ". . . If you want grief counseling, press three.
> If you want cremation, press four."

My Luddite blood boils.

Four

Waiting for Godot

WE TURN now to three fictions by, in turn, Beckett, Mann, and Kafka: *Waiting for Godot, The Magic Mountain*, and *The Metamorphosis*. Of course, there are many scores to be settled. To begin with, there is the matter of "application"—the demonstration of how existential phenomenology (or transcendental phenomenology on its own) may in some concrete manner illuminate a literary work of art, how phenomenology can do something which other theories or methods fail to accomplish. In turn, we are led to the question of whether phenomenology in any guise can act as a corrective to, not a replacement for, some other approach to literature which is found wanting in philosophical depth or range. If we focus upon these three books, can phenomenology clarify the relationship between philosophy and literature? Can we learn something useful, if not profound, about the meaning of style and its philosophical implications? Will our ruminations about transcendental subjectivity, intentionality, and irreality light up the landscape of that forlorn heath on which Estragon and Vladimir wait? Will our reflections on solipsism elucidate the sensuous pride of Clavdia Chauchat? Can reduction, bracketing, and epoché tell us convincingly why Gregor prefers to hang from the ceiling? Perhaps. But it would be just as well to confess at once that I doubt very much that answers which will be respected will come from posing questions in this way, reasonable as it may seem that after methodology there ought, in all justice, to come practical results. If not, what is the cash value of our strolls in the gardens of phenomenology? It is, by the way, interesting how often money and the image of "the ready" enter the otherwise pristine quarters of philosophy. It might appear that even in philosophy Balzac's dictum is sovereign: Money is the petrol of life. In vulgar parlance, do we wish to "invest" in a phenomenology which will not produce results? But what are results? Is bracketed cash a negotiable instrument? Must we remain content to heed the rumble of a distant drum?

To look for new insights into Beckett, Mann, and Kafka is not quite but almost to remove to the community of Chelm. After the libraries written about our books, the pickings must be lean. A deeper difficulty underlies the matter of old and new. It would be a reversion to an error we have already mentioned to think that phenomenological method—

the discernment of essence, for example—would yield critical treasures which less gifted methodologies have failed to disclose. The point of our analysis is to suggest that the relationship between philosophy and literature can be reapproached by way of phenomenology, that method here is not a device but a modality of comprehension. If, at first glance, it appears that we are offering apologies instead of claims which present fresh interpretive results, perhaps a more sustained view of our enterprise will show that existential phenomenology offers a new as well as productive conception of the boundaries and possibilities of both philosophy and literature. We shall have a number of ideas to offer about the three fictions, but underlying any one of them is the fundamental view that the current of human existence is taken for granted in the life-world, thematized in phenomenology, and reconstructed in transcendental subjectivity. To the fictions, then.

Among other concerns, Beckett's play is a study of balance. At some time or other during the two acts of *Waiting for Godot*, all the central characters in the play are on the ground. They fall. Sometimes it is difficult to get up; eventually they manage to regain "the upright posture," as Erwin Straus called it. For Straus, it is an axiom of the Lebenswelt that the maintenance of upright posture in human beings who are healthy and easily capable of walking is a victory of balance over chaos. "Human gait," Dr. Straus writes, "is, in fact, a continuously arrested falling."[64] For the rather remote and almost deserted scene of *Waiting for Godot*, falling seems to be unusually frequent. Tumbles are common, of course, in the vaudeville stage tradition which is so much a part of the play. And there is the madness with Pozzo the blind. But there is an almost "unbalanced" quality present throughout the action. Bowled over in their bowlers, Vladimir and Estragon are the drunken tramps of a sober planet. Theirs are not the purposeful pratfalls of the comedians but the calamities of the innocent. Do they drink? Or has deprivation removed the very meaning of liquor, quite apart from its unavailability? A round of drinks will not straighten up these hearties, for even in the upright posture they have entered a zone of despair, a "sickness unto death."

"Waiting" translates into "wanting," when the latter means missing or lacking. The Godot whom they lack confers purpose on the lives of Didi and Gogo. Why don't they leave? Because they are waiting for Godot. It is difficult to say what purpose their lives would have if Godot did come. The here-and-now presence of Godot might be an "insult" to the brain, in the language of neurology. Godot's absence is a mild insult, for it lends significance to the plight of the heroes in Beckett's play. But just as drinkers reel and fall when they have too much liquor, so Vladimir and Estragon fall when they have had too much absence, too much lack, too much "Godotlessness." The "unbalance" of the play is more than the falling down of its main characters; those characters lack, in diverse ways, typical functions of ordinary people in the life-world. Vladimir suffers from prostate trouble—an enlargement, cancer, or perhaps prostatitis. It may be that he has gonorrhea or some other venereal infection. What troubles him is the urgent and painful need to urinate—it hurts. But even his urination is unbalanced. It would seem that the urgent need to urinate is a sign of a full bladder; and so it is in a normal person. But in Vladimir's case, it is likely that his bladder is not full, that the urinary passage is constricted, and what the doctors call the "caliber" of his urinary flow is abnormally thin and dribbly. The final insult is that today—does it really matter when?—Vladimir could join a prostate support group. Yes, I've heard the announcement. Can you beat that?

Pozzo asks: "Which of you smells so bad?" Estragon answers: "He has stinking breath and I have stinking feet." No urology here: half the people in the world have stinking breath and the rest have stinking feet. Truths of the Lebenswelt! Odious as the stench might be to strangers, it is just as displeasing to the two tramps. Each is disgusted, in some degree and at some times, with the stench of the other. There is even stinking within stinking. In the scene when Pozzo calls for help and Vladimir goes to him only to fall himself, Estragon says: "Who farted?" We are back not only to the devices of burlesque and vaudeville, but to the ancient comics of the "Ur-Welt," with their pigs' bladders farting away in the merry-making of the kermis.[65] Didi and Gogo may lack the typical functions of ordinary people in the life-world, but they also suffer from exhibiting an excess of some of those functions. There is balance to be had: nothing to be done. Still, they carry on and carry on together—the last is the triumph of the play; the tramps not only prevail individually, they remain together. The unbalanced world of *Waiting for Godot* is only suggested by the falling of the characters; more fundamentally, the failure to achieve balance is to be understood as a disturbance in the temporal axis of the world that the characters inhabit. Theirs is a diurnal world. "Will night never come?" Vladimir asks again and again, but the nocturnal world is threatening—and worse. It appears that Estragon sleeps in a ditch at night, that bullies beat him, that *his* night comes with repeated danger to himself. Vladimir's night does not come in answer to his pleaful question but remains obscure. It is a time when he departs. The tramps are together during the day but not at night. What Vladimir experiences at night remains unknown to

Estragon and to us. Time has, it seems, undergone an inversion of an inexplicable character. One analyst, Günther Anders, suggests that *Waiting for Godot* presents a "life without time," that life is "treading water."[66] I would choose instead of "treading water" the song that Vladimir sings: "A dog came in the kitchen. . . ."[67] The song is endless and repetitive because it reenters itself ad infinitum (or as long as the singer sings it). The song goes on only by doubling back on itself. Stasis. Time has become irrealized. All that remains finally of Pozzo's watch is its description and provenance: "A genuine half-hunter, gentlemen, with deadbeat escapement. . . . Twas my granpa gave it to me!"[68] With the irrealization of time comes the temporal reality of the fictive. Now memories dim. Estragon says that he does not remember the story of the Crucifixion and of the Bible he remembers the maps of the Holy Land. And Vladimir, the gospel-rememberer, is not sure what he and Estragon did yesterday or even the day they were supposed to wait for Godot. But Vladimir is the one who remembers that they are to wait for Godot.

Irrealization takes several forms. There is a considerable list of what the tramps forget, including their names—or is it that they will answer to any name? Pozzo asks Estragon: "What is your name?" To which the reply is: "Adam." And when the Boy addresses Vladimir as "Mister Albert . . . ?" Vladimir answers "Yes."[69] Pozzo has not only forgotten what happened but also, it would appear, has lost the very sense of "yesterday." He says: "I don't remember having met anyone yesterday. But to-morrow I won't remember having met anyone to-day."[70] Not only name but age is placed in doubt. Pozzo asks Vladimir: "What age are you, if it's not a rude question? . . . Sixty? Seventy?" Receiving no answer, he asks Estragon "What age would you say he was?" to which Estragon replies "Eleven."[71] In his French text, by the way, Beckett has Estragon reply: "Demandez-lui."[72] Beckett has surpassed himself in his English version. But irrealization goes beyond seeming or purposeful amnesia. Names and ages do not matter; what matters is waiting for Godot. Irrealization uncovers a transcendental aspect: temporality has replaced time. If temporality is the noetic root of time and if time has been irrealized, then memorial consciousness, beyond being dimmed, has drained itself of the conception of thought. Vladimir says to Estragon: "What is terrible is to *have* thought."[73] "Have" is the critical word here. In English, Beckett gives emphasis to the word (but does not in the French text). What is clear about "have" is that it is ambiguous. "To *have* thought" refers first to have had it in the past, second to have historical reference (Vladimir: "A charnel-house! A charnel-house!"), and third to hold it, to think, to have a present. "Have" is absence abounding.

Temporal irrealization means that the noetic roots of the dimensions of time are altered in such a way that the intentional "rays" of consciousness fall short of their correlates. The noematic result is dispersion of any unities of meaning; the result is nothingness. In Sartrean terms, this nothingness is the "substance"—the ontological reality—of consciousness. However, a world is presupposed as well as a situation into which the individual is thrust. Within that "world" the imagination takes on its significance.[74]

Sartre's view of the imagination is indebted as much to Heidegger as to Husserl. We are given a hybrid phenomenology in the form of a fundamental ontology. We are left, then, with an existential phenomenology whose sources, in my judgment, are not in harmony with each other. Nevertheless, it is the case that the concept of "world" is the central issue in the matter of irrealization. The fictive world of *Waiting for Godot* is an irrealized world which has imagined characters. It is not enough to say that these figures are real in the reality of the play; they are irreal in the irreality of the play. In turn, this assertion permits us to examine more closely what is meant by "world" in phenomenological terms. For Husserl, "world" is the ultimate horizonal reference to which and within which all experiential claims are made. As Ludwig Landgrebe expresses it, "The world is the all-embracing doxic basis, the total horizon that includes every particular positing."[75] Husserl distinguishes between an inner and an outer horizon. Phenomenological reduction provides access to the inner horizon of temporality. What is signified by irrealization is not denial or negation but an abstention from believing-in the reality of the world as a "container" of everyday life. Vladimir and Estragon constitute their "world" by inventing each other:

> ESTRAGON: We always find something, eh Didi, to give us the impression we exist?
> VLADIMIR: . . . Yes yes, we're magicians . . .[76]

Within the temporally irrealized world, chronology is a suicide. "Time has stopped," Vladimir says.[77] Pozzo denies it, but his watch is soon to disappear. The "world" which remains, the world in which temporality has been irrealized—immanently irrealized—is itself a solipsism. How does it happen, then, that we, the audience of the play, the readers, find Beckett's characters real? What kind of "real" is *that?* It is the real of the life-world taking aim at itself—another term for philosophy, which considers everything in the world.

"Everything in the world." If we look closely, the "thing" will present itself as the world steps forth in the drama of irrealization. In *Waiting for Godot*, we are first given the boot; what follows is a considerable inventory of "things." Rubbish comes to our attention early in the play.

Vladimir has apparently made a note of the appointment with Godot.
Vladimir "fumbles in his pockets, bursting with miscellaneous rub-
bish."[78] Among the rubbish there are turnips and carrots—a carrot for
Estragon. Then this exchange:

> VLADIMIR: How's the carrot?
> ESTRAGON: It's a carrot.
> VLADIMIR: So much the better, so much the better . . .
> ESTRAGON: . . . I'll never forget this carrot . . .[79]

Everything else, it seems, is forgotten, including the reason for
Estragon (and Vladimir) not leaving. It is the "thing" quality of everything which wins out: "everything," including conversation, dreaming,
verbal games to pass the time, has a sticky side to it. Is that sticky side the
reason why Estragon will never forget that carrot? Everything special
seems to disappear: Vladimir's note about meeting Godot, Pozzo's pos-
sessions. Yet the adhesive side of things is insufficient for their identification. Supplication is needed for an act to have veracity and efficacy in the
ordinary world.

> POZZO: . . . I'd very much like to sit down, but I don't quite know how to go
>   about it.
> ESTRAGON: Could I be of any help?
> POZZO: If you asked me perhaps.
> ESTRAGON: What?
> POZZO: If you asked me to sit down.
> ESTRAGON: Would that be a help?
> POZZO: I fancy so.
> ESTRAGON: Here we go. Be seated, Sir, I beg of you.
> POZZO: No no, I wouldn't think of it! . . . Ask me again.[80]

And so on. Which means that the commonplace act needs the sticky
side replenished if it is to stand forth on its own, *present* itself in the
midst of the taken-for-granted life-world. "Have a seat" is not enough
for the emphatic quality to emerge. The more that is required is that the
"act-quality" of the act—the "thing" aspect of the thing—must be put
into relief, must stand out in its everydayness from its everydayness.
Pozzo the performer is outstanding; he has an equipage and a stage
presence. After one of his presentations, he asks the tramps for an evaluation of his performance: "How did you find me? . . . Good? Fair? Middling? Poor? Positively bad?" Reassured by his audience, Pozzo says:
"Bless you, gentlemen, bless you!" Vladimir answers Pozzo in Vladimir,
but Estragon replies in Estragon: "Oh tray bong, tray tray tray bong."[81]
Estragon, the master of tongues; Estragon, the linguist; Estragon, the
mocker of Beckett. Vladimir is not altogether fair when he says to

Estragon, during their theological conversation, "Come on, Gogo, return the ball, can't you, once in a way?" To which admonition, Estragon
sagely replies: "I find this really most extraordinarily interesting."[82] It is
said of Sartre, by the way, that his spoken English was far inferior to his
ability in reading the language. During his visit to the United States, he
claimed that he got by with two phrases: "Why not?" and "Another
Scotch!" Tray tray bong.

What connection is there between the concepts of "irrealization" and
the "current" of existence? As to Vladimir and Estragon, we may say
that the current is faint, intermittent, in short supply, fugitive to these
fugitives of the life-world. When the Boy asks Vladimir: "What am I to
tell Mr. Godot, Sir?" Vladimir replies, "Tell him . . . tell him you saw
us."[83] The message is not a communication but a report; not something
heard, really, but something seen. "They were there" is what Vladimir
tells the Boy to report to Godot—not even "They are there," for that
might not be true; they may have departed by the time the report is
received. For Vladimir, the essential fact of existence—the current felt,
however distantly—is that the fugitives' commitment has been met. As
Vladimir says: "We are not saints, but we have kept our appointment."[84]
Is there a current within the bracketed world of *Waiting for Godot*? I
have suggested that there *is* a pulsation, albeit a very diminished beat.
The rhythm of the current consists in a revival of improvisations: the
game of insulting each other, for example. That makes the time "go."
Or at least, go faster than it might have gone otherwise. But "going" is
irrealized throughout the play. The characters announce movement, say
they are going, but mostly remain still. Stasis rules, apart from the regu-
larity of Vladimir rushing off to urinate or the irregular "visitations" of
Pozzo and Lucky. Again, these are diurnal phenomena. Night envelops
the characters and blacks out the coherence of action. Night must be
inquired about, interrogated, catechized. Night anticipates the con-
founding of hell and death and returns us to the "theological" conversation between the tramps:

> ESTRAGON: Saved from what?
> VLADIMIR: Hell.

But a few lines later:

> ESTRAGON: From Hell?
> VLADIMIR: Imbecile! From death.
> ESTRAGON: I thought you said hell.
> VLADIMIR: From death, from death.[85]

Hell may be feared but death might mean deliverance. Vladimir says:
"Suppose we repented."[86] The transcending of their condition would

mean an escape from the bondage of even irrealized time but also—inevitably—the necessity of final judgment. The confusion between hell and death is the recognition of Last Things. Vladimir's longing, perhaps, is to replace (can he join?) the malefactor who said to Jesus, "Lord, remember me when thou comest into thy kingdom" and to whom Jesus said, "Today shalt thou be with me in paradise." "Hell" presupposes judgment; "death" still offers hope of heaven. Vladimir's passion is fear. Godot retains his hold on Vladimir:

> ESTRAGON: And if we dropped him? . . . If we dropped him?
> VLADIMIR: He'd punish us . . . [and then after looking at the tree] Everything's dead but the tree.[87]

Are we to say, then, that Estragon and Vladimir are also dead? That would be incorrect; they are correlates of the dead. Which is also to suggest, once more, that the tramps are imaginary characters in an imaginary landscape. What shall they fall back on? "While there's death, there's hope"? Sartre's "Hell is other people" does not hold for Gogo and Didi, who *are* "other people." One is tempted to new lines: "Neither tormentor nor tormented be." But it is too late. Night has fallen.

All four characters wear bowlers. Like books, they have their destinies. In particular, Lucky's hat is left behind. According to Pozzo, Lucky needs to have his bowler on in order to think. But on his second visit to the tramps, Lucky can no longer speak his thoughts: he is dumb.[88] It is easy to see why Vladimir and Estragon peer into the void of their hats. From where is meaning to come if not from nothing? "Do you think God sees me?" Estragon asks.[89] Apart from the presence of the Tree, there is nothing left but to pass the bowlers back and forth, from one to the other, as in the old vaudeville routine. If God sees Estragon, God does not descend upon the scene. He came much earlier and was crucified; all that is left is the Tree. "I'll look into the matter," we are often told. Well, the tramps do their own scrutinizing. "I'll get back to you," we are often told. Isn't that what Godot must have told Vladimir and Estragon?[90]

We are not done with passing the hat. To be sure, it is an old routine, but it is also one of the games common in *Waiting for Godot*. It is unwise to give a name to any of Beckett's games because *he* was there before us:

> VLADIMIR: Will you not play?
> ESTRAGON: Play at what?
> VLADIMIR: We could play at Pozzo and Lucky.
> ESTRAGON: Never heard of it.

Vladimir teaches Estragon the game:

VLADIMIR: I'll do Lucky, you do Pozzo . . . Go on.
ESTRAGON: What am I to do?
VLADIMIR: Curse me!
ESTRAGON: . . . Naughty!
VLADIMIR: Stronger!
ESTRAGON: Gonococcus! Spirochete![91]

The game of Pozzo and Lucky is continued a little later as the game of abuse:

VLADIMIR: Moron!
ESTRAGON: Vermin!
VLADIMIR: Abortion![92]

The reader of the Absurd may have his own games to recommend. For example the game of Questions and Answers:
Where do red blood cells go when they die?
Valhalla.
Games suggest childhood, and in some ways the tramps are playing the game of Childhood. When Estragon sleeps, Vladimir sings a cradle-song. Some lullabies are disaster songs ("when the bough breaks, the cradle will fall"). Vladimir takes no chances. He sings: "Bye bye bye bye" and repeats it.[93]

If the tramps are playing the game of childhood, they are enacting the terrors which accompany that game. Vladimir tries to comfort Estragon when he awakes from a nightmare (into a nightmare):

VLADIMIR: There . . . there . . . it's all over.
ESTRAGON: I was falling—
VLADIMIR: It's all over, it's all over.[94]

But Vladimir's comfort is partly self-protection. Earlier:

ESTRAGON: I had a dream.
VLADIMIR: Don't tell me!
ESTRAGON: I dreamt that—
VLADIMIR: DON'T TELL ME!
ESTRAGON: . . . It's not nice of you Didi. Who am I to tell my private night-mares to if I can't tell them to you?
VLADIMIR: Let them remain private. You know I can't bear that.[95]

The nightmare may be part of the game of childhood but there is no game of nightmare. At least Vladimir will not play it. The games, after all, are played within the nightmare of reality. Time has stopped; the tramps are on the move, except for the fact that they cannot move; they are waiting for Godot. Yet to say that "they cannot move" is not to say that they are paralyzed. Obviously, they leave each other at night. There *is* movement but they are motionless. How is that? We are reminded of Zeno's paradoxes. There is movement evident in the life-world, but the inverted world which is philosophy's realm proves that motion, thought in everyday terms to signify movement, in reality is an illusion. What we have instead is stasis. And so we have returned to Beckett's world in *Waiting for Godot*. When Vladimir says that "Time has stopped," Pozzo rejoins: "Don't you believe it, Sir, don't you believe it. . . . Whatever you like, but not that."[96] Of course, during this speech Pozzo has been attending to his watch. Time as watch-time goes on; at least there is chronology even if the chronometers vanish. Inner time has ceased. Night has come for the children of the Lebenswelt. We are *in* the mythic story of the children who have gotten lost in the forest. They are *there*; but they are stricken there. And night has fallen.

The transcendental in *Waiting for Godot* lies in the bracketing of the axioms of existence which everyday life otherwise takes for granted as "real," "true," and "reliable." The quality of impermanence or undecidedness which permeates the current of life in the play is not an achievement of the characters but rather their point of departure in every act. Let us consider this puzzle: If reality is damaged, how is it possible for someone whose reality it is to make that determination? Reality may be mixed—here smooth, there rough. But damage is not equivalent to unevenness; it is a *fault*, and how can that fault be discovered if "fault" is what is given to the being-in-reality? To say to a child: "I don't much care for your mother" is to utter a very strange pronouncement. What is the child to make of it? The essential reply, whether overtly expressed or not, is "Well, after all, she *is* my mother." One's mother is one's mother is not a tautology but an expression of nature; it is a moral cry. Reality is not only what we have, what we are "given," but also what we *are*.

I have seen a number of stage performances of *Waiting for Godot*. But the one performance I missed, to my lasting regret, was the opening of the play in the United States. That was the company which included Bert Lahr as Estragon. Lahr, a legendary comic, started in burlesque and made a great hit as the Cowardly Lion in the movie, *The Wizard of Oz*. His face had that wondrously bewildered expression—perfect for Estragon. However, from the outset Lahr honestly confessed utter lack of comprehension of Beckett's play. The play opened in Miami! Michael Myerberg, the producer, advertised the coming attraction: "Bert Lahr, the star of *Burlesque*, and Tom Ewell, the star of *The Seven Year Itch* in the laugh sensation of two continents—Samuel Beckett's *Waiting for Godot*."[97] The result was a disaster. "Lahr found himself living through a comedian's nightmare. He met a complete stone wall. 'I have never experienced anything like this in the American theater. I don't think anyone has. Two thirds of the audience left after the first act.'" The Miami *Herald's* headline the following day was:[98]

MINK CLAD AUDIENCE DISAPPOINTED IN
WAITING FOR GODOT

Later, Lahr recalled: "Playing *Waiting for Godot* in Miami was like doing *Giselle* at Roseland."[99] Although Lahr understood nothing of the play at the beginning, he came to comprehend a great deal of it in the course of his experience playing Estragon. After the Miami fiasco, Lahr acted in a New York production that was directed by Herbert Berghof. It was a vindication of Lahr, whose performance was a theatrical glory. If, at the outset, he understood nothing of the play, Lahr came to recognize in Estragon the roots of Lahr's own experience in life as well as in the theater; ultimately, he mastered the entire play with an instinctive depth that was remarkable. Berghof said of Lahr's grasp of *Waiting for Godot*: "I think he understands it better than any critic I've ever read, better than anybody who has ever read about it, and I think he understands it better than Beckett."[100] Of course, Lahr had his detractors. Walter Winchell, that leper's bell of his time, babbled chaotically about Beckett's play. I recall reading a newspaper account of Winchell in his decline, years after the New York production of *Waiting for Godot* had closed its run, wandering the streets of Miami and being accosted by an old friend who said something like: "Walter, I haven't seen you in years. How are you?" To which Winchell muttered: "I'm going to get a haircut." The equivalent dialogue could be found in *Waiting for Godot*.

For a page or two I have moved from the text of *Waiting for Godot* to its performance on stage. I feel no guilt in having done that. After all, how do we read a text anyway? If our lips don't move, the ventricles of our brain quiver. A play is a to-be-imagined affair, and we have already had something to say about the imaginary. But now I must return to my older procedure. Indeed, we return just in time to ask of Beckett's play, What about love and death? If, as I have suggested, the characters of *Waiting for Godot* are figures in a landscape of nothingness, then the polarities of human consciousness—love and death (at least suicide)—are encapsulated in negation. First love. Estragon asks: "How long have we been together all the time now?" Vladimir replies: "I don't know. Fifty years maybe."[101] There is no reason to doubt what is said. And if it is true, as we think, then Didi and Gogo have been companions for fifty years. What kind of love is theirs? Certainly, they have affection for each other, despite the doubts that are expressed about remaining together. Estragon says: "I sometimes wonder if we wouldn't have been better off alone, each one for himself. . . . We weren't made for the same road."[102] Yet, in the time of the dead present within the play, the tramps occasionally embrace. The embraces are sometimes fussy, sometimes warm (though brief), somehow nonchalant—companions of the road who have tramped it for fifty years, what should we expect? Ecstasy? Are Vladimir and Estragon sexually alive? Dubious but still interested:

> ESTRAGON: What about hanging ourselves?
> VLADIMIR: Hmm. It'd give us an erection.
> ESTRAGON: . . . An erection!
> VLADIMIR: With all that follows. Where it falls mandrakes grow. That's why they shriek when you pull them up. Did you not know that?
> ESTRAGON: Let's hang ourselves immediately![103]

But the time for suicide is over. The rope that won't hold and the belt that's too short merely point back to a lost past; the tramps have moved beyond the time of suicide. Vladimir says: "Hand in hand from the top of the Eiffel Tower, among the first. We were respectable in those days. Now it's too late. They wouldn't even let us up."[104] There was a time, long ago, when Estragon did try:

> ESTRAGON: Do you remember the day I threw myself into the Rhone?
> VLADIMIR: We were grape harvesting.
> ESTRAGON: You fished me out.
> VLADIMIR: That's all dead and buried.[105]

Hope is gone but the desire for life remains. Vladimir says: "Hope deferred maketh the something sick." The "something" is the heart (Proverbs 13:12). Vladimir continues a line later, after Estragon's appeal for help. "Sometimes I feel it coming all the same. Then I go all queer."[106] What follows the words from Proverbs is: "but a desire fulfilled is a tree of life." *The New Oxford Annotated Bible* suggests that the tree of life "is a metaphor for life itself."[107] Old hope is recalled in an exchange which follows:

> VLADIMIR: Do you remember the Gospels?
> ESTRAGON: I remember the maps of the Holy Land. Coloured they were. Very pretty. The Dead Sea was pale blue. The very look of it made me thirsty. That's where we'll go, I used to say, that's where we'll go for our honeymoon. We'll swim. We'll be happy.[108]

That was the hope of a poet; what homosexual has ever longed for a honeymoon at the Dead Sea? Or heterosexual of Estragon's time, for that matter. But wait: although the Dead Sea "supports no life," according to *The Columbia Encyclopedia*, in contemporary Israel "the Dead Sea coast . . . is the site of beaches, spas, and tourist hotels."[109] O prescient

Estragon! But we have also reached the limit of language. I have called Estragon "homosexual" (the same would hold for Vladimir). I have no more evidence for that claim than the play itself. But what strikes me as undeniably evident is that it is inappropriate to call Gogo and Didi "gay." I have plenty of reasons for saying that, but for the moment, one reason calls for citation: Estragon and Vladimir aren't *anything*; in being themselves, they are beyond labels. Still, they are recognizable:

> ESTRAGON: . . . We're not from these parts, Sir.
> POZZO: . . . You are human beings none the less. (*He puts on his glasses.*) As far as one can see. (*He takes off his glasses.*) Of the same species as myself. (*He bursts into an enormous laugh.*) Of the same species as Pozzo! Made in God's image![110]

Not being "anything," the tramps are beyond the reach of the natural attitude of the life-world; they have achieved a kind of negative sanctity which leaves them forever fixed, not only beyond "movement" but in the eye of the ontological storm. Homosexuality says nothing about Vladimir and Estragon. What does it have to say anyway, about anybody?

A matter of preference
An attitude
A predilection
A caprice
A conceit
Counting the cost

It is in the rhythm of their serenades that the love between Didi and Gogo is to be heard:

> ESTRAGON: It's the rope.
> VLADIMIR: It's the rubbing.
> ESTRAGON: It's inevitable.
> VLADIMIR: It's the knot.
> ESTRAGON: It's the chafing.[111]

And in eloquence:

> ESTRAGON: All the dead voices.
> VLADIMIR: They make a noise like wings.
> ESTRAGON: Like leaves.
> VLADIMIR: Like sand.
> ESTRAGON: Like leaves.[112]

And the summation of love expressed by Estragon: "Don't touch me! Don't question me! Don't speak to me! Stay with me!"[113]

What I find most moving in *Waiting for Godot* is the play's dispossession of mundane life. Unbalance reigns, characters fall, what seem mad-people intrude, villains of the night lie in wait, games are played and played out, the horizon of finality is anguish. And in the midst of this lunacy, Estragon and Vladimir persist, keep their appointment. The question is not, Why are they there? The question concerns "there." "There" is the place of Estragon and Vladimir. We all know where it is; only the tramps are uncertain about it. There was one troupe that did a performance of *Waiting for Godot* before a male prison audience. The authorities had doubts about the occasion: prisoners who might hoot and whistle and worse; not any women in the cast. In the event, Beckett's play proved to be an enormous success. The audience behaved, responded perfectly. After the performance, some of the prisoners were questioned: Who is Godot?—that old misadventure. But this time, a prisoner, speaking in effect for everybody in the audience, had the right answer: "The outside."

As with prisoners, sentence has been passed on the tramps. In phenomenological terms, a reduction has taken place. We are not speaking of reduced circumstances but of an abstention from believing-in the current of everyday life: epoché has suspended the characters of the play in a world, as we have suggested, of stasis. But the wax museum is furious with the illusion of action. Regarded in a purely Husserlian manner, *Waiting for Godot* is the bracketed consciousness of belief. The most trivial items of human behavior are put into thematic relief: from taking off a tight boot to pulling on your trousers. Between the being of the tramps and the language they utter stands a third force: mime. Let us say that mime is the art of virtual expression. The tramps are miming themselves and often using spoken language as an interposition of being between nothing and pseudo reality. The third force is instantiated in the play itself:

POZZO: . . . Do I look like a man that can be made to suffer? Frankly? . . .
    What have I done with my pipe?
VLADIMIR: Charming evening we're having.
ESTRAGON: Unforgettable.
VLADIMIR: And it's not over.
ESTRAGON: Apparently not.
VLADIMIR: It's only beginning.
ESTRAGON: It's awful.
VLADIMIR: Worse than the pantomime.
ESTRAGON: The circus.
VLADIMIR: The music-hall.
ESTRAGON: The circus.[114]

If sex is no more than a useless label, what about love? There are moments in *Waiting for Godot* of great tenderness between Didi and Gogo.

And we have already quoted the "stay with me" speech. Is there more to report? Yes, there is the very beginning of Act I. In his first lines, Vladimir turns to Estragon and says: "So there you are again." "Am I?" replies Estragon.[115] It is Vladimir who *sees* Estragon, who gives him his alterity. The tramps—they have also been referred to in the critical literature as "hoboes," does it matter?—reassure each other of their existence. For Estragon, the only other "reassurance" he receives is from the gang of brutes who beat him in the ditch at night. Vladimir's "night life" is left a mystery not only to the reader of the play (or to its audience during performance) but to Estragon as well. Vladimir keeps waiting for night to fall. Why? As Estragon points out, morning will always follow. What will night produce? One possibility in explanation is that Godot does not come at night, and so it would seem that Godot and night are strange alternatives. In a speech interrupted by cries of "Ah!" (from Estragon) and "Help!" (from Pozzo), Vladimir says: "We are waiting for Godot to come—. . . Or for night to fall."[116] It is invariably Vladimir who reminds Estragon that they are waiting for Godot. And it may be that although Vladimir has a stronger memory than his companion, the reason for Vladimir's remembering is that he thinks that Godot will either punish them or save them—both are mentioned by Vladimir. At the same time, Vladimir has a commonsensical attitude regarding Godot: "I'm curious to hear what he has to offer. Then we'll take it or leave it."[117] But there had been some exchange with Godot earlier:

ESTRAGON: What exactly did we ask him for?
VLADIMIR: Were you not there?
ESTRAGON: I can't have been listening.
VLADIMIR: Oh . . . Nothing very definite.
ESTRAGON: A kind of prayer.
VLADIMIR: Precisely.
ESTRAGON: A vague supplication.
VLADIMIR: Exactly.[118]

Can I help it if Beckett has the best lines? The truth is that Vladimir and Estragon have reached extremity. There is only rubble left; they stand on nothing. And having come to this end, they confess that they cannot go on.

VLADIMIR: . . . We have time to grow old. The air is full of our cries. . . . I can't go on! . . . What have I said?[119]

And near the very end of *Waiting for Godot*:

ESTRAGON: Didi.
VLADIMIR: Yes.

ESTRAGON: I can't go on like this.
VLADIMIR: That's what you think.[120]

We are at the still point of anguish. Our being has exhausted itself and we are beyond suicide; we are alive in death. Is this hell then? Or is human exhaustion an infinite process? "I die of not dying." If dying is thought of as *leaving*, then we are in trouble:

POZZO: I must go.
. . .
ESTRAGON: Then adieu.
POZZO: Adieu.
VLADIMIR: Adieu.
. . .
VLADIMIR: Adieu.
POZZO: Adieu.
ESTRAGON: Adieu.
. . .
POZZO: And thank you.
VLADIMIR: Thank *you*.
Pozzo: Not at all.
ESTRAGON: Yes yes.
POZZO: No no.
VLADIMIR: Yes yes.
ESTRAGON: No no.
. . .
POZZO: I don't seem to be able . . . to depart.
ESTRAGON: Such is life.[121]

With pre-reflective intuition of the truth, the characters are immersed in the Parmenidian plenum. Nothing moves, nobody departs, cries wheel in the air: intentions, suppositions, admonitions. It is another day but nothing changes. Godot has not come and we are beyond endurance. It is that "beyond" that interests Beckett. It is not perseverance, which presupposes not only hope but expectation. We are beyond finality, and that is where belief begins. Nothing has changed; we do not have a congregation: it is as though the cross were given and the Crucifixion only intimated. Beckett is often spoken of as a playwright of the Absurd, a Tertullian poet. But the familiar admonition of Tertullian that to believe is absurd is questioned by Paul Tillich: "It would be unnecessary to confront the paradoxical with the absurd if it were not for the confusing phrase, *credo quia absurdum*, which has been wrongly attributed to Tertullian, and if it were not for the fact that the paradoxical has been identified with the absurd."[122] We are left with a false attribution, but as with Plato's Seventh Letter, *somebody* wrote it. A more nearly (and genuinely) existential use of "The Absurd" enters Beckett's scene. Vladimir and Estragon have been socially phlebotomized, to call language out, remove its eyeglasses, and mix it up a bit: they have been bled, drained, challenged, pushed around somewhat. All right, we are guilty of playing fast and loose, as they say, with medical terminology. There may be rules for playing; we have transgressed those rules. But are there *laws* for playing with language? How discouraging. We *have* returned the ball; what if it's a yellow ball instead of a white one? Well, we seem to have arrived at a muddle. Absurd! Forget Tertullian. We are stuck in the midden. Our companions of the road, Vladimir and Estragon, are here with us. How are we to be extricated? Of one thing I'm certain: our "analytic" friends are nowhere in sight; they inhabit quite different regions. As I write, Queen Elizabeth and President Mitterand have made the journey beneath the Channel, in the "chunnel." In Luna Park it was called the Tunnel of Love. Men who looked like younger versions of Didi and Gogo operated the machinery. Has the new tunnel brought Unity? As Pozzo would say, "Don't you believe it!" English philosophy still clings to its reserve. Oxbridge graduates and those under their sway do not speak of death. Philosophy can do without bedpans. In *The Encyclopedia of Philosophy*, in the entry on "Death," we find: "most contemporary Anglo-American analytic philosophers probably regard the paucity of materials on death as evidence of the subject's resistance to serious philosophical inquiry. In general, they wish to exclude the subject of death from the area of legitimate philosophical speculation, either as a part of their campaign against metaphysics or on the grounds that the subject can be more adequately dealt with by psychologists and social scientists."[123]

Paucity of materials on death? *Paucity of materials?*

VLADIMIR: Where are all these corpses from?
ESTRAGON: These skeletons.[124]

The turn toward death is not sudden in our discussion. It has been explicit in *Waiting for Godot* from the outset of the play in the profound reference to the Crucifixion and in our emphasis on a phenomenological approach to the examination of everyday life. The current of existence in the life-world is diminished in Beckett's play, as we have suggested, to a point of stoppage: stasis. It takes artificial techniques—games, improvisations—to retain the very sense of movement or flow in mundanity. The typified lines stand forth throughout the play:

Let's go.
We can't.
Why not?
We're waiting for Godot.
Ah!

Reconstructed in transcendental subjectivity, the stasis of the play reveals the signification of stoppage: temporality has ended, the interior life of what makes Vladimir and Estragon human beings has become estranged from what we have come to think of as the vitality of life: the tramps are simulacra of the living; they are in eternity. They cannot move because there is nowhere to move *to*. They cannot bear to stay where they are and they cannot leave. They cannot stand more but they persist. There is no distance between their predicament and the question of what that predicament "means." The cry of "nothing to be done" reverberates in dead air. "Christ have mercy on us!" says Vladimir, and soon after he observes: "Everything's dead but the tree."[125] The play, we recall, begins with the "theological discussion":

VLADIMIR: Ah yes, the two thieves. Do you remember the story?
ESTRAGON: No.
VLADIMIR: Shall I tell it to you?
ESTRAGON: No.
VLADIMIR: It'll pass the time. . . . Two thieves, crucified at the same time as our Saviour. One—
ESTRAGON: Our what?
VLADIMIR: Our Saviour. Two thieves. One is supposed to have been saved and the other . . . damned.[126]

The story of the Crucifixion has entered the ordinary world where the events constituting that story are said to have taken place. Transcendental subjectivity seizes upon the essential form of that occurrence: what are for the believer the supernatural moments of transfiguration which stand apart from the current of the mundane. That, in Christian doctrine, Christ dies in the world in his human aspect but lives in his Godly aspect presupposes that the mundane world may be "penetrated," as it were, so that what is alive in its bodily form may be transformed in miracle. The transcendental is the possibility of the actual. In different terms, the actual—that which is simply about us and contains us—is irrealized in miracle. It hardly follows that every act of irrealization involves miracle; but every miracle involves irrealization. Transcendental subjectivity, for the phenomenologist, is not a domain of faith or a haven of belief. If, however, we consider the Christian sense of the Cross, we are led to the dual meaning of "the Tree" as made of wood and possessing transcendence. Obviously, I am not interested here in Christian or religious exegesis but in the phenomenology of *Waiting for Godot*. For the two thieves who are crucified on either side of Christ, the mechanics of murdering them is, at a naturalistic level, the same inventory of wood and nails. The thief who railed against Jesus, saying "If thou be Christ, save thyself and us," demanded release, not salvation; he was a man of wood and nails. The thief who "said unto Jesus, Lord, remember me when thou comest into thy kingdom" saw Christ in his transcendental quality, not because he believed, but because his belief set aside *his* suffering in his awareness of the Crucifixion. Again, I do not aim at exegesis but at the clarification of the sense in which the transcendental may be distinguished from the mundane.

There are two "conclusions" to Beckett's theological conversation, the first leading into the second. Vladimir's statement that "everything's dead but the tree" announces the miracle of rebirth and tacitly suggests that *Waiting for Godot* is a "mystery" play. At the start of the play, when Vladimir introduces the Crucifixion and mentions the two thieves, he says, as we know, that one thief was saved.

> ESTRAGON: Saved from what?
> VLADIMIR: Hell.
> ESTRAGON: I'm going.
>   *He does not move.*[127]

Near the end of the first act of the play, Estragon takes off his boots in order to leave them for someone else:

> VLADIMIR: Your boots, what are you doing with your boots?
> ESTRAGON: . . . I'm leaving them there. . . . Another will come, just as . . . as me, but with smaller feet, and they'll make him happy.
> VLADIMIR: But you can't go barefoot!
> ESTRAGON: Christ did.
> VLADIMIR: Christ! What has Christ got to do with it? You're not going to compare yourself to Christ!
> ESTRAGON: All my life I've compared myself to him.[128]

In fact, we know very little about either Estragon or Vladimir. They are muted miracles of the play. And the tramps know little or nothing about their present situation (their eternal situation, I have suggested). About Godot, they are uncertain even of his name; they are confused about the meeting with Godot, with what was arranged. Even the place is uncertain. Yet the boy knows where to find them. Godot is consistent: he is a postponer, he is a promiser. Didi and Gogo are accepters; what do they have to lose? Nor is Pozzo to be excluded from this list of ambiguities. Two of the more dramatic speeches in *Waiting for Godot* come toward the end of the play. One is Pozzo's after Vladimir has questioned him about Lucky being dumb:

> VLADIMIR: Dumb! Since when?
> POZZO: . . . Have you not done tormenting me with your accursed time! It's abominable! When! When! One day, is that not enough for you, one day

he went dumb, one day I went blind, one day we'll go deaf, one day we were born, one day we shall die, the same day, the same second, is that not enough for you? . . . They give birth astride of a grave, the light gleams an instant, then it's night once more.[129]

Vladimir makes his speech soon after Pozzo's declamation. In some ways, the two speeches are copies of each other:

VLADIMIR: Astride of a grave and a difficult birth. Down in the hole, linger- ingly, the grave-digger puts on the forceps. We have time to grow old. The air is full of our cries.[130]

Both Pozzo and Vladimir in these speeches have broken through in- ventions, games, and the caresses of language. They are final declara- tions. Pozzo is dispossessed of his pipe, his watch, his atomizing spray. The performances are over. Vladimir is meditating on what *happens* in this world, what *happens* in it. That is the great ganglion of the taken for granted:

VLADIMIR: Was I sleeping, while the others suffered? Am I sleeping now? To- morrow, when I wake, or think I do, what shall I say of to-day? That with Estragon my friend, at this place, until the fall of night, I waited for Godot?[131]

What happens in this world. And that is the great theme of phenome- nology: the "natural attitude" of which Edmund Husserl wrote, the pri- mal epistemic assumption, the grand presupposition of daily life, which is that our world is real, self-subsistent, intersubjective, lasting, as it ap- pears to be, the same for all of us more or less, perdurable. The guide- lines of naive realism hold good and may be counted on to see us through the world. You can bet your life on the reliability of the senses, more or less—and that "more or less" is still another assurance that the life-world is a reliable home. And, in common-sense terms it *is*. Philoso- phy may end by reassuring us that what seems real *is* real, that what ap- pears to be the case in ordinary experience is the case, that law and order and justice underlie our venture in the Lebenswelt. But philosophy can also be a spoiler. Phenomenology is a proven spoilsport, for its most fundamental activity consists in placing in doubt the very foundation stone of our believing-in the world. Reduction, in phenomenological method, does not imply denial or obliteration but rather a bringing to light of what common sense is content to leave in the twilight of con- sciousness. For many, phenomenology is an obscurity which is itself hid- den by forbidding terminology. For some, however, phenomenology is the demon of philosophy.

If phenomenology has illuminated *Waiting for Godot*, it has done so by entering the play's own taken-for-granted world of everyday existence. If the tramps are not in time but in eternity it might be thought that stasis rules out mundanity. This is not so. What remains is the rhythm of the everyday. I have stressed the importance of the diurnal and the nocturnal in the play, but it is also true that whether it is the day which we read about or see (in performance), the night too has its style, its rhythm. We hear that rhythm only by indirection yet its force cannot be denied. If Vladimir and Estragon are in eternity, it may follow that what envelops them is eternal night.

What is the play about? Bert Lahr was first sent *Waiting for Godot* in book form. "What's it about?" asked his son as his father read it. "Without looking up he mumbled, 'It's about two bums.'"[132] Lahr's précis is as ultimately wrong as it is ultimately vindicated.

Five

The Magic Mountain

WAITING FOR GODOT is a "horizontal" fiction; *The Magic Mountain* is a "perpendicular" novel. Beckett's play takes place on level terrain. Whatever the uncertainties of place for the tramps, there is no doubt about what's below or what's above. The terra is firm and it's flat. There is neither time nor need to point out that "assuming the horizontal"—taking the position of the rest cure at the Berghof—has nothing whatever to do with the "horizontal" in *Waiting for Godot*. Nor has the perpendicular of Mann's novel anything to do with height. The antonym of the perpendicular on the Mountain is "the flat-land." Thus are we girded to do battle with one of the most formidable fictions of the twentieth century, having just arrived in Time after a stay in Eternity.

In years of lecturing, I have started off my remarks on *The Magic Mountain* with: "This is a *Bildungsroman*." When I teach the novel again, I will say instead: "This is a great chunk of magic realism." It is, fortunately, not altogether clear what is meant by "magic realism," but I am like the United States Supreme Court Justice who said of obscenity: "I know it when I see it." Of course, the "magic" of *The Magic Mountain* and the "magic" of magic realism are hardly the same, but there is an affinity between them; both share in the uncanny. We shall see that magic at work in the course of our inquiry. Certainly, Mann is unsparing in his mention of the uncanny in his novel. Indeed, there is something uncanny in the entire experience of both the reading and the read in the course of the journey through that immense alchemy. We are in for it!

Hans Castorp, the hero of *The Magic Mountain*, is referred to in the English translation of *Der Zauberberg* as "a 'delicate child of life'" ("ein 'Sorgenkind des Lebens'").[133] The English version is interesting. Indeed, Hans *is* "Life's delicate child." But there is another way of understanding the German, not a better but another interesting way. Let us imagine a scene in the living room of an upper-class, well-to-do, German family in the time before the First World War. The mother of the family is introducing her children to a guest:

> Let me see. This is Georg, he is our scientist, always dissecting frogs and mice, forever making charts of the weather variations. Georg will be a physician. And here is Lisa, our artist. Lisa is coming along beautifully with her piano

training and plans to enter the conservatory in a year or two. Max will be our banker, our man of affairs, perhaps our man of politics; he speaks well. And yes, here is Hans; Hans is our "problem child," solid, reliable, not quite as strong in health as we would like but getting there. We have confidence in Hans; we have hope.

"Life's delicate child," life's "problem child," offers "hope" for resolution of his disparate qualities, for becoming the Bürger son and grandson of his forebears. The "great—great—great . . ." of the Baptismal Bowl is the echo within him, his desire for continuity, his expectation of taking his place in the line of his descent. There are several ways of understanding Hans Castorp: as the future of his past, as the rebel against expectation (his own and that of others), and as a kind of cosmic dropout. His story cannot be told quickly but early impressions are fateful. Most crucial: orphaned over and over again, from parents and grandfather, Hans has a familiarity as well as a resonance with illness and death. As he says, late in the novel, "There are two paths to life: one is the regular one, direct, honest. The other is bad, it leads through death—that is the *spirituel* way."[134] In the current of existence in the life-world of his childhood and youth—the flat-land, as he will come to call it—Hans passes muster despite early symptoms of bodily weakness: "A little anaemic he had always been, so Dr. Heidekind said, and had him take a good glass of porter after third breakfast every day, when he came home from school. This, as everyone knows, is a hearty drink—Dr. Heidekind considered it a blood-maker."[135] Resonance with illness and death is also resonance with time—time as uncanny. Again and again, to his grandfather's delight, the child asks to see the baptismal vessel: "The little one looked up at Grandfather's narrow grey head, bending over the basin as it had in the time he described. A familiar feeling pervaded the child: a strange, dreamy, troubling sense: of change in the midst of duration, of time as both flowing and persisting, of recurrence in continuity—these were sensations he had felt before on the like occasion, and both expected and longed for again, whenever the heirloom was displayed."[136] This early imprinting is itself "constituted" in phenomenological language, that is, Hans' resonance with illness and death is a function of time, memorial and patient, exacting and warming. Much later, Castorp will not only recognize that imprinting during his stay on the Mountain but will embrace it like a lover: time as the secret activity which binds love and death. His protracted stay at the Sanatorium Berghof is good for Hans as it is "good" for the Berghof. Just as we learn that the remarkable, therapeutic air on the Mountain is good not only as a curative agent but is "good" for the disease itself which the patient seeks to overcome and the physician seeks to cure, so we come to realize that love, for Hans, is inextricably bound to death. The history of his disease and passion is the *Bildungsroman*, the humane education of the novel's hero but, better perhaps, it is the *formative* which is the force of Hans' life, from obscurity to obscurity.

Here is a novel of formation, and there is a lot to trace, even in outline: the overarching movement—so that we may see it from the first—is from problem child of the flat-land to the achiever of the Mountain. This may be the appropriate place to acknowledge a debt to the philosopher and authoritative phenomenologist, Dr. Fritz Kaufmann (who wrote his doctoral dissertation under the direction of Edmund Husserl), a most learned thinker, who was also an expert on the work of Thomas Mann as well as one of Mann's correspondents. Some of Kaufmann's writing on Mann appeared in 1944 in two numbers of the journal *Philosophy and Phenomenological Research* and was given its final form in his book, *Thomas Mann: The World as Will and Representation*. Alas, for my present purposes, Kaufmann does not present in his book any discussion of Husserl's phenomenology and its possible relationship to Thomas Mann. Kaufmann writes:

> Hans Castorp comes from the Hanse town of Hamburg and the family of the blond Hanses. . . . But he is more than this. He is also "Hans the dreamer," a figure out of the German fairy tale. In him life has overcome its own bluntness, its indifference to the spirit, but is also giving up the shelter of time-honored conventions. A child of life, he is to become its problem child. And, as so often happens with problem children, it may be that life is kindly disposed toward the young man just because he boldly embarks on the perilous course of the spirit.[137]

Although I read the book when it was published and must have absorbed the use of "problem child" (Kaufmann did his own translations from the German for the book), I must confess that my careful reading of Kaufmann's work at best left an unconscious trace of his "problem child." As I write now, his version of the original is not self-consciously before me. But if it is true that nothing is ever lost, then I delight in crediting the late Fritz Kaufmann with Hans Castorp's usage as an early influence on me. More important, however, is the fact that in his book, Kaufmann does not mention Husserl's phenomenology. Aristotle, Buber, Descartes, Pascal, Hegel, Kant, Kierkegaard, Leibniz, Russell, Scheler, Nietzsche, Plato, Heraclitus, Schopenhauer—but not Husserl. The closest Kaufmann comes is Max Scheler, "who may have been the connecting link between Thomas Mann and phenomenology."[138] But those interested in that link would do as well to read Kaufmann's essay on "Art and Phenomenology." There Kaufmann writes: "Husserl him-

self noticed the close affinity between the artistic and the phenomenological inhibition: both illustrating, though in different ways, a univer-
sally possible modification of consciousness—that of the neutralization
of the thesis of being. The reductions, methodically carried through in
phenomenology, happen to find an automatic fulfillment in art."[139] I
think that the connecting link between Thomas Mann and phenomenology is Fritz Kaufmann.

"The overarching movement" is sustained by means of the leitmotiv.
In traditional terms, the leitmotiv is a technique within musical composition, a mode of repetition of theme and variation which brings the lis-
tener the past in a present which, magically, is alive to what follows. The
leitmotiv is at once a gatherer, a displayer of what has been gathered,
and an initiator of what is to come, given a particular complex of moments. The leitmotiv is the magician of technique in Mann's novel; but
all of this is hardly new. Nevertheless, it is necessary to recall, from time
to time, what indeed we know. One of the phenomena which Hans Castorp experiences during his stay on the Mountain is that of forgetful-
ness. In fact, not long after he has arrived at the Sanatorium Berghof and
has met Settembrini, that worthy inquires of him: " 'Will you permit me
to ask how old you are?' And behold, Hans Castorp could not tell! At
that moment he did not know how old he was, despite strenuous, even
desperate efforts to bethink himself. In order to gain time he had the
question repeated, and then answered: 'I? How old I am? In my twenty-
fourth year, of course. I'll soon be twenty four.' "[140] And what is eventually forgotten is Hans' entire life on the flat-land. His associations fall
away, just as his treatises on technical subjects, too heavy for the hand,
one by one fall to the floor. Correspondence, newspapers—all diminish
and fade to almost nothing. *Ocean Steamships*, his railroad companion,
lies at last neglected and forgotten. Even his pocket watch, faithful companion on his skiing adventure—a momentous achievement—eventually
fails. "He no longer carried a timepiece. His watch had fallen from his
night-table; it did not go, and he had neglected to have it regulated."[141]

We know about the standard, well-used leitmotivs of the "Kirghiz"
eyes which Clavdia possesses and which remind Hans of his young acquaintance of long-ago school days, Pribislav Hippe, and the continual
sprinkling of certain numbers to titillate the sense of the magical: the
clutch of "sevens" which tend to tedium after a few hundred pages. We
are well acquainted with the leitmotiv of bodily stance and gesture:
Hans has long been accustomed to rest his head against his hand, supported by his arm, his elbow resting, in turn, on the table. The older
imagery of the head inclined against the ruff comes back to us, the incli-
nation of grandfather's head. When, toward the end of the novel,

Naphta challenges Settembrini to a duel, "Hans Castorp was imitating his grandfather's famous attitude, for his neck was all a-tremble."[142] And we should not fail to mention the motiv of the hands flailing across the hips, which Mann describes several times, as the "gathering-in" sign of death as the "grim reaper." Think of Joachim's death-scene as well as the séance scene with the medium, Ellen Brand:

> Elly, bent forward, her face almost in her lap, slumbered. She was busy too, absorbed in the oddest activity, with which the others appeared familiar, but which Hans Castorp watched with attentive wonder. For some minutes together she moved the hollow of her hand to and fro in the region of her hips: carried the hand away from her body and then with scooping, raking motion drew it towards her, as though gathering something and pulling it in.[143]

The movement described is that of the scythe, the German word for which is *Hippe*. It should also be recalled from the reading of *The Magic Mountain* that one leitmotiv can lead to another. The chapter entitled "Hippe" includes the account of the borrowing of the pencil, famously repeated in the "Walpurgis-Night" chapter, but also carries mention of another motiv, that of the hand supporting the chin:

> When, his nerves being tolerably restored, he got to his feet again to continue his walk, he found his neck trembling; indeed his head shook in precisely the same way, at his age, in which the head of old Hans Lorenz Castorp once had shaken. The phenomenon so freshly called up to him the memory of his dead grandfather that, far from finding it offensive, he took a certain pleasure in availing himself of that remembered and dignified method of supporting the chin, by means of which his grandfather had been wont to control the shaking of his head, and to which the boy had responded with such inward sympathy.[144]

Thomas Mann's declared use of the leitmotiv as the bonding matter of *The Magic Mountain* and the pains he takes to utilize his method, leads us almost inevitably to ask whether there is a phenomenological analogue. "I have the honour," as Joachim Ziemssen says to Hofrat Behrens, when he announces his intention to leave the Berghof and to join his regiment,[145] of suggesting Edmund Husserl's concept of "horizon." There is a plethora of leitmotivs that I have not mentioned as well as different forms of the leitmotiv that remain unexpressed, but it must remain your privilege to know them and my right to resist their mention. We are in this together! Well, then, what does Husserl mean by "horizon?"

Before I turn to quotations from Husserl and others and before I begin speaking in phenomenological terms, I wish to present a piece of my remembered past that may set the discussion in more humane terms than philosophy often permits itself. In my first year of college I had a wonderful instructor in English composition who inspired me to write what I hesitate now to call a "treatise." How I loved her! How inadequate I was to express my love. A seventeen-year-old boy pleading his case to a young woman working on her doctoral dissertation—impossible. She read poetry to the class:

> I weep for Adonais—he is dead!

I collapsed. But I was resolved! I wrote my treatise for her as my secret gift. Not a word of what was in my heart but one hundred pages of what was in my head. I wrote a miniature book on a group of poems by Stephen Crane: *The Black Riders*. The edition of Crane's poetry which I borrowed from the college library was excellent: volume 6 of *The Work of Stephen Crane*, edited by Wilson Follett, New York: Alfred A. Knopf, 1926. But the book carried the message: "This group is substantially a reprint of *The Black Riders and Other Lines* published 1895 and dedicated to Hamlin Garland." I *had* to see the first edition; our library did not have it. When I applied at the New York Public Library I must have been sized up as either a book thief or trash of some other kind. I was informed that in order to inspect the first edition of *The Black Riders* I would have to bring the library official a testimonial, indicating that I was upright and that I presented no threat to the New York Public Library. Fortunately, I had an uncle—a favorite uncle—who was a Manhattan lawyer and who practiced literary law. I presented my case and quickly was rewarded with what I needed. The librarian was impressed.

A uniformed guard was summoned. He accompanied me to some hidden place at the end of complex stairways. There I was instructed to enter a wire-meshed room with pragmatic furniture: a small desk and a small desk chair. A little later, the guard entered and placed before me, on the desk, the treasure: the Stephen Crane "first." No exchange of words; no "there you go!" from the guard. Nor did I venture anything. When the guard left the wire cubicle to wait outside the cage, I heard a tiny sound: the lock snapped into place. More or less, I was incarcerated with *The Black Riders*. By God, this was research! I had been warned in advance that I could bring nothing in with me: no briefcase, no other books, no manuscripts, no notebooks, no ink or pencil. I was vaguely reminded of snatches of a burial service: "for we bring nothing into this world." And we certainly don't take anything out of the New York Public Library. I communed with the late nineteenth-century book for quite some time, then took my leave escorted by the guard. When I left the building, the blaze of light on Fifth Avenue shattered the tenseness of my being into epiphanies of dazzlement. I had entered the world of *The*

Black Riders, Stephen Crane was my companion of genius, my treatise would transfigure the world! My all was in the entry numbered XXIV:

> I saw a man pursuing the horizon;
> Round and round they sped.
> I was disturbed at this;
> I accosted the man.
> "It is futile," I said,
> "You can never ——"
>
> "You lie," he cried,
> And ran on.[146]

Now let us follow the road back. Crane's poem, the Library, my class, my teacher—my first year in college. We move back along a horizon of givenness and of intention. Husserl writes: "I am conscious of a world endlessly spread out in space, endlessly becoming and having endlessly become in time."[147] And Husserl goes on to say:

> *what is given at any particular time is usually surrounded by a halo of undeter-mined determinability*, which has its mode of being brought closer "*explica-tively*" in becoming separated into a number of intendings . . . ; at first it still may be in the realm of obscurity, but then within the sphere of givenness until what is intended to comes into the sharply illuminated circle of perfect givenness.[148]

We are recommending that the phenomenological concept of "hori-zon" may be understood as the equivalent of the notion of the leitmotiv. It must be kept in mind that Mann's leitmotiv looks both forward and backward; it portends and it retains. Also, and most pressingly, the leit-motiv *presents* itself in immediacy. In Husserlian language, the leitmotiv is itself Evidenz. So, what we are given is something which all at once *is*, *remembers*, and *portends*. Just as important: this triple function is not thought through self-consciously; suddenly, all in a moment, in the twinkling of an eye, in an *Augenblick, plötzlich*—the triple play is accom-plished. The leitmotiv in Mann is not of the kind: this reminds me of that. Hans Castorp's nosebleed at the bench—the *red* warning—near the beginning of his stay on the Mountain, is *re-presented* in the blood at the scene of the duel near the end of the novel—again, near the bench. The essence of the leitmotiv resides in its valence, its capacity to present itself *in person* (as the phenomenologist might say) at the same moment that it pirouettes.

Husserl writes: "The joy . . . which begins and ends, and during the interval endures, I can first gaze at as it is in its purity, following all its temporal phases. But I can also pay attention to its mode of declaring itself: to the modus of the actual 'Now,' and to this feature also that with this very 'now,' a new and continuously new 'now' links up in necessary continuity."[149] In the thoroughfare of its gaze, the leitmotiv moves along what we have referred to as a phenomenological horizon. But the identification is even more intimate: the concepts of leitmotiv and horizon are interchangeable without being identical. That means that particular ways in which moments of experience are seized upon in consciousness as the individual moves along the horizons of his experience are not the precise ways in which the leitmotiv operates. For example: It makes sense to ask whether in the course of the many events of Hans' experience on the Mountain, there is a "still point" which can be located. I believe that there is. It is found in the scene when the cousins, in their role as gallants to the dying, escort Karen Karstedt to the graveyard:

> No soul was to be seen or heard, the quiet remoteness and peace of the spot seemed deep and unbroken in more than one sense. A little stone angel or cupid, finger on lip, a cap of snow askew on its head, stood among the bushes, and might have passed for the genius of the place—the genius of a silence so definite that it was less a negation than a refutation of speech.[150]

There may be a resting place or a stopping point along Husserl's "horizon," but there is no still point to be found, no magical moment which encompasses the whole of the horizon. We move *along* a horizon, *toward* a horizon—and that is all; we do not "become" the horizon. Yet it must be recognized that the horizon of consciousness includes the trail or record of anticipation as well as that of memory. The leitmotiv functions in *The Magic Mountain* in a manner which is captured by Husserl's discussion of temporality—its protential and retential character. In a section of his lectures on the phenomenology of inner-time consciousness, Husserl discusses "The Continua of the Running-Off Phenomena." He writes:

> We would prefer to avoid . . . the use of the word "appearances" for the phenomena that constitute immanent temporal objects; for these phenomena are themselves immanent objects and are "appearances" in an entirely different sense. We speak here of the "running-off phenomena," or better still, of the "modes of temporal orientation"; and with respect to the immanent objects themselves, we speak of their "running-off characters" (e.g., now, past). We know that the running-off phenomenon is a continuity of constant changes. This continuity forms an inseparable unity, inseparable into extended sections that could exist by themselves, into points of the continuity. The parts that we single out by abstraction can exist only in the whole running-off; and this is

equally true of the phases, the points that belong to the running-off continuity. We can also say of this continuity, with evidence, that in a certain sense it is immutable; that is, with regard to its form.[151]

The form of continuity is, for Husserl, immutable. This is the way the matter may be put: The equivalence of "horizon" and leitmotiv consists of an immutable continuity. *Form* proves to be the phenomenological essence of change. But didn't Hans say that "Form is folderol"?[152] Yes, Hans did say that to the Hofrat but Thomas Mann didn't. What Thomas Mann *did* say (in his talk on "The Making of *The Magic Mountain*") was:

> The book itself is the substance of that which it relates. It depicts the hermetic enchantment of its young hero within the timeless, and thus seeks to abrogate time itself by means of the technical device that attempts to give complete presentness at any given moment to the entire world of ideas that it comprises. It tries, in other words, to establish a magical *nunc stans*, to use a formula of the scholastics. It pretends to give perfect consistency to content and form, to the apparent and the essential; its aim is always and consistently to *be* that of which it speaks.[153]

If I have made my case, then form, phenomenologically understood, far from being rigid is rather quite the opposite: form is mobile; it is horizontal. In turn, we may see that Husserl's conception of "essence," rather than being eternally fixed, is also dynamic: "Plato, the reddened flower . . . ." Style, in our existential phenomenology, is the embodiment of mobility as form. In different terms, mobility and form—but now "style" transposed—are the components of the concept of love in *The Magic Mountain*. Of course, it is Dr. Krokowski who poses the primordial question: "what then was this form, this mask, in which suppressed, unchartered love would reappear? . . . And Dr. Krokowski answered his own question, and said: 'In the form of illness. Symptoms of disease are nothing but a disguised manifestation of the power of love; and all disease is only love transformed.' "[154]

From almost the moment Castorp arrived at the Sanatorium Berghof, met by his cousin Joachim, he heard about Dr. Krokowski and his specialty. Indeed, his lectures on psychoanalysis are mentioned in the brochure which advertises the Berghof. But now, we may recall, Hans receives the information directly. Joachim says of Krokowski that "He psycho-analyses the patients." " 'He what? Psycho-analyses—how disgusting!' cried Hans Castorp; and his hilarity altogether got the better of him. He could not stop. The psycho-analysis had been the finishing touch. He laughed so hard that the tears ran down his cheeks; he put up his hands to his face and rocked with laughter."[155]

But the man who arrives for a three-week visit is not the man who later becomes, secretly and slyly, Dr. Krokowski's patient. Hans never realizes that he has been found out by Joachim.[156] Castorp's "duplicity" involves more than being a stealthy or secret patient of Krokowski. To be sure, Hans has attended Krokowski's lectures, has stared at the back of Clavdia's neck, has listened to Krokowski's message along with Lawyer Paravant, who flicks his ear with his forefinger to make him hear better—the same Paravant who, later on, devotes his energies to trying to square the circle. It is Krokowski who shakes Hans Castorp's hand in congratulations when Behrens's "sounding" shows that Hans is one of "them": "Dr. Krokowski arose from his place and strode up to Hans Castorp. With his head tipped back sideways, and one hand on the young man's shoulder, smiling so heartily that the yellowish teeth showed in his beard, he shook him warmly by the hand."[157]

Initiated, Hans now has the spark, the impulse to ascend in his new life on the Mountain. But what does it mean to say that he is duplicitous? Is Joachim remarking solely on his discovery by chance that his cousin is undergoing psychoanalysis? That may be the case for Joachim but there is quite another issue at risk for Hans. Duplicity means, more fundamentally (whether Joachim suspects it or not), that Hans has given up not only the life of the flat-land but has entered the ambiguous and treacherous existence offered by magic and alchemy. X-ray or not, fever or not, catarrh or not, it is most dubious that Hans Castorp is infected with the disease of the Mountain. He is enchanted, yes; he is in love, yes; he is formatively ascending, yes; he is pursuing his pedagogic-humanistic grail, maybe; but at bottom, Hans is rather mystified, a bit muddled, somewhat self-divided, dozing as it were. In the phenomenological vocabulary which, as Mann would say, has been vouchsafed us, the current of life on the Mountain has changed for Castorp. He is alive in a new "key."

It is prudent to doubt the absolute sincerity and authenticity of everything to do with *The Magic Mountain*. The author, the narrator, the central characters, the minor characters—pretty much the whole of it must be questioned. I would say the safest figure in the book—the most reliable, the most honest—is obviously Hans Castorp's cousin Joachim Ziemssen. But because practically everything must be questioned, it does not follow that everything and everyone in the book is a trickster or a charlatan or a deceiver. Still, it would be wise to be on guard. I said that Joachim was trustworthy; is not Settembrini equally reliable, and without qualification? The answer must be no, though the character is closest in so many ways to Thomas Mann's own humanism. "No" because the very presentation of this humanist is dubious in the text itself. Settembrini is a most sympathetic character; why, then, does Clavdia

Chauchat hold him in a kind of contempt? She is, at least, highly suspicious of him. The answer, I believe, is that we tend to like people who like us. Settembrini distrusts Clavdia and tries to shield his "student" from her. A dozen good reasons may be given to explain Settembrini's action. Clavdia's power is sensual—at least in the beginning. Her sensuous being is opposed essentially to reason as embodied in Settembrini. That opposition is evident in Hans' response to his "mentor." Settembrini is a great humanist but he is also an "organ-grinder man," one who chirrups at the girls. "Carducci-Latini-humani-spaghetti," Hans mutters behind Settembrini's back.[158] There is a "high" explanation for Settembrini's dislike for Clavdia: "it was the love of woman which the crippled Leopardi was condemned to renounce; that this it prinicipally was which rendered him incapable of avoiding the embitterment of his soul."[159] And there is also a "low" account of the matter—the one which I have offered, banal as it appears: we tend to like people who like us. The prime issue is Hans himself, Hans who stands between Settembrini and Clavdia—among others.

Both Clavdia and Settembrini have a great deal to teach Hans Castorp—and they do. Most noteworthy, however, is the fact that Hans ingests without comprehending and absorbs without digesting. That is true for a very long period of initiation on the Mountain. He goes through an "encyclopedic" of learning; the sciences, among other considerations, are swallowed with zest. Hans is changed but the change is not "formative," only cosmetic, so to speak. It is essential to the hermetic process that time refine the raw material—the base metals—before true change may take place. For years, in effect, Hans listens and reads but cannot speak in his own voice. He is taught by his mentors the privilege of silence, its genius. Or better: Hans comes to understand silence by way of a transformation which takes place in his being in the course of alchemic weathering. He is transformed from a good-natured flatland equivalent of a "goose" into the "brother" of Mynheer Peeperkorn, able to converse with Mynheer in an efficacious manner, with insight and with honor. This is no small testimonial. Hans Castorp has undergone an education.

Although the doctors at the Berghof have much to teach Hans, they cannot be counted as his major mentors. Rather, it is four figures—two and two—who qualify for eminence: Clavdia and Mynheer Peeperkorn on the one hand, Settembrini and Naphta on the other. Despite his muttering, Hans is closest to Settembrini. Naphta, an incendiary intellect of spectacular learning, vies with the humanist over Hans. Naphta is the only Jew of stature in the novel and he is a Jesuit. Or, more precisely, Naphta was born a Jew and becomes a convert to the Society of Jesus: he is a marginal Jew and an incomplete Jesuit. The illness of the Mountain has stopped him in his Jesuitical ascent; the Society has arranged for him to become a professor of Latin in a secondary school in the high country. The two intellectuals wrestle over Hans. Settembrini, never one to underestimate the acumen and power of his opponent, warns Hans against Naphta: "His form is logic, but his essence is confusion."[160] Naphta is a dialectician, a revolutionary, and an intellectual terrorist. It has been suggested that Thomas Mann took as his model for Naphta Georg Lukacs. Be that as it may (as authors love to say), the figure of Naphta represents to me the portrait of Trotsky as a Jesuit. Hans is entranced with both Naphta and Settembrini; his mind is entangled in their debates. In fact, the more heated the debates become with the presence of Hans Castorp as a kind of oxygen feeding the fire of the combatants, the more incomprehensible they become, for at times in the most intense of their battles toward the end, they take each other's positions, their arguments vanish into each other, and their language is lost in a din of conceptual screeching. Only death ends the debate; it leaves Castorp under the tutelage of Settembrini, but also under the sway of what Hans has gained from Clavdia and Peeperkorn.

With the development of the novel, we come to see as well the growth and diversity of the mechanism of the leitmotiv. The horizon which phenomenology locates in temporal terms permits the movement of one leitmotiv into another. When Hans takes his first strenuous walk on the Mountain, his head begins to shake "in precisely the same way now, at his age, in which the head of old Hans Lorenz Castorp once had shaken."[161] Having returned to the leitmotiv of his childhood, Hans now moves on to a new motif: "He mounted still higher on the zigzag path, drawn by the sound of cow-bells, and came at length upon the herd, grazing near a hut whose roof was weighted with stones. Two bearded men approached him, with axes on their shoulders. They parted, a little way off him, and 'Thank ye kindly, and God be with ye,' said the one to the other."[162] The hut reappears in Hans' "Snow" adventure, when his ski trip takes him into the storm and he finds "the hay-hut with the weighted roof" to lean against.[163] And the "Thank ye kindly, and God be with ye" re-echoes in the novel. The scene in which Joachim tells Hofrat Behrens that he is leaving, the scene in which the Hofrat "in a towering passion"[164] dismisses the cousins, ironically contains the leitmotiv (transposed a bit, to be sure) of the words between the two bearded rustics:

"Your family knows what you are doing—do they consent?"

"My mother—yes. It is all arranged. The first of October I join the seventy-sixth regiment as cornet."

"At all hazards?" Behrens asked, and fixed him with his bloodshot eyes.

"I have the honour," Joachim answered, his lips twitching.

"Very good, Ziemssen." The Hofrat's tone changed; he abandoned his position, he relaxed in every way. "Very well, then. Stir your stumps, go on, and God be with you."[165]

Duplicity in *The Magic Mountain* is sometimes doubled, that is, the character is self-divided and divided still again. It is possible to trace the horizon of diremption through the "history" of the leitmotiv. Naphta, for example, is on surface view divided as Jew and Catholic, as Jesuit and revolutionary, but he is also something of a sybarite: "'you get such a surprise when you first enter his room and see all that silk . . . the beautiful old furniture,' Hans Castorp went on, 'the *pietà* out of the fourteenth century, the Venetian lustre, the little page in livery—and such a lot of chocolate cake, too.'"[166] It is Settembrini who summarizes: "I will characterize this man for you with a single word. He is a voluptuary."[167] Yet the "doubling" leads to still another motiv. When Hans first visits Naphta's rooms, he is struck by an early and raw art work—a "pious horror," as Hans first perceives the wooden group, identified by Naphta as being from the fourteenth century. Hans inquires further:

"What is the name of the artist?"
Naphta shrugged his shoulders.
"What does it matter?" he said. "We should not ask—for in the time when it was made they never did. It was not created by some wonderful and well-advertised single genius. It is an anonymous product, anonymous and communal."[168]

In the spirited argument which follows between Naphta and Settembrini, Naphta claims insistently that a genuine individualism "sorts very well with the most binding communism." To which Hans adds: "Anonymous and communal." Settembrini glares at him. "'Be quiet, Engineer,' he said, with a severity probably due to nervous irritation. 'Inform yourself, but don't try to express your views.'"[169] But the horizon of the leitmotiv leads on and reaches its apogee in the mystical experience recounted in the episode called "Snow." At the center of the experience, Hans acknowledges: "Now I know that it is not out of our single souls we dream. We dream anonymously and communally."[170] At the same time, in the same dream, Hans Castorp brings to fusion his experience with Clavdia's "predecessor," Pribislav Hippe, the meaning of the body, disease, and death. Castorp perceives, finally, that in himself lies the essence of what is human. Life's delicate child is no longer simply Hans but man altogether. The dream-poem he has dreamed in "Snow" presents as its center "the position of the Homo Dei" and as its conclusion, "Man is the lord of counter-positions." But in that balance, Hans perceives that "it is love, not reason, that is stronger than death."[171] None of these powerful centralities—the body, disease, love, death—is reducible to the instantiations they represent. The individual deaths on the Mountain are recorded, but the sovereignty of death remains untouched by its exemplifications. In this way, the transcendental is introduced into the life, disease, and death of the individuals who are caught up in the movement of existence—its current of illness, decline, and very occasional recovery. "Horizon," in its phenomenological force, shows itself as the clue—Husserl would say "the transcendental clue"—to the meaning of the substance of *The Magic Mountain*: the essence of time. Time undergoes phenomenological reduction on the mountain: it is bracketed not only from the chronology of the flat-land but also from death itself. Oddly enough, it is talk about death which is as unwelcome on the Mountain as it is on the flat-land. One does not talk about death at table. It is worse than gauche to talk about death to the dying; it is vulgar and base, neither correct nor gentlemanly. Talk of death, one might say, lies somewhere in the neighborhood of psychoanalysis.

Death is in the horizon of time; it is that toward which we move. Helmut Kuhn has written a most perceptive essay on "The Phenomenological Concept of 'Horizon.'" We shall borrow a few sentences from it: "Horizon is the ultimate circumference within which all things, real and imaginable, are bound to appear. . . . While limiting the totality of given things, the horizon also frames it. . . . By its very nature every horizon is 'open.'"[172] In its transcendental aspect, then, horizon bounds, frames, and opens experience for the individual who is capable of "enjoying" the phenomena which consciousness reveals. Within the fictive reality of Mann's novel, it is Hans Castorp who is equipped to experience such "enjoyment." And it is clear that this is so because from early childhood on, Hans has been sympathetic to illness, disease, and death. In being "life's delicate child," he is open to experimentation—the *placet experiri* of Settembrini. This openness includes, most profoundly, the *spirituel* principle, as Hans explains to Clavdia, the *spirituel* way which leads to love and death.[173] For Hans the *spirituel* is the reverse side of the honor to which Joachim is bound. That is part of the reason for Hans' revolt in the final séance scene. A curiosity-dominated love may have been responsible for Hans asking for Joachim in the séance, but it is the same love which leads Hans to ask for forgiveness when the damage of the séance has been done. Hans has followed his experimentation to its end—and beyond. His alchemic transformation has led beyond the *spirituel* to the demonic.

In arriving at the demonic, Hans Castorp has repeated an earlier venture when he went skiing: he has come full circle. This time, he has regained his acquaintance with the uncanny. Consider that Hans' education has taken him through Settembrini, Naphta, Clavdia and—although we have had little time to examine an important part of his apprenticeship—Mynheer Peeperkorn. Drs. Behrens and Krokowski are by the way. Through the leitmotiv of memory, Castorp has brought himself back to Hippe, to the crush Hans had as a schoolboy, to the homoerotic propensity which led Hans to borrow that pencil from Pribislav and return it to another "slav" with Kirghiz eyes, to the three red shavings he secretes in an inner drawer of his desk.[174] There are, indeed, leitmotivs within leitmotivs. The shavings are red—a signal of danger, of the occult, and of the uncanny in *The Magic Mountain*. We need only recall the red light which goes on during the X-ray procedure and the red lamp of the séance. The inner horizon of temporal development includes the warnings of danger for the magicker. We transubstantiate ourselves: *we* are the base metals which are in need of purification and transmutation. The alchemist's goal is not to make gold but to transform himself. The very idea of such a procedure is uncanny: to leave oneself in becoming another. The very theme of the double is itself uncanny. When that theme is developed in terms of mental illness (as it is in Dostoyevsky's *The Double*), the account of the illness is uncanny.[175] And so, the uncanny becomes a complex leitmotiv in *The Magic Mountain*. The motiv is not only complex but far-reaching. "Even the puzzle of life itself . . . was easier to approach by uncanny, even morbid paths than by way of health."[176] It is hardly surprising that the motiv of the uncanny reaches the pitch of the séance. Music has prepared the way. Hans Castorp is the guardian of the new record player, its monitor, its supervisor, its "intelligencer." No wonder that the uncanny presents itself first in the story and music of Gounod's *Faust* and second in the spectral presence of the record which has Valentine's Prayer in the séance room. Magic, yes. Artifice of the fictive, certainly. But the deeper moment in the leitmotiv of the uncanny resides in the willingness of "life's delicate child" to risk this final experiment: to sunder time in the discipline of the paranormal.

The apotheosis of the uncanny comes in the séance when Hans asks for his cousin Joachim. The return of the dead is perhaps the most elemental aspect of the uncanny. Before the manifestation of Joachim, however, another piece of mischief presents itself:

> Hans Castorp made on his own account a most singular discovery, which might be regarded as a personal attention on the part of the dark powers here manifesting themselves with such childish perversity. A light object lay in his lap; he discovered it to be the "souvenir": . . . the glass diapositive of Clavdia Chauchat's X-ray portrait. Quite uncontestably he, Hans Castorp, had not carried it into the room.[177]

With the playing of the record of Valentine's Prayer, the image of Joachim is finally conjured: "There in the background . . . Joachim sat. It was the Joachim of the last days, with hollow, shadowy cheeks, warrior's beard and full curling lips . . . but there was no change in the mildness of the great dark orbs, whose quiet, friendly gaze sought out Hans Castorp, and him alone."[178] Joachim is in the uniform of a German soldier of the First World War; he wears the characteristic helmet of that time and carries a saber and pistol. On his chest is discerned a cross. It is not a decoration but presumably a religious emblem. Yet there is nothing in Joachim's appearance to indicate that he carried the title of an officer. Rather, his dress seems to indicate that of "an old-fashioned foot-soldier." What Hans Castorp sees, I think, is not Joachim but himself. The superficial resemblance is that of his cousin but the prescient image is that of himself. Castorp has reached the end of his "experimentation." In truth, he has exceeded his mission in tampering with time. The end of the séance marks the transformation of Hans: "Hans Castorp went up to the protesting Krokowski, close up to him. He tried to speak, but no words came. He put out his hand, with a brusque, imperative gesture. Receiving the key, he nodded several times, threateningly, close into the other's face, turned and went out of the room."[179]

Time has been accelerated; the uncanny has been penetrated. To the figure who has been summoned in this frantic hour, Hans whispers: "Forgive me!"[180] Valentine's prayer has become Castorp's prayer. We are approaching the end of our story. It would appear that we have run out of time but that is not yet the case. Time undergoes change but it is essentially perdurable. The idea that time has been accelerated is paradoxical with respect to Thomas Mann's method. *Steigerung* is an alchemic principle but it cannot be applied to the essence of time, for time itself is the agent of acceleration. In this way we arrive at the proposition: Time is uncanny. Thomas Mann has Hans say to his cousin: "I shall never cease to find it strange that the time seems to go so slowly in a new place. I mean—of course it isn't a question of my being bored; on the contrary, I might say that I am royally entertained. But when I look back—in retrospect, that is, you understand—it seems to me I've been up here goodness only knows how long; it seems an eternity back to the time when I arrived."[181] The commonplace observation that time seems to pass slowly on certain occasions or else to fly is transcended in the meditation of Hans Castorp and his remark to Joachim. What is uncanny about time in Davos is that it defies measure or calibration; it has its own nature, constituted out of the transformation of disease into love. The alchemistry of time arises out of the choice of the *spirituel* way, which Thomas Mann calls "unreasoning love."[182] The time of chronology—flat-land time—includes death as facticity, as a "thing" of the life-world; temporality involves *my* death or the death of the Other grasped as mine, as integral to my life. One can regret a statistic but a person cannot grieve for it. Grief is the daughter of love, not knowledge.

We come by way of existential phenomenology to the meaning of death as the transcendental aspect of negation. Can the death of Joachim Ziemssen be "regretted," let alone mourned? A fictive death is required by aesthetic criteria; only those on the Mountain—those fictive beings— who knew, admired, or loved Joachim can mourn his death. Where is the reader left, then? Mann writes:

> We let the curtain fall for the last time but one. While it rustles down, let us take our stand in spirit with Hans Castorp on his lonely height, and gaze down with him upon a damp burial-ground in the flat-land; see the flash of a sword as it rises and falls, hear the word of command rapped out, and three salvoes, three fanatical salutes reverberating over Joachim Ziemssen's root-pierced grave.[183]

The reader is a mediator between the fictive and the "real" world, the life-world. Phenomenological reduction has placed the "really real" aspect of ordinary existence between transcendental brackets. The ascent of Hans Castorp on the Mountain is not essentially remote from the movement each individual experiences as a phase of his lived life. The fictive may be not only comprehensible but moving for the reader precisely because the lineaments of change are present in the intentional rays of consciousness. Husserl's intentional objects are neither real nor imaginary; they are irreal. Thus the realm of the fictive is at once close to actual human existence and released from particularity and objectification. Essence is appropriated fictively without the "real" giving way to the imaginary. Having concerned ourselves with a novel, we have immanently assumed that essence and the fictive are the center of our work. It has been suggested that Husserl's central metaphor was the visual. Yet it might now be said that the most powerful metaphor, though internal to the novel, is the auditory. This is so not because the source of the leitmotiv is music but because the auditory is the interior meditation on what is *spirituel*. Alfred Schutz reminds us of Leibniz's definition of music: "music is a hidden arithmetical activity of a mind that does not know it is counting." Schutz continues: "And Schopenhauer proposes to sum up his own conception of music in another definition: . . . Music is a hidden metaphysical activity of a mind that does not know it is philosophizing."[184] But it is in the text of *The Magic Mountain* that we find the most decisive statement of the primacy of music in Mann's creation. It is unavoidably evident that of the recordings in Hans' keeping, the one most dear to him is Schubert's "Linden-tree":

> Let us put it thus: a conception which is of the spirit, and therefore significant, is so because it reaches beyond itself to become the expression and exponent of a larger conception, a whole world of feeling and sentiment, which, whether more or less completely, is mirrored in the first, and in this

wise, accordingly, the degree of its significance measured. Further, the love felt for such a creation is in itself "significant": betraying something of the person who cherishes it, characterizing his relation to that broader world the conception bodies forth—which, consciously or unconsciously, he loves along with and in the thing itself.[185]

Without the terminology or the obvious techniques of phenomenology, Mann's description of the various levels of significance in Hans' experience of Schubert's *Lied* resonate with Husserl's vision. First, there is the song itself; second, the song "appresents" the larger conception of "world"; third, love of the entire conception which emanates from the song is itself significant. The whole of Hans' experience has become internalized, rendered lucid and resolved at last. "May we take it that our simple hero, after so many years of hermetic-pedagogic discipline, of ascent from one stage of being to another, has now reached a point where he is conscious of the 'meaningfulness' of his love and the object of it? We assert, we record, that he has."[186] It is this alchemic internalization of his experience on *Der Zauberberg* that is the substance of the uncanny. "Life's Problem Child" has fulfilled the positive side of his being; although he has not become illumined, he has learned the significance of love through the transformations of the stages of love. Hans Castorp has achieved what it was in him to achieve: he has moved from a rather ordinary, middling fellow to a *spirituel* being. On the verge of the Great War, Hans Castorp has dreamt out his magical dream with dignity and with honor. Still, it is necessary for the reader to be on guard. The entire novel dissembles; "don't trust me altogether," it says. But this element of distrust is present in most of Thomas Mann's work. It is the moment of danger, the red light of the X-ray scene once again, but even more deeply, the threat of the artist, who cannot be trusted completely. This threat manifests itself to Hans in a dream:

> he stood trying to shoulder Settembrini away from the spot where they stood, the Italian smiling in his subtle, mocking way, under the full, upward-curving moustaches—and it was precisely this smile which Hans Castorp found so injurious. "You are a nuisance," he distinctly heard himself say. "Get away, you are only a hand-organ man, and you are in the way here." But Settembrini would not let himself be budged; Hans Castorp was still standing considering what was to be done when he was unexpectedly vouchsafed a signal insight into the true nature of time; it proved to be nothing more or less than a "silent sister," a mercury column without degrees, to be used by those who wanted to cheat.[187]

And, of course, we have learned to interpret dreams, to look for their latent as well as manifest content. Hans' dream is fundamentally untrustworthy. Settembrini *is* ultimately a friend; at the end, he is the only one to cry at the departure of Hans Castorp. But he is also equivocal: he is at once a wind-bag and a gentleman. Settembrini sees in Hans' face the danger that resides in music; it has the Devil's share:

> "Music quickens time, she quickens us to the finest enjoyment of time; she quickens—and in so far has moral value. Art has moral value, in so far as it quickens. But what if it does the opposite? What if it dulls us, sends us to sleep, works against action and progress? Music can do that too; she is an old hand at using opiates. But the opiate, my dear sirs, is a gift of the Devil; it makes for lethargy, inertia, slavish inaction, stagnation. There is something suspicious about music, gentlemen."[188]

The quickening of time is woven into the fabric of the occult. We shall see a bit more of it. But Hans' dream is untrustworthy for still other reasons. The image of the "silent sister" has been smuggled into the dream, for time cannot be measured by space. Time cannot be trusted to the calibrated measure which the silent sister requires to determine the true temperature of the cheater. In any case, Hans Castorp cheats in the opposite direction: without realizing it, Hans wants to be ill, to have "temperature," to place the mercurial cigar between his lips and under his tongue, to become "one of them." The price of such early longing is that Hans' meditations on time, his philosophical insights, his *aperçus* are all lost in quick order. Nothing sticks. Mann writes:

> Despite his benumbed condition he felt it incumbent upon him to be polite, to make conversation, and to this end he sought to recall those brilliant ideas he had previously had, on the subject of time. Alas, they had fled, the whole "complex" of them, and left not a trace behind: on the subject of time not one single idea, however insignificant, found lodgment in his head.[189]

If the novel cannot be completely trusted, where does that leave the narrator? Finally! Finally we come to the narrator. We shall not linger long. He calleth to me out of Seir, Watchman, what of the narrator? Let him call! Let him call! Whatever the narrator may be, let us also be wary of the author. He is not to be trusted altogether. This view may seem to be unreasonable. After all, the author has recounted a long journey, seven years of a magical stay. Still, we should not trust him. The reader may think me ungrateful or paranoiac and be tempted to say, "Rather, keep your eye on Natanson!" Fair enough. Let us say: keep your eye on author, narrator and me. Why so suspicious? It is partly Thomas Mann who has given the reader fair warning. Of *The Magic Mountain*, Mann writes that "it employs the methods of the realistic novel, but actually it is not one."[190] Is it necessary to remind the reader that I have used the phrase "magic realism" in describing Mann's novel? But I said also that "magic realism" is uncertain—rather vague. And perhaps that vagueness is just what is needed in speaking of the Mountain. Just as the heroes of the Mountain undergo transformation, so the language of the flat-land must change to be adequate to the milieu of the Berghof. Hans and Clavdia speak French in the Walpurgis-Night chapter. The language of love requires more than the use of the intimate or familiar form of address. Clavdia understands Hans: "*Petit bourgeois!*" she said, "*Joli bourgeois à la petite tache humide. Est-ce vrai que tu m'aimes tant?*" And Clavdia is given the classiest exit line in contemporary literature: "Over her shoulder she said softly: '*N'oubliez pas de me rendre mon crayon.*'"[191]

Let us now join Hans Castorp and "take stock." Let us now join Edmund Husserl and "take stock." Let us now join forces with existential phenomenology and "take stock" And let us proceed backward: existential phenomenology, Edmund Husserl, and Hans Castorp.

A necessary distinction must be made between existential phenomenology as a philosophic method or theoretical position and the work or conceptual material to which it is applied. In my judgment, *The Magic Mountain* is not an "existential" novel. It may be concerned with such themes as death but it would be extremely difficult to think of any historical figure in existential thought who could be said to exemplify Mann's novel. Kierkegaard, Heidegger, Sartre—certainly, they are alien to the scheme of Thomas Mann. Apart from Schopenhauer, Nietzsche, and Freud, Mann's influences and sources are literary and cultural.

We have employed an existential method to explore a nonexistential work. There is no paradox at issue in this procedure. Also, it should be remembered that "existential" in my usage is linked to "phenomenological," and I have tried to show that *The Magic Mountain* lends itself to phenomenological treatment. Again, this does not make the novel itself "phenomenological." It is all the more important to consider these cautions because *The Magic Mountain* is sandwiched between *Waiting for Godot* (traditionally called a play of the "Absurd") and *The Metamorphosis* (how far can one keep Franz Kafka from existential thought?). Could I have used another novel in place of *The Magic Mountain*? Although I am not saying that *The Magic Mountain* is the only piece of fiction which would "work" in the present context, I am less sure about alternatives. I would have to think about it. Perhaps another pedagogical-alchemic work would do: Gabriel García Marquez's *One Hundred Years of Solitude*. Perhaps.

Earlier, I quoted from Husserl's work on inner-time consciousness. In bringing Thomas Mann's concept of time to closure, it is appropriate to return to Husserl's discussion. He says:

> Let us now distinguish between "phenomena of consciousness," time-constituting phenomena, and (on the other side) such phenomena that constitute *objects in immanent time*. We can scarcely use the language of "appearances"

for these temporal-objects-in-their-running-off-modes. For it indeed becomes apparent that immanent objects are themselves appearances, and yet appearances in an entirely different sense—in some cases, for example, they are appearances of external objects. The best thing we could do would be to say "*running-off phenomena*" and, with respect to the immanent *objects* themselves, to speak of their "running-off characters" (e.g., now, past).[192]

The contrasts are those of *The Magic Mountain*: the "running off" of the dimensions of time—now, past—is comprehensible only within the immanent unity, the immutable form, of temporality itself. The phenomenological foundation of time, including its bizarre involution—its uncanny aspect—is form. At one time, Hans calls form "folderol."[193] By the end of the fiction, Hans may be said to recognize form, I would say, as "the fundamental adventure of his life."[194]

Now, final stock-taking with Hans Castorp. In his seven years on the Mountain, Hans has made the circle of himself as well as his surroundings. "Our hero had sat at all seven of the tables in the dining-room, at each about a year, the last being the 'bad' Russian table, and his company there two Armenians, two Finns, a Bokharian, and a Kurd. He sat at the 'bad' Russian table, wearing a recent little blond beard, vaguish in cut, which we are disposed to regard as a sign of philosophic indifference to his own outer man." No longer are serious questions about his well-being addressed to him by the staff. And because he was left alone, "he was like the scholar in the peculiarly happy state of never being 'asked' any more."[195] He is a tubercular emeritus, still active, as it were, but as a kind of scholar in residence, a presence rather than a force. A far greater force, the earthquake that shatters the Mountain forever, intervenes and ends the tenure of the scholar. Mann brings down the final curtain:

> What is it? Where are we?
> Whither has the dream
> snatched us?[196]

I told you not to trust him! The old magician has made the elephant disappear right before our eyes. Who is left to summarize it all? If it is correct to say that the village cemetery is the "still point" of *The Magic Mountain*, then the novel's temporal being is characterized by Holger, the playful familiar, who leaves us with a grand horizontal flush: "A hastening while."[197]

Six

The Metamorphosis

NOTHING in the ample literature on *The Metamorphosis* can change the fact that the central event in Kafka's story is the transformation of Gregor Samsa into a hideous insect.[198] The transformation is inescapable for any reader or critic, no matter what philosophical predilections are involved. How or even whether this metamorphosis can be understood is part of the mystery of Kafka's story, but there is no doubt about the finality, the irrevocability of Gregor's transformation. Everything begins with that: in the beginning was the metamorphosis. Kafka insisted that the insect cannot be depicted. With what abhorrence would Kafka have regarded Vladimir Nabokov's discussion of *The Metamorphosis*.[199] A monomaniacal obsession saturates Nabokov's brilliant criticism. I would say that apart from the important training he had in entomology and the discipline of precise and demanding drawing—a dissection of the most extraordinary kind—Nabokov's criticism was accomplished under the sign of the *blueprint*. How everything was, where everything was, how the floor plan of the fiction was managed—all this was essential nourishment to Nabokov's critical mind. The drawings of Gregor's body resemble plans for a boat-building project. The questions that Nabokov poses arise out of the physics of bodily motion: how did Gregor manage to get out of bed? That rocking motion which finally succeeded in landing him on the floor of his room demanded a beetle back of definite shape and proportions. Gregor can not only be depicted, he can be displayed in detail enough to cover walls. Those butterflies never had a chance!

In the presence of Kafka's writings, one is tempted to quote Gregor's father: "get a locksmith at once!" In *The Metamorphosis* it is Gregor who manages to turn the key to his room, manages to grasp the key with his mouth, manages to turn the key with his toothless jaws, which he damages in the effort: "a brown fluid issued from his mouth, flowed over the key and dripped on the floor."[200] The family no longer needs a locksmith; instead the reader has come. In truth, it is only Gregor who can unlock his door. And he can unlock it only from within, at precious cost. Thus Gregor Samsa presents himself to the world. In a letter to Max Brod, Kafka quoted Kierkegaard:

> As soon as a man appears who brings something of the primitive along with him, so that he doesn't say, "You must take the world as you find it," but

rather "Let the world be what it likes, I take my stand on a primitiveness which I have no intention of changing to meet with the approval of the world," at that moment, as these words are heard, a metamorphosis takes place in the whole of nature. Just as in a fairy story, when the right word is pronounced, the castle that has been lying under a spell for a hundred years opens and everything comes to life, in the same way existence becomes all attention. The angels have something to do, and watch curiously to see what will come of it, because that is their business. On the other side, dark, uncanny demons, who have been sitting around doing nothing and chewing their nails for a long time, jump up and stretch their limbs, because, they say, here is something for us.[201]

It is not the word "metamorphosis" in this passage which attracts us; it is the word "primitive" which is commanding. The transformation has taken place before "the right word is pronounced." The primitive is what is self-defining. The individual who presents himself is not he who is seen but he, like Father Abraham, who has withstood testing—not in comparison to others but in the covenant of his inwardness. "Fire!" Pascal wrote. That "fire" constitutes the central and generative question of *The Metamorphosis*, a question posed soon after the beginning of the story: "What has happened to me?" This apparently simple question has the force of consciousness undergoing upheaval. "What has happened to me?" is never answered in Kafka's story; the "real" Gregor is unchanged. His circumstances have altered. Others have changed. If Gregor has been transformed, others have been blasted to their roots. And still others are shocked. Flannery O'Connor writes of her mother:

> Regina is getting very literary. "Who is this Kafka?" she says. "People ask me." A German Jew, I says, I think. He wrote a book about a man that turns into a roach. "Well, I can't tell people *that*," she says.[202]

Still, the idea of a "key" to the story persists. Nabokov did not have to raise such a question, for he was concerned solely with the "style" and space of *The Metamorphosis*. The dialectic of ideas is replaced by the force of language. And, as I have said, Nabokov's criticism is brilliantly done. It leaves the reader grateful, but with the impression: let the dogs and cats fight over the scraps of ideas, I have the only substance which literature possesses: style—the final victory of language. If Nabokov does not satisfy, then we are left where we were: in search of a key. The search has been concluded for a number of Kafka critics in the "metaphor." Kafka is reported to have said: "To be a poet means to be strong in metaphors."[203] How this statement is to be interpreted remains a problem; what is unproblematic is the inevitable battle of the metaphors. One target which can hardly be ignored in *The Metamorphosis* is the metaphor of the newspaper illustration of the woman with the muff, which Gregor has cut out of a magazine. It comes in the second paragraph of the story, soon after Gregor thinks, "What has happened to me?" Kafka writes:

> Above the table on which a collection of cloth samples was unpacked and spread out—Samsa was a commercial traveler—hung the picture which he had recently cut out of an illustrated magazine and put into a pretty gilt frame. It showed a lady, with a fur cap on and a fur stole, sitting upright and holding out to the spectator a huge fur muff into which the whole of her forearm had vanished![204]

Not much later we learn through Gregor's mother (in defense of her son): "The only amusement he gets is doing fretwork. For instance, he spent two or three evenings cutting out a little picture frame; you would be surprised to see how pretty it is; it's hanging in his room."[205]

Later, the metaphor is deepened. Gregor's sister and mother remove furniture from his room. Gregor is greatly agitated: "he was struck by the picture of the lady muffled in so much fur and quickly crawled up to it and pressed himself to the glass, which was a good surface to hold on to and comforted his hot belly. This picture at least, which was entirely hidden beneath him, was going to be removed by nobody."[206] Had Gregor cut out the illustration because of its erotic aspect or had he discovered or deciphered its erotic meaning after his transformation? Or is the metaphor to be interpreted in some other way? Certainly, it has been interpreted differently. Heinz Politzer writes: "He creeps up to the picture and covers it with his body when mother and sister threaten to remove it. The body of the animal covers the body of an animal-like woman who is clad threefold in fur. A ludicrously dissonant variation of the main theme of metamorphosis is developed here when the insect presses himself against the glass."[207]

It has also been suggested that the newspaper on which the picture is printed (as well as newspapers throughout the story) is metaphorically important to the meaning of *The Metamorphosis*.[208] The smallest unit of the word—the individual letter of the alphabet—would be metaphoric material—the metaphor within. Late in his life, Kafka studied Hebrew. There was talk of going to Palestine. Perhaps it was the number-laden Hebrew alphabet that beckoned him. In metaphor country, nothing can be ruled out. But Palestine was, if remote, not altogether improbable. Several members of Kafka's circle of friends ended up as Zionists or at least in Palestine. One of them, in fact, is a link between Kafka and phenomenology. Hugo Bergmann, an old friend of Kafka (going back to secondary school) studied philosophy under a student of that great Viennese presence, Franz Brentano; the student was Anton Marty. In 1908, four years or so before *The Metamorphosis* was accomplished, Bergmann published a monograph entitled, *Untersuchungen zum*

Problem der Evidenz der inneren Wahrnehmung.[209] The study was dedicated to "Prof. Dr. Anton Marty." In 1891 Husserl published his *Philosophie der Arithmetic,* dedicated to *his* teacher in philosophy, Franz
Brentano.[210] Bergmann's work is replete with substantial discussion of
the early Husserl, informed and critical. At the same time, the author
attends to a number of other thinkers in the broad phenomenological
tradition of the time. It is likely that Kafka heard the names, at least, of
the phenomenologists. Probably he heard something of their doctrines.
Such historical linkage is not what drives me to think of Kafka in connection with phenomenology. But, for philosophers, history needs to be
attended to occasionally.

I am moving toward *The Metamorphosis* in my own metamorphical
direction. Perhaps another historical note might be of help. From 1911
through 1913, in one way or another, Kafka took a most serious interest
in a troupe of Yiddish actors playing in Prague. Fortunately, there is no
need to gather evidence for this assertion. In an excellent and carefully
documented book, Evelyn Torton Beck has done the work for us: *Kafka
and the Yiddish Theater: Its Impact on His Work.*[211] The final fact of this
book is that Kafka was profoundly influenced by Yiddish theater. Why?
Because in its primitive way, the actors in this minor troupe tore open
the wound of what was Jewish in Kafka's being. "Primitive" because the
most basal characteristics of theater were exposed in the performance of
these artists—above all, *gesture.* The body itself became theatrical. For
Gregor, Gregor as insect, there is an "immediacy of 'human gesture.'"
Left with language which cannot communicate, Gregor's bridge to the
world is his body, its movement, its whereabouts. In his portentous "interview" with the chief clerk, Gregor "asks," "Will you give a true account of all this?"[212] In his metaphorical being, Gregor is already dying.

After Gregor's death, the charwoman, who swept "it" up, comes to
give her report to the family:

> "Well?" said Mr. Samsa. The charwoman stood grinning in the doorway as if
> she had good news to impart to the family but meant not to say a word unless
> properly questioned. The small ostrich feather standing upright on her hat,
> which had annoyed Mr. Samsa ever since she was engaged, was waving gaily
> in all directions. "Well, what is it then?" asked Mrs. Samsa, who obtained
> more respect from the charwoman than the others. "Oh," said the char-
> woman, giggling so amiably that she could not at once continue, "just this,
> you don't need to bother about how to get rid of the thing next door. It's
> been seen to already."[213]

The charwoman at the end of *The Metamorphosis* says to the Samsas:
"Bye, everybody."[214] Were she in America, she would have said: "Have
a nice day!" And the Samsas do.

It is difficult to "know" or even hypothesize what Gregor's future might have been had he not undergone transformation. Metamorphosis is not so much his destiny as his mode of existence. In Sartrean terms, Gregor is real in the unreality of the world. His "gesture" is himself. In Husserlian terms, Gregor is the irreality within Kafka's fiction. But it is in Schutzian terms that we are able to make a significant phenomenological advance. In his essay "On Multiple Realities"—one of his strongest and most illuminating studies—Schutz takes as his point of departure the chapter in William James' *The Principles of Psychology* on "The Perception of Reality." Schutz reminds us that for James, "reality . . . means simply relation to our emotional and active life. The origin of all reality is subjective, whatever excites and stimulates our interest is real. To call a thing real means that this thing stands in a certain relation to ourselves. 'The word "real" is, in short, a fringe.'"[215] Moreover, the "real" is multiple in its essential character, that is to say, the nature of reality consists of many levels of interpretation, attitude, and action. William James lists the "most important sub-universes commonly discriminated from each other and recognized by most of us as existing"[216] in the following way:

1. The world of sense, or of physical "things" as we instinctively apprehend them, with such qualities as heat, color and sound, and such "forces" as life, chemical affinity, gravity, electricity, all existing as such within or on the surface of the things.

2. The world of science, or of physical things as the learned conceive them, with secondary qualities and "forces" (in the popular sense) excluded, and nothing real but solids and fluids and their "laws" (i.e. customs) of motion.

3. The world of ideal relations, or abstract truths believed or believable by all, and expressed in logical, mathematical, metaphysical, ethical, or aesthetic propositions.

4. The world of "idols of the tribe," illusions or prejudices common to the race. All educated people recognize these as forming one sub-universe. The motion of the sky around the earth, for example, belongs to this world. That motion is not a recognized item of any of the other worlds; but as an "idol of the tribe" it really exists. For certain philosophers "matter" exists only as an idol of the tribe. For science, the "secondary qualities" of matter are but "idols of the tribe."

5. The various supernatural worlds, the Christian heaven and hell, the world of Hindoo mythology, the world of Swedenborg's *visa et audita*, etc. Each of these is a consistent system, with definite relations among its own parts. Neptune's trident, e.g., has no status of reality whatever in the Christian heaven; but within the classic Olympus certain definite things are true of it, whether one believe in the reality of the classic mythology as a whole or not. The various worlds of deliberate fable may be ranked with these worlds

of faith—the world of the *Iliad*, that of *King Lear*, of the *Pickwick Papers*, etc.

6. The various worlds of individual opinion, as numerous as men are.

7. The worlds of sheer madness and vagary, also indefinitely numerous.

Every object we think of gets at least referred to one world or another of this or of some similar list.[217]

This statement by William James is fundamental to the understanding of what follows in our discussion of Schutz's theory of "multiple realities." Schutz points out that James speaks of a "sense of reality" which, Schutz writes, "can be investigated in terms of a psychology of belief and disbelief." But here an important distinction is made: "In order to free . . . [James'] important insight from its psychologistic setting we prefer to speak instead of many sub-universes of reality of *finite provinces of meaning* upon each of which we may bestow the accent of reality. We speak of provinces of *meaning* and not of sub-universes because it is the meaning of our experiences and not the ontological structure of the objects which constitutes reality."[218] The shift is from ontology to phenomenology. Husserl's "natural attitude" is transposed in Schutz's presentation into "the world of working" as the paramount reality.

> The world of working as a whole stands out as paramount over against the many other sub-universes of reality. It is the world of physical things, including my body; it is the realm of my locomotions and bodily operations; it offers resistances which require effort to overcome; it places tasks before me, permits me to carry through my plans, and enables me to succeed or to fail in my attempt to attain my purposes. By my working acts I gear into the outer world, I change it; and these changes, although provoked by my working, can be experienced and tested both by myself and others, as occurrences within this world independently of my working acts in which they originated. I share this world and its objects with Others; with Others, I have ends and means in common; I work with them in manifold social acts and relationships, checking the Others and checked by them. And the world of working is the reality within which communication and the interplay of mutual motivation becomes effective.[219]

In Schutz's terms, it is the paramount reality of daily life in which Gregor undergoes metamorphosis—the world of working. And this holds true for Gregor's sense of that world: "Oh God, he thought, what an exhausting job I've picked on! Traveling about day in, day out. It's much more irritating work than doing the actual business in the office, and on top of that there's the trouble of constant traveling, of worrying about train connections, the bad and irregular meals, casual acquaintances that are always new and never become intimate friends."[220] The elements of the world of working as they affect Gregor go far beyond traveling and making train connections. There is his salary which sup- ports his family and helps toward paying back his father's loan; there are Gregor's plans to pay for his sister's musical education; there is Gregor's concentrated effort to *do* his job. And there are the "fringes" of meaning associated with his occupation: the other commercials who "live like harem women," the hard-of-hearing chief in the office, who sits at a high desk and talks down to employees.[221] All of these factors are part of Gregor's world of working. But leaving that world, even in a temporary way, is not accomplished by going home. In that somnolent abode of "home" Gregor is the awake insect; the others in the family are in a strange kind of Sartrean "Bad Faith"; altogether, the Samsa household is locked in a familial stupor. It is the metamorphosis of Gregor which "shows forth" the family, arouses them from their mediocrity long enough to crucify their son and brother.

In the midst of the paramount reality of daily life, at the center of the world of working, Gregor becomes—in contrast to his family—a kind of hero. Vladimir Nabokov writes: "The Samsa family around the fantastic insect is nothing else than mediocrity surrounding genius."[222] I have not suggested that the natural attitude is a torpor or that mundane existence is an inferior mode of being—inferior to a life of intellect or art, say. To the contrary, the paramount reality *is* paramount because it is the ground of all other provinces of meaning. In transcendental terms, all structures of the life-world are constituted as unities of meaning from their foundation in what Schutz has termed the "paramount" reality. William James speaks of "the paramount reality of sensations": Alfred Schutz speaks of "the world of working as paramount reality." James is caught up in a psychology of the Lebenswelt; Schutz is concerned with its "meaning-constitution." These are complementary missions. They do not conflict; they serve different purposes and utilize different meth- ods. Schutz spoke of his work as being a "phenomenology of the natural attitude." It would be a mistake, however, to think that he is solely con- cerned with the world of working or even that the paramount reality is the one from which we always begin and to which we always return. The many finite provinces are not set in concrete. They are mobile, dialecti- cal realms through which the mundane traveler, the Lebenswelt's Leo- pold Bloom, moves. Schutz writes:

> A word of caution seems to be needed here. The concept of finite provinces of meaning does not involve any static connotation as though we had to select one of these provinces as our home to live in, to start from or to return to. That is by no means the case. Within a single day, even within a single hour our consciousness may run through most different tensions and adopt most

different attentional attitudes to life. There is, furthermore, the problem of "enclaves," that is, of regions belonging to one province of meaning enclosed by another. . . . To give an example of this disregarded group of problems: any projecting within the world of working is itself . . . a phantasying, and involves in addition a kind of theoretical contemplation, although not necessarily of the scientific attitude.[223]

Still, the phenomenological status of "the world of working" is primary. Schutz reminds us that "The world of working in daily life is the archetype of our experience of reality. All the other provinces of meaning may be considered as its modifications."[224] The urgent question is that of how movement from one province of meaning to another is accomplished. The necessary condition for movement is a shock. The reality of the natural attitude "seems to us to be the natural one, and we are not ready to abandon our attitude toward it without having experienced a specific *shock* which compels us to break through the limits of this 'finite' province of meaning to shift the accent of reality to another one."[225] As Schutz would have said: thus Schutz. In Kafka's story the specific shock is the metamorphosis of Gregor Samsa into a gigantic insect. Gregor wakes from uneasy or troubled dreams. I do not think that it can be justly said that those dreams were the "shock" and that the consequence was the transformation of Gregor. Here we must proceed cautiously, for there are readings of Kafka which maintain that *The Metamorphosis* is the recounting of a dream. And it is evident that many critics find the "atmosphere" of the story to be dreamlike. The fact is that disturbing dreams, even nightmares, do not often result in metamorphoses. They are, rather, everynight occurrences, more or less. It would be safer psychologically to say that dreams may be transformations. Indeed, one psychoanalyst, Dr. John N. Rosen, considers dreams and psychosis to be profoundly related: "Over the whole course of his psychoanalytic career, Freud maintained the conviction that psychosis, dreams and nightmares are essentially similar; ultimately (1940) he said that a dream *is* a psychosis. We say that a psychosis is not only similar to dreams in general, but closely related to the protracted and relentless nightmare in particular."[226]

This, perhaps, is an extreme position, as is Dr. Rosen's contention that psychoanalysis may be used in the treatment of psychotics. It is not my responsibility to pass judgment here. Nor is it within my competence to do so. Instead, let us consider the case of Gregor. Even if real nightmares can be psychotic, can fictive dreams satisfy the same criteria or theory? We do not know Gregor's dreams, apart from being told that on the night before the metamorphosis those dreams were uneasy. How troubled were they? We are not told; we cannot say.

Whether or not those dreams were a psychotic episode, the account we have of Gregor's life points to the shock which vibrates in his question, What has happened to me? In that question is the moment of shock. But what finite province has Gregor moved to from his world of working? Although James' list of sub-universes does not include that of dreams, he discusses dreams in a most interesting footnote.[227] Schutz devotes Part IV of "On Multiple Realities" to "the world of dreams." He distinguishes sharply between the dreaming self and the "phantasying" self:

> The dreaming self neither works nor acts. . . . We have . . . to show briefly the principal modifications which the "bracketing of the world of working" undergoes in the provinces of phantasms on the one hand and in the province of dreams on the other. I suggest that the worlds of imageries are characterized by . . . the freedom of discretion, whereas the world of dreams lacks such freedom. The imagining self can "arbitrarily" fill its empty protentions and anticipations with any content and, strictly speaking, it is these fillings upon which the imagining self bestows the accent of reality. It may, as it pleases, interpret its "chances" as lying within its mastery. The dreamer, however, has no freedom of discretion, no arbitrariness in mastering the chances, no possibility of filling in empty anticipations. The nightmare, for instance, shows clearly the inescapableness of the happening in the world of dream and the powerlessness of the dreamer to influence it.[228]

It must be recognized that when we speak of the understanding or interpretation of dreams, the experience of the dream is directly available only to the dreamer. And even then, the dreamer may recall his dream in a fragmentary or distorted way. Some dreams are lost, it would seem, even to the one who dreamt them. The psychoanalyst has his patient's report of a dream, not the dream itself. The penetration of the Other's dream is achieved through the arts of indirection. The metaphysical implications of dreaming are immense. In the solitude of the dream, the dreamer cannot communicate his dream. In telling his dream after awakening, the dreamer is at distance from his dream and remains at distance from the Other. Joseph Conrad's Marlow says to his circle of listeners on board ship, in *Heart of Darkness*:

> "I did not see the man [Mr. Kurtz] in the name any more than you do. Do you see him? Do you see the story? Do you see anything? It seems to me I am trying to tell you a dream—making a vain attempt, because no relation of a dream can convey the dream-sensation, that commingling of absurdity, surprise, and bewilderment in a tremor of struggling revolt, that notion of being captured by the incredible which is of the very essence of dreams. . . . No, it is impossible; it is impossible to convey the life-sensation of any given

epoch of one's existence—that which makes its truth, its meaning—its subtle and penetrating essence. It is impossible. We live, as we dream—alone."[229]

It may be odd to use one fiction to illuminate another, but indirection occasionally makes mischief. In Schutz's terms, the dreamer is the solipsist of the dream; his communication with the Other can only be indirect. He writes:

> Are we sure that the awakened person really can tell his dreams, he who no longer dreams? It will probably make an important difference whether he recollects his dream in vivid retention or whether he has to reproduce it. Whatever the case may be, we encounter the eminent dialectical difficulty that there exists for the dreamer no possibility of direct communication which would not transcend the sphere to which it refers. We can, therefore, approach the provinces of dreams and imageries merely by way of "indirect communication," to borrow this term from Kierkegaard, who has analyzed the phenomena it suggests in an unsurpassable way.[230]

Indirection also leads us to suggest a parallel of sorts between the solitude of Gregor and that of the phenomenologist in the reduced sphere. The question of communication which Schutz raises regarding the dreamer and the Other has its analogue in the situation which Husserl describes of the paradox of phenomenological communication: how can one who has achieved transcendental reduction communicate his findings to another who remains in the paramount reality of everyday life? How is Gregor's transcendental question to be answered? We do not know Gregor the dreamer; we know Gregor as Gregor. Phenomenology illuminates his being to the extent that the coherence of Gregor's situation is revealed. That coherence is both established and inwardly challenged the first time he tries to communicate after the metamorphosis has taken place. Kafka writes:

> "Gregor," said a voice—it was his mother's—"it's a quarter to seven. Hadn't you a train to catch?" That gentle voice! Gregor had a shock as he heard his own voice answering hers, unmistakably his own voice, it was true, but with a persistent horrible twittering squeak behind it like an undertone, that left the words in their clear shape only for the first moment and then rose up reverberating round them to destroy their sense, so that one could not be sure one had heard them rightly.[231]

Through that revolting radar, Gregor learns what has happened to his voice; he also learns that no one else will understand him. It might be thought that a phenomenology of the body would be relevant at this point. Instead, I turn to a much smaller part of Gregor's story which I believe illuminates "the body" without employing large schemes. In savage vaudeville language, let us present Gregor taking a "turn":

> He had only begun to turn round in order to crawl back to his room, but it was certainly a startling operation to watch, since because of his disabled condition he could not execute the difficult turning movements except by lifting his head and then bracing it against the floor over and over again.[232]

Gregor's turn, managed by his bracing his head against the floor, is a forewarning of the moment which soon follows when "his head sank to the floor of its own accord"—the moment of death.[233]

Movement through different finite provinces of meaning requires a shock of a specific sort. What about the notion of movement itself? It would appear that the motive power which permits movement has still to be uncovered. And Schutz is not slow to offer an explanation. Its source lies within the compass of the natural attitude:

> the whole system of relevances which governs the natural attitude is founded upon the basic experience of each of us: I know that I shall die and I fear to die. This basic experience we suggest calling the *fundamental anxiety*. It is the primordial anticipation from which all the others originate. From the fundamental anxiety spring the many interrelated systems of hopes and fears, of wants and satisfactions, of chances and risks which incite man within the natural attitude to attempt the mastery of the world, to overcome obstacles, to draft projects, and to realize them.[234]

It—Kafka, the story, the characters, the action, the conclusion—all comes to this: Gregor Samsa asks two transcendental questions which no one can answer. First, "What has happened to me?"; second, "Will you give a true account of all this?" There is enough mystery without another explication; there is enough guilt without another theory of guilt. There is nothing altogether false which can be said about *The Metamorphosis*. Here we should listen to Isaac Bashevis Singer's version of Spinoza: "There are no falsehoods, there are only distorted truths."[235]

If literary theory is of limited use in trying to understand the story Kafka has told, then what about phenomenology? In fact, phenomenology has just arrived at the Samsa threshold. Having knocked, it enters. What a shambles it finds! Nevertheless, there is something to go on: Gregor has awareness, language he understands although he cannot be understood when he tries to speak. That failure to be understood is the wound within the metaphor.

The movement of Gregor is toward death; in this he retains his common humanity. We are not in a conveyance, advancing from one station to another, with death as the terminus; we are en route back as well as forth, in complicity with a variety of levels of existence. And this variable transit is shown in *The Metamorphosis* from the beginning. Transformed into a monstrous insect, Gregor is nevertheless, early in the morning, trying to dress so that he can make a train. Incredibly incapable of human movement, Gregor is nevertheless ready to carry his sample cases to the railroad station. He is well aware of the time and aware as well of a double truth: he has been transformed into an insect and he has his regular job to do as a commercial. What impedes him is not the recognition that an insect cannot perform the duties of Gregor's job but the blockage he confronts in his new state or condition. The pathos of this double awareness is that Gregor persists in being Gregor, that his transformation has not absolved him of his duty. Despite the appalling evidence, Gregor at first believes that what has happened will be put right, that what he has become *is not*:

> His immediate intention was to get up quietly without being disturbed, to put on his clothes and above all eat his breakfast, and only then to consider what else was to be done, since in bed, he was well aware, his meditations would come to no sensible conclusion. He remembered that often enough in bed he had felt small aches and pains, probably caused by awkward postures, which had proved purely imaginary once he got up, and he looked forward eagerly to seeing this morning's delusions gradually fall away. That the change in his voice was nothing but the precursor of a severe chill, a standing ailment of commercial travelers, he had not the least possible doubt.[236]

What inevitably becomes clear to Gregor is not that he has moved from one finite province of meaning to another—from, say, the paramount reality to the realm of delusion, even temporary delusion—but that the world of working has suffered an involution, that all at once intersubjectivity has fallen into disrepair, that he, Gregor, can understand still but can no longer be understood. Under what rubric is Gregor's transformation to be understood phenomenologically? In Schutz's terms, it might be suggested that Gregor has become caught in an "enclave" of meaning. "Enclaves," as already indicated, are "regions belonging to one province of meaning enclosed by another." Schutz has a further word to say about enclaves. In a discussion of what George H. Mead called "the manipulatory zone" of human agency, Schutz writes:

> The manipulatory zone is that portion of the outer world upon which I can actually act. In a certain sense it might be said that the part of the world within my reach which does not belong to the manipulatory zone transcends

it; it constitutes the zone of my potential manipulations or, as we prefer to call it, of my potential working acts. Of course, these realms have no rigid frontiers; to each belong specific halos and open horizons, and there are even "enclaves" within "foreign territory."[237]

". . . and there are even 'enclaves' within 'foreign territory.'" Gregor, we are told at the beginning of the story, had recently cut out of an illustrated magazine a picture which he had framed and hung in his bedroom. "It showed a lady, with a fur cap on and a fur stole, sitting upright and holding out to the spectator a huge fur muff into which the whole of her forearm had vanished!"[238] The muff is a metaphor for Gregor's enclave. The lady has on three pieces of fur; she is covered on her upper body with fur. In Stanley Corngold's translation, "stole" is replaced by "boa." The essential covering is the cap or hat on the lady's head and the muff which conceals her hand and forearm. Brain and writing organ seem to have been covered over, appear to have receded. Held out to the spectator is a "huge fur muff into which the whole of her forearm had vanished." There may be little point in associating the three pieces of fur with the other "threes" in *The Metamorphosis*. But there is significance in noting the retreat of the hand and forearm. The size of the muff is impressive; it suggests that the hand and forearm are well concealed, that there is *depth* to what has vanished. The "foreign territory" to which Gregor has fled is the banishment-place of transgression. Gregor's life appears to be utterly contained by his job and his family, but the apparently innocent amusement he permits himself in making the frame exposes the fringes of his world of working. The eroticism of the picture of the lady with the muff reveals the "metastability" of the metaphor; that picture not even Grete—especially Grete!—shall have. Gregor presses his hot belly on it.

Was Gregor an exception to the life of the commercial, the traveling salesman, the drummer? So many shady stories begin with the traveling salesman, but Gregor finds the life unsatisfactory. Is Gregor's libido cathectic only toward Grete? Is that his trouble, his guilt? Were his uneasy dreams of his sister? And is his metamorphosis a punishment for unsanctioned love? Obviously, the psychoanalytic approach to *The Metamorphosis* is one way of interpreting its central metaphor. There are other approaches. The loneliness of the writer, the anguish of being blocked in one's art, perhaps the interior paradox of the metaphor being itself a metamorphosis, as Stanley Corngold has suggested, are alternative ways of trying to understand the story. The phenomenological concept of "enclave" is not offered as still another entrance. Rather, we are trying to comprehend a "piece" of a writer "strong in metaphors." The muff as enclave is the emblem of withdrawal to the limit of the paramount reality. The muff overlaps its representational sense when Gregor covers it with his insect-body; he finds the framed cooling surface congenial. At the same time, Gregor announces his intentions: the lady with the muff is *his* and he will not allow its removal from his room. The metaphor of the muff is itself "foreign territory." It is Gregor Samsa's "shady story."

The movement to an enclave is an intrinsic feature of the Lebenswelt. Continuity and interruption are as much a part, a priori, of our existence in the life-world as are familiarity and strangeness. Yet these conditions are far from being esoteric findings by Husserl and his associates. In a way, these events are so familiar that they are strange. Paul-Louis Landsberg has expressed this insight with precision in his remarkable essay on *The Metamorphosis*.

> According to our custom, each morning on awakening we take up our old selves again, unchanged. However, there is no doubt that our body and all that we are have been transformed a little, even during the short space of our sleep. The most modern psychological science is now discovering the truth of the most ancient superstitions. Conditions during our sleep fix the disposition of our being, which in turn influences the character of each one of our days. In truth, everyone who has learned self-observation well knows that every morning it is by means of a certain and peculiar process that we take up our body and soul again and readjust ourselves to the surrounding world. When we have gone to bed the night before in unfamiliar surroundings, it is with a certain difficulty that we realize this fact as we find ourselves once more in the middle of "reality." [Here Landsberg adds a footnote: "This little experience occurs over and over again in the unstable life of a commercial traveler. It is not by chance that Kafka gave his hero this vocation, which like no other tends to render impossible any continuity in life."] Each morning we are a little like travelers who are coming back from far away; each morning we set out once more "in quest of lost time." I myself believe that in this unconscious or subconscious negligence of the transformation, however slight, of our selves and our world during sleep, there is a tendency, a deep rooted instinct calculated to stabilize our coherence and our identity. According to the habits of the world, and according to the laws which science has discovered, it would be quite impossible for us to awake one morning and find ourselves transformed into repulsive insects. But in our customary certainty of the identity of our being and world in general, there is just enough of artificiality, enough will, enough fragility so that Kafka's fiction touches an unacknowledged but anguishing reality, nourished from sources deeper than those of rational reflection and scientific knowledge. This is the only way in which such an incident could be validly introduced. It is on awakening "from a

troubled dream" that the person in question would discover himself transformed. He would discover his metamorphosis in the miscarrying of his daily expectations and the shattering of his effort to re-achieve customary but unconscious continuity.[239]

To be caught in a phenomenological enclave is to be immersed in a "midrash" of meaning and counter-meaning to which there is neither end nor resolution. What has served Gregor in the world of working, in the paramount reality of job and home, no longer exists; it has never existed. The love his family supported him with is as illusory as the "light" that enters his room just before he dies. "He thought of his family with tenderness and love."[240] How is that possible? Gregor accepts his "disappearance"—his death—with the certitude that his death is required not only by his family but himself as well. Does Gregor ever object to anything? Certainly. But it is necessary to see Gregor in the midst of his world. His crawling around his abused room has resulted in his defilement: his insect body has collected the fluff and dust and detritus of his captivity. Gregor carries with him, embedded, transfixed on him, the stuff of battle. His wounds are bandaged not with gauze but with the grime of the floor and the putrefaction of the remains of his feedings: bits, fragments of corruption. Gregor remains alarmingly human. Along with the love he retains for his family are his resentments of them. The "foreignness" of his enclave may be identified by the transtemporal quality of Gregor's life as an insect. For his family, Gregor metamorphosed is Gregor "gone away." In his place is a vast "heuristic" of interpretation. Surely our son and brother would never do this terrible thing to us; it cannot be Gregor who allows his family to suffer such torment. And just as Gregor has made it unnecessary for the locksmith to come by turning the key to his room at excruciating cost, so it appears that the call for a doctor has had no result. Nobody attends Gregor as a patient, as wounded, as a victim of the implacable demands of the natural attitude. He is fought at the same time that he is essentially abandoned.

The shock which signals the movement from one finite province of meaning to another is accompanied, according to Schutz, by a change in the time perspective of the individual who is in movement. In general, the complex time perspectives of the finite provinces of meaning is a central part of their significance. Movement from one finite province to another is not, as Schutz has warned, a simple piece of traffic. The time reality at issue is as involuted as it is directional. The one constant which emerges from this analysis is what Schutz terms the "vivid present" which may be shared between persons in the "we-relation," that is, in situations in which two individuals face or confront each other in the intimacy of shared experience. In a curious but penetrating passage, Schutz writes:

> All of these time perspectives can be referred to a vivid present: my own actual or former one, or the actual or former vivid presence of my fellow-man with whom, in turn, I am connected in an originary or derived vivid present. All this occurs in the different modes of potentiality or quasi-actuality, each type having its own forms of temporal diminution and augmentation and its appurtenant style of skipping in a direct move or "knight's move."[241]

Movement from province to province is not always directly forward or directly to any other side. The "knight's move" is oblique. The meaning of the knight's move in this context is that comprehending the Other may demand "indirect communication," rather than straightforward assault or maneuver. As Schutz has emphasized, in the course of days or even of hours, the individual may move through heterogeneous ranges of experience, each moment of activity demanding different time-perspectives and indirect as well as direct modes of communication.

Yet two phenomenological constants remain: "time" is interpreted in Bergson's terms as *durée*; and the metaphysical consideration which Schutz emphasizes, "*We grow older together.*"[242] The first constant cautions us that "time perspectives" are not features of the world of chronology. *Durée* is inner time, experiential time, *temps vécu*, the time which we live rather than the time which marks the number of hours or minutes an event lasts. It is only by intuition, Bergson maintains, that time as *durée* can be grasped. It is only by the surrender of concepts that the inner life of experience can be approached. He writes: "By intuition is meant the kind of *intellectual sympathy* by which one places oneself within an object in order to coincide with what is unique in it and consequently inexpressible."[243] Intuition here is the true "empiricism," for Bergson. "A true empiricism is that which proposes to get as near to the original itself as possible, to search deeply into its life . . . by a kind of *intellectual auscultation*, to feel the throbbings of its soul; and this true empiricism is the true metaphysics."[244] With the advancement of this view, Bergson is able to say that "*Metaphysics . . . is the science which claims to dispense with symbols.*" Finally, Bergson reminds us: "There is one reality, at least, which we all seize from within, by intuition and not by simple analysis. It is our own personality in its flowing through time—our self which endures."[245] Looking backward, Bergson has entered the passion of *The Magic Mountain*; looking toward the phenomenology of the finite provinces of meaning, we find the philosopher—even before Schutz discovered Husserl—whose doctrine of *durée* is the clue to the meaning of "Multiple Realities." But it is Schutz himself who is responsible for the idea of "growing older together." That concept is, for him, a "metaphysical constant." The one with whom we share a vivid present is also, perhaps, the one with whom we grow older together. Two quite different cases present themselves. When I drop off at the tobacconist's to purchase something, the vivid present we share is brief. The tobacconist goes on living just as I do when I leave his place of business and proceed to my office. Whether I am an old customer or not, the case is the same. The time I spend with my family or with a single member of my family is radically different in its time perspective. Those I live with and those I love are "consociates," in Schutz's language, those "contemporaries" with whom I share space and time. But the implications reach further. Not only my relatives but my friends are, in certain vital ways, consociates. So also, I would say, are the consociates who transcend space and time: certain individuals whose birth I await and certain people who have died but who still share my world. But the time perspectives are different from what is ordinary in the world of working.

And here we come to the crux of Schutz's phenomenology as it applies to *The Metamorphosis*. Gregor transformed into an insect ceases to "grow older" with his family or anyone else. His outward appearance to others, the noises he makes, his "getting loose" in the apartment, his abandonment of the routine of Gregor, the commercial—all this is not the phenomenological clue to Gregor's existential condition. What has reordered the Samsa household is a metamorphosis of time: Gregor and the family are no longer growing older together. The communication closed to Gregor because he cannot be understood by others is but a part of his isolation. More important, perhaps, is Gregor's realization that his family believes that Gregor cannot understand *them*. The infant can make its wants known, though in a limited way. Still, if one thing does not work, another will be tried. The situation does not prevent adults from talking or singing or playing with the infant. Moreover, it is recognized that such efforts are important; the infant needs attention just as it is the pleasure, most often, of those responsible for the well-being of the infant to do their part. Within the natural attitude, "growing older together" is not self-consciously understood as being part of the vitality of life. Hidden in the fens, as it were, is the temporal force which drives the individual, entrapped in the life-world.

"Growing older together" presupposes the "We-relationship" in mundane existence. If, as Schutz believes, the vivid present is the source of the various time-perspectives of lived experience, it must be recognized that, in turn, the vivid present is rooted in the primordial "We-relationship" which is at the root of sociality. The "we" is severed at the outset of *The Metamorphosis*. Whatever the metaphor of the "we" may be—family, association, the sociality of any life—its reversal in Kafka's story reveals the opaque side of the metaphor: the solipsism of a divided if not shattered love, the pathology of the body but, still more important, the heroism of persistence in the face of hostility, overt attack, and the pathos of willed neglect. Gregor maintains his affection, let alone love, for a family which can grasp only what can be given it and nothing of what is required of it. In his descent to obscurity in the world of home, Gregor suffers his fate with grace. *There* is his final victory: grace which cannot be grasped by those he loves or even by himself.

Charles Neider attempts a psychoanalytic interpretation of the story. "In *The Metamorphosis*, the most masochistic piece of his mature period, Kafka portrays himself as a gigantic bug which plagues a decent family. The autobiographical inferences are inescapable." Neider goes on to say of the story: "There is implicit everywhere the neurotic's horror of losing control, and there are hints of fear of the lower depths of sleep, night and dream."[246] *Traum* and "trauma" are too obvious for anyone to make claims. I am of the opinion that Gregor undergoes the latter but has ceased to be capable of the former. At least we can hold to this: no dreams are reported or alluded to after the first sentence of the story. To be sure, there are many people who remember their dreams; are there any individuals who do not have the capacity to dream? How could that be determined? In the case of those who cannot remember dreaming, there is generally the recognition: I had a dream but I cannot remember it. Nothing has happened to Gregor's capacity to remember; but something has happened to his capacity to dream. The transformation has meant thievery. The implications are momentous: Gregor has undergone an upheaval.

If it is not possible to speak of a "current of existence" in the case of Gregor, it is permissible to inquire into his "daily life." Kafka writes:

> During the daytime he did not want to show himself at the window, out of consideration for his parents, but he could not crawl very far around the few square yards of floor space he had, nor could he bear lying quietly at rest all during the night, while he was fast losing any interest he had ever taken in food, so that for mere recreation he had formed the habit of crawling crisscross over the walls and ceiling. He especially enjoyed hanging suspended from the ceiling; it was much better than lying on the floor; one could breathe more freely; one's body swung and rocked lightly; and in the almost blissful absorption induced by this suspension it could happen to his own surprise that he let go and fell plump on the floor. Yet he now had his body much better under control than formerly, and even such a big fall did him no harm.[247]

Gregor the *Luftmensch* is soon grounded. Even then, he is bombarded. But the bombardier, Gregor's father, has lapsed into lassitude. As he is pulled up from his armchair by the women of the house, he comments: "This is a life. This is the peace and quiet of my old age."[248]

The days of clear spaces for Gregor in his room give way to filthy clutter:

> It had become a habit in the family to push into his room things there was no room for elsewhere . . . many things could be dispensed with that it was no use trying to sell but that should not be thrown away either. All of them found their way into Gregor's room. The ash can likewise and the kitchen garbage can. Anything that was not needed for the moment was simply flung into Gregor's room.[249]

The change in the room is not, of course, Gregor's doing, but others have transformed it into the quarters of a miser or an obsessive. In effect, the room has become a kind of attic, a place for life's leftovers. At the same time, we are also able to consider that which presses against perception without mediation and with ultimate conviction: we are returned to Husserl's conception of *Evidenz*. There is a fatality, an unavoidability in Kafka's presentation. We can easily imagine ourselves in a theater seat during a performance of *Waiting for Godot*; we can comfortably settle into an armchair for reading *The Magic Mountain*; but when it comes to *The Metamorphosis* we are already on tiptoe, trying to see over someone's shoulder; the crowd is overbearing, oppressive. And what is there to see? What's the fuss about? Nothing is out of the ordinary. That's just it; it is the ordinary which is strange. Has Gregor changed? Day by day, you can't tell a thing. Suddenly, you find yourself changed. Landsberg said it best:

> Once, years ago, very late at night, I was in my native village. I was climbing a stairway which led to a restaurant on the second floor of a house. It was impossible to climb the stair without seeing oneself in several mirrors. It was surprising, and all the more so for Germany, where mirrors in restaurants are much less common than they are in Paris. As I ascended, I could see my image from the rear, in a great mirror. Suddenly I noticed that there was a small round bald spot on my head which had formerly been abundantly covered with hair. All at once this slow metamorphosis, for certainly I had lost my hair little by little, shocked my sense and my conscience. The feeling which overcame me at that instant was not wounded vanity, nor, as a psychoanalyst would have it, a manifestation of the castration complex, but was, without doubt, a mortal anguish, the anguish of living, a fear of its rapidity, of its incessant progress, and like all fear of life, a fear of its ripe fruit—death.[250]

"I'm being crowded out!" is the speech of the life-world, not phenomenology, but what is signified by that statement has to do with the pressure of life, of living.

Perhaps it is time to renew our contact with the phenomenological concept of Evidenz. The "giving of something-itself" is at the center of Husserl's notion.[251] The immediacy of Evidenz is of vital importance to phenomenology because consciousness inspecting its cargo is concerned with what "originarily" (to use Husserl's term) presents itself—not with representations or copies but only with "first editions," as it were. The grasping of something intentionally *meant* is an assurance not of truth but rather of the ineluctable character of what presents itself to the gaze of consciousness. Nor is Evidenz the full story. "Adequacy," for Husserl, must be considered. Let us say that as a phenomenologist I have faithfully described the Evidenz-presenting phenomenon; that does not assure that I have described all of it. Adequacy calls for fullness. Yet Evidenz itself is perhaps the most rousing conception which Husserl brings to our attention. It must be appreciated in its full force. Husserl writes: "*The concept of any intentionality whatever*—any life-process of consciousness-of something or other—and *the concept of evidence, the intentionality that is the giving of something-itself, are essentially correlative . . . evidence is a universal mode of intentionality, related to the whole life of consciousness.*"[252] In this sense, what is perceived, as it is perceived (the percept qua percept), the noema as it is *meant* is the most critical feature through which consciousness informs perception. In some severe forms of dementia, the patient may see giant insects crawling toward him— see, not "see." To say, as an observer of the scene, that there is, in empirical fact—in actuality—no such insect, that the patient is hallucinating, is not to touch the intentional givenness of a nauseating fear. "It's all in his mind." Yes, where else are precious belongings kept? In the alchemic storehouse of the mind. In what we are pleased to call the lifeworld of normality, what is given in immediacy is the ordinary, the commonplace, the taken for granted, the everyday world of getting up early to meet trains and fulfill the life of the commercial traveler. When that routine existence is halted for some unexpected reason, the weight of its traditional performance crashes through the "membrane" of consciousness and presents in Evidenz the guilty party. The phenomenologist surveys the scene of disaster and scrutinizes the damage. It is an error of vast proportions to suggest that he is insensitive and merely scrupulously describes, as would a perverse anatomist summing up a scene of human butchery with disinterest. Neutrality tells its story. While we have been concerned with some of Husserl's ideas, we have not bracketed Gregor's two questions. Gregor is before us in full Evidenz and adequation; it is his questions which are retreating at an alarming pace. Gregor is the visual equivalent of someone who is shouting so loudly that we cannot understand what is being said.

Along with Evidenz, we have spoken of Husserl's insistence on the "irrealization" of the particular in the comprehension of essence. The *fictive*, once again, is the sovereign sign of phenomenology. Concomitantly, it is the subjunctive which is the preferred mode of phenomenological discourse.[253] Were there more room in the story, we would be able to step back and survey Gregor. As it is, we are herded, jostled, pounded by Kafka's account. The little we can make out of Gregor appears to be indistinguishable from all the rest of the crew. What exactly are we *supposed* to see? We seem to be asking, How is Gregor supposed to behave? Toward the end of the story, the answer to our question is provided clearly enough by Grete:

> "He must go," cried Gregor's sister, "that's the only solution, Father. You must just try to get rid of the idea that this is Gregor. The fact that we've believed it for so long is the root of all our trouble. But how can it be Gregor? If this were Gregor, he would have realized long ago that human beings can't live with such a creature, and he'd have gone away on his own accord."[254]

Grete should know. She should be able, if anyone, to recognize her brother. Or is it only the creature which occupies her thoughts? Near the end of the story, Gregor is trapped in his room:

> Hardly was he inside his room when the door was hastily pushed shut, bolted, and locked. The sudden noise in his rear startled him so much that his little legs gave beneath him. It was his sister who had shown such haste. She had been standing ready waiting and had made a light spring forward, Gregor had not even heard her coming, and she cried "At last!" to her parents as she turned the key in the lock.[255]

The tower clock strikes three in the morning as Gregor breathes his faint, final breath. What terrible punishment must await Grete and her parents!

Gregor's death leaves us desolate. Is phenomenology anodyne? The transcendental reduction leaves Gregor's two questions intact and still burning, but we are left just below the floorboards; not in a human crawl space but in a diminished insect crawl space, populated by roaches, beetles, spiders, and centipedes. They are in their insect life-world, going about their entomological business. The dictionary's last listing for "insect" is: a small, trivial or contemptible person. We have no reason to believe that Gregor is any of these; how, then, can he be considered an insect? That, of course, is not Kafka's question. It may remain a phenomenological question, however. What has happened in *The Metamorphosis* is that the floor, the foundation has crashed altogether. It is well that the Samsas are thinking, at the end of the story, of moving to a different apartment. Their old one is victimized by an invasion of lowlife. The phenomenologist also speaks of "foundations"; indeed, phenomenology is announced as a "foundational" discipline. Has it been regularly fumigated? What lies beneath its inmost floorboards?

Philosophy, it is sometimes maintained, does not concern itself with sentences; its interest is propositions. A proposition is the meaning of a sentence. Following this theory, what propositions do we find in the sentences of *The Metamorphosis?* We are not asking about messages, morals, or platforms, but about meaning. What is the meaning of Kafka's story? The phenomenologist, like Gregor Samsa, is solitary. Is Gregor a methodological or metaphysical solipsist? A comical element in the story is sometimes suggested by critics. In order to determine who the joke is on, we have to know what the joke is. Do we have something like a bad joke here? Is Kafka a jokester? I do not understand what the answer "yes" would mean in these circumstances. The story is not cathartic; it is pitiful. Terror and pity without catharsis. Despite the subjunctive mood, there is nothing Aristotelian about Kafka. But then phenomenology was always closer to Plato, that discerner of essences— "Plato, the erotic bird!"

If there is a moment of fond recollection a reader may have from a story of immense cruelty and the deepest suffering, it may be Gregor's enjoyment in hanging upside down, suspended from the ceiling. That, of course, is what philosophy is, as I have hinted: the enjoyment of what Hegel called the "inverted world." However, Gregor's bequest is not philosophical and it is not regenerative. The bequest is revealed in the final sentence of the story. The reference is to the Samsa family: "And it was like a confirmation of their dreams and excellent intentions that at the end of their journey their daughter sprang to her feet first and stretched her young body."[256]

Grete rises from the debris of her brother's corpse. What, finally, are we to make of Gregor? If phenomenology has not provided an interpretation of Gregor, it has perhaps given aid in understanding his "territory," his placement in the world. The overbearing reality of *The Metamorphosis* may not yield answers, but it has—I believe with phenomenological help—distilled the most penetrating, the most aching questions. Gregor, of course, dies, but it remains problematic as to whether he has starved himself to death, in effect (committed suicide; and if so, for altruistic reasons?), been starved to death, in effect (murdered; death by benign neglect?), or died of still more ancient rites. Have we been given, as has been suggested, a version of the sacrifice of Isaac in which God does not provide the ram? Has Grete been the effective instrument of her parents' will or has she imposed her own will on the family? Whether or not it is the story of Abraham and Isaac, I believe that Kafka has given us in *The Metamorphosis* a primal story of nobility and martyrdom.

Seven

Action

I ABHOR reunions, retreats, and recapitulations. And so, there will be no summaries in these final pages, no reviews. We will simply continue and deepen what we have done. However, I do wish to return to the beginning of this essay, to the discussion of Danto's remarks on the metaphor of the "I." At the outset I wrote that for Danto, truth proves ultimately to be a metaphor of consciousness: the metaphor of the "I" of the consciousness of the reader. What our discussion of the phenomenology of the self attempted to show is that the empirical self, conscious of the world, percipient of the sensory realm, is built upon a transcendental stratum of consciousness, which is the ground for the constitution—the intentional meaning-constitution—of social reality. It follows, if our analysis has been profitable, that the metaphor of the "I" has a deep structure, one which Danto's argument does not reach or take into account. The "I" which is the metaphor of consciousness has no living address, no social security number or card of identity, no bank account, no family relations, no property. But the metaphor of the transcendental "I" is rich in the possibilities of the current of existence, the a prioris of horizon and of the uncanny. It should be emphasized that there is no conflict between the realm of the empirical and that of the transcendental. What I have expressed, then, is not a criticism of Danto's views regarding the metaphor of the "I" but rather an exhortation for more radical analysis. In these terms, it is possible to make good sense of the "I" as both a psychological-empirical metaphor of consciousness and as an intentional-transcendental realm which consciousness reveals upon appropriate phenomenological reduction. Understood in different terms, "good" solipsism is an anatomy of the entire range of the a priori—that "enormous a priori in our minds" which Jean Wahl mentioned to Wallace Stevens in connection with Edmund Husserl.

It is not only helpful but completely necessary to understand the relationship between the empirical and the transcendental, whether in psychology or in the relationship between phenomenology and the natural sciences. There can be no contradiction (or agreement, for that matter) between physics and phenomenology. The two operate at qualitatively different levels, a difference illustrated in the relationship between empirical psychology and phenomenological psychology. In Husserl's early

writings, *Logical Investigations,* before pure phenomenology as a transcendental discipline of intentionality emerged, there was an effort to
distinguish between phenomenology of consciousness and empirical
psychology.[257] At the time the *Logical Investigations* was first published
(1900), Husserl was deeply involved in trying to disentangle his emerg-
ing phenomenological psychology from the views developed in the work
of his teacher, Franz Brentano, especially the latter's important and
influential book, *Psychology from an Empirical Standpoint.* In his late period (the 1920s and 1930s), Husserl had freed himself of Brentano's
constraints and was able to set forth his transcendental results with full
force.[258]

In terms of the ego, the distance between empirical consciousness and
transcendental consciousness is philosophically vast and the difference
qualitatively absolute. The metaphorical "I" of the reader in phenomenological terms leads to the inscription of a priori origins: what is "primal" about the death of Gregor, for example, is that solitude and alone-
ness—the three o'clock in the morning of the soul—are foreordained in
his occupation, in his work, but most importantly, in the two questions
which Gregor asks: "What has happened to me?" and "Will you give a
true account of all this?"

The distinction between the empirical-psychological and the phenomenological-transcendental is vital to the understanding of all of the
major concepts which we have presented and considered, in particular
"current," "horizon," "familiarity" and "uncanniness." Generally understood, the problem with each of these concepts in terms of interpretation is that the temptation to reduce them to their psychologistic level
of meaning appears to be quite inviting to critics who are bent on translating meaning into brain activity. For Husserl such a conversion was
"psychologism," the "naturalization of consciousness." So, for example,
the "current of existence" may be traceable to a particular area of the
brain. I think that the source for this approach to meaning lies in nineteenth-century neurology. More specifically, the fundamental discoveries of Paul Broca regarding the correlation of aphasia with pathology of
the brain and the subsequent work of Carl Wernicke on aphasia led to
the theory of "localization," that is, the association of particular or dis-
crete parts of the brain with the function of language.[259] Husserl's phenomenology is in no position either to support or oppose neurological
theory or neurological findings. Phenomenology operates on a different
level from natural-scientific work. However, "psychologism," in Husserl's view, conflates the two or, more broadly, seeks to ground intentional consciousness in the neurophysiological activity of the brain. Such
conflation does a disservice to any attempt to comprehend consciousness, for it leads the inquirer to search for correlations instead of search-

ing out the presentations of consciousness in neutral or straightforward fashion, without assumptions and presuppositions concerning causation. Husserl's opposition to psychologism is that an insidious philosophical cargo is carried by what is otherwise a value-neutral vessel.

Apart from some generalized reference to the cortex, what area of the brain is to be associated with Ivan Ilych's surmise: "At the law courts . . . Ivan Ilych noticed, or thought he noticed, a strange attitude towards himself. It sometimes seemed to him that people were watching him inquisitively as a man whose place might soon be vacant"?[260] In still larger terms, what area of the brain is to be associated with fictive reality altogether? If significant portions of the human cortex are damaged, presumably stuporous watching will win out over acute reading, but why this is so is quite a different issue from the significance of the "current of existence" in Tolstoy's story.

"Horizon" appears to be the most easily graspable term in Husserl's vocabulary. Illustrations of horizon are easy to come by. So, for example, Alfred Schutz begins his *Reflections on the Problem of Relevance* with a common-sense formulation of the idea:

> Having decided to jot down some thoughts on the matter of relevance, I have arranged my writing materials on a table in the garden of my summer house. Starting the first strokes of my pen, I have in my visual field this white sheet of paper, my writing hand, the ink marks forming one line of characters after the other on the white background. Before me is the table with its green surface on which several objects are placed—my pencil, two books, and other things. Further on are the tree and lawn of my garden, the lake with boats, the mountain, and the clouds in the background. I need only turn my head to see the house with its porch, the windows of my room, etc. I hear the buzzing of a motorboat, the voices of the children in the neighbor's yard, the calling of the bird.[261]

At this level of the natural attitude, horizon may be understood (in its outward reach) simply as one thing in my perceptual field following another, or as zones of intimacy and distance. The a priori underlying this order of horizon involves the possibility of continuation and the possibility of repetition. The a priori of continuation suggests that narratives are conceivable: first this happened, then that happened, followed by still other events. But these are not merely lists of occurrences; it is what connects, what binds events together which is essential to the narrative. For a thematic sequence to be possible there must be the a priori conception of a chain of happenings in which what links the elements of the chain may be said to be capable of supporting the narrative line.

I have made ample use of the term "a priori" throughout these pages. It is important to be clear about its meaning. The literal translation "prior to" inevitably raises the question, Prior to what? And the traditional response is, Prior to experience. But the a priori goes far deeper. Historically, it is essential in modern philosophy to return to Kant. In his *Critique of Pure Reason*, Kant says that "any knowledge that professes to hold *a priori* lays claim to be regarded as absolutely necessary."[262] In his commentary on *The Critique*, Norman Kemp Smith writes:

> The fundamental presupposition upon which Kant's argument rests—a presupposition never itself investigated but always assumed—is that universality and necessity cannot be reached by any process that is empirical in character. By way of this initial assumption Kant arrives at the conclusion that the *a priori*, the distinguishing characteristics of which are universality and necessity, is not given in sense but is imposed by the mind; or in other less ambiguous terms, is not part of the matter of experience but constitutes its form.[263]

Smith's thesis that the fundamental presupposition of Kant's argument—that, in effect, the universality and necessity of the a priori can never be empirically achieved—itself presupposes a deeper assumption on Kant's part: that we have a priori knowledge. That we *have* such knowledge is the deepest assumption of all. However, W. H. Werkmeister argues that much discussion of the a priori in Kant is vitiated by mistranslation in such a way that Kant's a priori is understood as an adjective instead of what it should be—an adverb.[264] It would be a mistake for us to be drawn into a Kantian engagement. It is the case that there are affinities (but also differences) between Kant's use of the a priori and that of Husserl.[265] What emerges as the central result of our discussion at this point is that the a priori for Husserl and for phenomenology is bound to what Husserl terms "eidetic" analysis and is characteristic of an "eidetic method." The method at issue is that of "free variation." Kant's "universality" and "necessity" return in Husserl's eidetic discipline as "*essential universality*" and "*essential necessity*." What is distinctive about the "essential" in this context is that in "free variation" a phenomenon is changed in imagination—varied—so that it becomes possible to see, for example, that in visualizing a green balloon, the color may be varied and the balloon still remain a balloon. In the course of imagining, the phenomenon is intended in its possible (we might say its *fictive*) manifestations. The imagining is a mode of perception in which "every *fact can be thought of merely as exemplifying a pure possibility.*"[266] What is deemed a priori here is not the result of a theoretical construct or a definition which leans on negative qualifiers but rather an intentional seeing which reveals the impulse of empirical perception without utilizing it in any way.

We have considered the external but not the internal horizon, phenomenologically understood. Perhaps that is because the internal horizon, being, I think, a more subtle notion, is more difficult to penetrate and to present. Nevertheless, we will try. Husserl ends his *Cartesian Meditations* with a quotation from Saint Augustine: "Do not wish to go out; go back into yourself. Truth dwells in the inner man."[267] The "inner man" is, above all, a temporal being. The root of the phenomenology of inner-time consciousness may be found in Augustine as well—in the great statement he makes about time in his *Confessions*. Husserl's formulation of "protentions" and "retentions" with respect to the temporality of intentional consciousness is anticipated by Augustine's conception of the "present." But before detailed considerations, Husserl salutes Augustine at the outset of *On the Phenomenology of the Consciousness of Internal Time*:

> The analysis of time-consciousness is an ancient burden for descriptive psychology and epistemology. The first person who sensed profoundly the enormous difficulties inherent in this analysis, and who struggled with them almost to despair, was Augustine. Even today, anyone occupied with the problem of time must still study Chapters 14–28 of book XI of the *Confessions* thoroughly. For in these matters our modern age, so proud of its knowledge, has failed to surpass or even to match the splendid achievement of this great thinker who grappled so earnestly with the problem of time.[268]

In fine, the entire field of inner-time analysis is opened up in Augustine's "proto-phenomenological" examination of the threefold character of time in the *Confessions*. The theme of a temporal or "inner" horizon of perception is carried through in Husserl's reflections from his work on time to his final lectures and manuscripts which comprise *The Crisis*.[269] Alfred Schutz provided us with a very clear illustration of "external horizon"; can we do something similar for "inner horizon"? I am sitting in my study, at home, typing out these words on an old Olivetti Studio 44 portable. Every stroke should but does not remind me that I am manual in an electronic, technological age. As I pound out these sentences, I can pause to remember the occasion in 1962 when I turned in another manual—a Smith-Corona—which had died after living a long and most useful life: I traded for my present machine when it was new. In the more than thirty years which have passed since that trade-in, I can if called upon recite the major events of my life. But the indicators of years, places, personal and family events may be seen as moving back along an inner temporal horizon to what occurred before. The purchase had its history, its horizon.

Horizons are metaphors for the movement of perceptual consciousness. Like all metaphors, horizons are activators of the imageries of space and time; they are journeymen of the a priori. In one of his poems, Dylan Thomas writes that "Death is all metaphors." The line is impressive but perplexing. It is difficult to "cultivate" metaphors; they are not like pearls. Accordingly, adding metaphors or subtracting metaphors is an unlikely procedure. What would *all* metaphors be? *Where* would they be? How would it be possible to know if some metaphors were missing? To be "strong in metaphors" does not mean to possess all metaphors, including the good and the bad. Perhaps the line in Dylan Thomas means that a radical loss of discrimination signals death. "To be strong in metaphors" means that the selective process which yields the most brilliant metaphors is the path toward poetic glory, and "letting everything in" is the negation of poetry, the entrance of death. Anyway, does metaphor have place at all? Is not intense language (or moments of intense language) more like "existence" in a more nearly mathematical sense? Do numbers "exist?" Metaphors are condensations of language in which words *become*, in which words escape their bounds and reverse our perception of what is real. "To be strong in metaphors," then, means on this reading to track the normal for the sake of misleading it, discomforting it, and, in that almost lost word, to alienate it. If metaphors are misleaders, then poets are warriors of another battle, "passionates" of another love.

Horizons may lead to deception but the uncanny appears to be univocal. Freud's essay on "The 'Uncanny,'" which we have had recourse to earlier, places the concept in the sphere of aesthetics, in the domain of feeling. His approach to the meaning of the uncanny is first by way of language: he cites dictionaries, goes into etymologies, and moves from there into folklore and literature. Psychoanalytically, Freud's emphasis turns to what he calls "repetition-compulsion." His own example:

> We of course attach no importance to the event when we give up a coat and get a cloak-room ticket with the number, say 62; or when we find that our cabin on board ship is numbered 62. But the impression is altered if two such events, each in itself indifferent, happen close together, if we come across the number 62 several times in a single day, or if we begin to notice that everything which has a number—addresses, hotel-rooms, compartments in railway-trains—always has the same one, or one which at least contains the same figures. We do feel this to be "uncanny," and unless a man is utterly hardened and proof against the lure of superstition he will be tempted to ascribe a secret meaning to this obstinate recurrence of a number, taking it, perhaps, as an indication of the span of life allotted to him.[270]

Freud turns to "look for undeniable instances of the uncanny."[271] However, we already have our own instances: the séance held by Dr. Krokowski, the mysterious appearance of the record of Valentine's Prayer at that occult meeting, the manifestation of the dead Joachim Ziemssen, and the chilling sense, in my judgment, that the manifestation of Joachim is a prescient image of Hans Castorp. Any of these moments in *The Magic Mountain* qualifies as "uncanny." The uncanny, we must recall, is the reverse side of the familiar. And that reference to the familiar is the reason for our being concerned with the uncanny. The familiar is an a priori of the life-world. That our familiar surroundings and routines *are* familiar is simply taken for granted in daily life. The phenomenologist is interested in the "taken for granted" because the reconstruction of mundane experience is a central concern of a philosopher who stubbornly seeks to uncover the presuppositions of experience. It is a gross simplification to say of familiarity that it reduces to repetition. What does repetition reduce to? If the essence of familiarity lies in the intentional rather than psychological activity of consciousness in constituting the unity of an element of experience, then the essence of the uncanny consists in its sudden and radical departure from the familiar. The experience of the uncanny cannot be planned by the individual who is seized by what is primordially strange. The dread which so often accompanies the uncanny is related to death, to the dead, and to the dying, although the particular way in which such a relationship manifests itself may be an example of the uncanny. I believe that I can illustrate what I mean here by telling a story involving my own experience.

At one period during my college days, I worked the night shift as an orderly in a small, private hospital. Although I had no training in the duties of an orderly, I had read a good bit of medical literature, had spoken to medical personnel in that hospital, and picked up what I had to know rather quickly, one way or another. In addition to preparing male patients for operation (shaving parts of their body), doing catheterization, giving enemas, and performing a considerable variety of minor medical procedures, I was also responsible for preparing the dead for the funeral home personnel, who would ultimately come to carry these corpses away. In a small hospital there were not a great many dead for me to handle. The routine was not complex. After attending to orifices of excretion, I had to place the cadaver on a narrow, rather short gurney. Unlike standard gurneys, the one used for the dead had, in this hospital, sections at both ends which were hinged. During the night shift, few precautions had to be taken regarding other patients in their rooms. I was instructed to close the doors of patients' rooms which were along the path I would follow from the dead man's room to a special elevator I had to use. Most of the patients were asleep. It was usually one or two or three o'clock in the morning when I transported the dead. It was all rather eerie, but not uncanny. Like Hans Castorp, I had a certain resonance with death. However, there came a time (as the lawyers say) when the uncanny crashed through the eerie. The special elevator I was required to use in moving the corpse to the morgue in the basement of the building was barely able to accommodate the gurney and me. With the gurney set alongside one wall, I just managed to squeeze in sideways between the gurney and the other wall; I faced the panel of buttons to be pushed for stopping at the various floors.

The disaster which struck happened in this way. I was escorting a corpse to the morgue. I closed the metal extension door of the elevator and punched the button for the basement. The elevator started its descent. One of the hinged portions of the gurney unaccountably gave way. With its sudden drop, the corpse shifted violently, partially leaving its place on the gurney and pinning me against my side of the wall, while at the same time coming into contact with the operating panel and causing the elevator to stop between floors. The corpse's head and one arm were tight against my face and upper limbs. Even if there had been a telephone in the elevator, I would not have been able to reach it. I was, in effect, sealed in space and in silence; my cries could not possibly be heard. I was impressed with the language of "dead weight." I found it impossible to move in any direction and it was three o'clock in the morning. Only in Dance of Death books could a more bizarre scene be imagined. The corpse's face was hard on mine, his arm was stiff against my arm; it was stifling, and there was nothing I found it possible to do. The special elevator was seldom used and rarely at the hour of my entrapment. In fine: I experienced the uncanny in the smothering desperation of the upset. If I had been frozen in that moment when I lifted the corpse onto the gurney, the scene would have approximated what I experienced in the elevator—an approximation which, in imagination at least, would have been less anguishing. Again, I can only guess at the reports of those who were victims of mass executions but who were wounded, not killed, but left for dead by their executioners and survived by lying motionless beneath the bodies of the dead. This is not a "How did I survive?" story but an account of the onslaught of the uncanny in extremity. The uncanny expressed itself as the loss of all metaphors.

The current of existence, the concept of horizon, familiarity and the uncanny are all aspects of the life-world, but we have not given the life-world its due. It is Alfred Schutz who is phenomenology's spokesman of the Lebenswelt. But Schutz is quick to indicate that the concept of the life-world is not restricted to phenomenology; a host of philosophers of different persuasions have come to the same essential idea. Schutz writes:

> Philosophers as different as James, Bergson, Dewey, Husserl, and Whitehead agree that the common-sense knowledge of everyday life is the unquestioned but always questionable background within which inquiry starts and within which alone it can be carried out. It is this *Lebenswelt*, as Husserl calls it,

within which, according to him, all scientific and even logical concepts originate; it is the social matrix within which, according to Dewey, unclarified situations emerge, which have to be transformed by the process of inquiry into warranted assertibility; and Whitehead has pointed out that it is the aim of science to produce a theory which agrees with experience by explaining the thought-objects of science. For all these thinkers agree that any knowledge of the world, in common-sense thinking as well as in science, involves mental constructs, syntheses, generalizations, formalizations, idealizations specific to the respective level of thought organization.[272]

Although the concept of the life-world has been tacitly acknowledged by a variety of philosophers, it is Husserl who has given it pride of place in his thought and it is Schutz who points out why this is so. Proceeding from a consideration of Max Weber's use of the notion of *Verstehen* as interpretive understanding, Schutz comes to the problem of other minds and the more general issue of intersubjectivity. Alluding to Kant, Schutz says it may be a "scandal of philosophy" that the problem of other minds and of the intersubjectivity of experience has not as yet been solved, "but the solution of this most difficult problem of philosophical interpretation is one of the first things taken for granted in our common-sense thinking and practically solved without any difficulty in each of our everyday actions."[273] But "practically solved" in that passage from Schutz means resolved in the course of mundane experience, not "almost solved" philosophically. The way common-sense thinking "practically solves" the problem of intersubjectivity is by "taking it for granted." In other words, by not recognizing it as a problem at all. This is one way of saying that the natural attitude, for Husserl, assumes intersubjectivity. More fundamentally, the natural attitude tacitly accepts the epistemology of naive realism: *of course* there is a world "out there," and *of course* there are others with whom we communicate. The Other may present a problem in aphasia but not in normality. We may be hard of hearing but we are not hard of intersubjectivity. The life-world is fundamentally characterized, according to Schutz, by its implicit epistemic allegiances, and he goes on to say in what I think is a statement characteristic of his inner style: "And since human beings are born of mothers and not concocted in retorts, the experience of other human beings and of the meaning of their actions is certainly the first and most original empirical observation man makes."[274]

In a major essay on "Phenomenology and the Social Sciences," Schutz promulgates Husserl's intellectual project:

Phenomenological philosophy claims to be a philosophy of man in his life-world and to be able to explain the meaning of this life-world in a rigorously scientific manner. Its theme is concerned with the demonstration and explanation of the activities of consciousness . . . of the transcendental subjectivity within which this life-world is constituted. Since transcendental phenomenology accepts nothing as self-evident, but undertakes to bring everything to self-evidence, it escapes all naive positivism and may expect to be the true science of mind . . . in true rationality, in the proper meaning of this term.[275]

In the passages which follow this statement, Schutz discusses the problems and objections inherent in and traditionally voiced about Husserl's conception of philosophy and the life-world. The problems and objections regarding intersubjectivity stayed with Schutz throughout his professional life and are finally addressed in strength in his essay on "The Problem of Transcendental Intersubjectivity in Husserl."[276] An essential point in Schutz's criticism of Husserl in this context is that the phenomenological concept of "constitution" (which, strictly speaking, has to do with meaning) has subtly shifted into an ontological notion of "creation" (which, strictly speaking, has to do with Being). Schutz considers this shift to be inimical to the original purpose of Husserl's thought:

> At the beginning of phenomenology, constitution meant clarification of the sense-structure of conscious life, inquiry into sediments in respect of their history, tracing back all *cogitata* to intentional operations of the on-going conscious life. These discoveries of phenomenology are of lasting value; their validity has, up to now, been unaffected by any critique, and they are of the greatest importance for the foundation of the positive sciences, especially those of the social world. For it remains true that whatever is exhibited under the reduction retains its validity after return to the natural attitude of the life-world. But unobtrusively, and almost unaware, it seems to me, the idea of constitution has changed from a clarification of sense-structure, from an explication of the sense of being, into the foundation of the structure of being; it has changed from explication into creation . . . The disclosure of conscious life becomes a substitute for something of which phenomenology in principle is incapable, viz., for establishing an ontology on the basis of the processes of subjective life.[277]

In the discussion which followed the original presentation of Schutz's paper on transcendental intersubjectivity (especially the remarks made by Eugen Fink), it becomes quite clear that the basic point made about constitution has to do with Schutz's view of Husserl's treatment of the subject. In that discussion Schutz says: "I strove to show that Husserl's failure to find a solution to this problem [transcendental intersubjectivity] is due to his attempt to interpret the *ontological* status of social reality within the life-world as the constituted product of the transcendental subject, rather than explicating its transcendental *sense* in terms of opera-

tions of consciousness of the transcendental subject."[278] Fink's part of
the discussion is very impressive on its own and most incisive. Two
points which he makes demand attention: his discussion of death and his
references to certain final manuscripts of Husserl's which speak of a primal ego and a primal subjectivity. Fink says:

> The finitude of my life as related to death also belongs, in a fundamental way,
> to [the] intramundaneity of myself and my fellow-men. Can the transcenden-
> tal Ego die? Or is death only an objective fact which belongs to its objectiva-
> tion in the world and which has not truth for its final transcendental inward-
> ness? Consequently, in a way, is not the intramundane human situation
> under-determined when one does not keep in view such determinations of
> human existence as finitude, that is, the fate of death? Does this not concern
> transcendental subjectivity, too?[279]

Regarding Husserl's concern with the primal, Fink says: "According
to Husserl's ideas in these very late manuscripts, there is a primal life
which is neither one nor many, neither factual nor essential; rather, it is
the ultimate ground of all these distinctions: a transcendental primal life
which turns itself into a plurality and which produces in itself the differ-
entiation into fact and essence."[280]

These are indeed dense comments—"dense" in the sense of com-
pacted and not easily penetrated. But if we take a step back, as it were,
and think of what Fink has said in the context not only of our discussion
of phenomenology and of the life-world but of the three fictions we
have tried to understand, it may be somewhat easier to approach him as
the bearer of transcendental questions as well as the carrier of news of
still further depths in Husserl's phenomenology. Death is mysteriously
but cogently present in *Waiting for Godot*:
"Where are all these corpses from?"
"These skeletons."
Obviously, *The Magic Mountain* is death-saturated. And *The Metamorphosis* is a study in transcendental death. Is Gregor simply dead—
dead and nothing more—when he is swept into the dustbin? The answers to his questions have been given: "What has happened to me?"
Answer: You have died. "Will you give a true account of all this?" Answer: Yes, the account will be called *The Metamorphosis*. The third question is self-generated: "Who is giving these answers?" Answer: Franz
Kafka. As to "a transcendental primal life," what other life does Gregor
have? I have suggested that Kafka has, in *The Metamorphosis*, given us a
primal story. I believe that I have at least made a start in elucidating the
phenomenological meaning of the primal.

Hegel said: "The owl of Minerva flies only at dusk." The ideas we
have examined and the notions we have entertained all presuppose what

Schutz terms "the wide-awake adult." We might add: the experienced adult—the person who has "at dusk" looked into the scalding turmoil of life and who has risked exploring its disgraces and pathologies. What image do philosophers have of their readers? It is very hard, in my opinion, to answer that question because it assumes that philosophers do indeed have some conception of their reader. It may well be that the reader in question conforms to an ideal type. Or it may be that the reader is a metaphor which introduces a phantom audience. If it were possible for the author to ask, "Reader, do I know you?" the answer might be lunatic: "'Strangler' Lewis here!" The deciding metaphor of this book is consciousness constituting its world. We might profit by returning still again to Arthur Danto's metaphor of the "I" as the consciousness of the reader. I have suggested that Danto's "I" stands in need of phenomenological enhancement. Danto has told the truth, but he has not told the whole truth. What needs amplification is the status of the dynamic with respect to the "I." Husserl stresses the motility of consciousness, the streaming-forth of intentionality unfolding as the world. The metaphor of the "I" is incomprehensible if that "I" is static; the inwardness of the metaphor is *action*.

One of the most pungent philosophical expressions of human sensibility made in our time was the assertion by George Herbert Mead that "The percept is a collapsed act."[281] Taken flatly, this statement may be ignored; most contemporary philosophers, I hazard, could make no immediate sense of it. The setting will bring forth the sense. Mead is usually understood as part of the pragmatic movement in the United States; in particular, he is associated with the "Chicago School." It is also the case that Mead has had as much impact on the development of sociology as on philosophy. The school of "symbolic interactionism" is profoundly indebted to him. In the past, I have interpreted the thought of Mead in broader, more nearly Continental terms than most writers who undertake an inquiry into his thought. I have no intention of taking the present occasion to settle scores with other students of pragmatic philosophy. My present concern is with Mead's conception of action. What does it mean to say that "The percept is a collapsed act"? It should be indicated at the outset that it is not altogether clear what precisely Mead means by an "act." One aspect of the act, for Mead, comes from the biological idea of a span defined by stimulus and response, which in turn is fundamentally linked to the meaning and status of a "specious present." "The unit of existence is the act, not the moment," Mead writes.[282] But our task at present is not to undertake an examination, in a critical sense, of Mead's thought but to provide some clarification of what he means by his terms. Regarding the act, Schutz—who introduced me to Mead's thought—once said to me that Mead's theory was modeled on the eating of a piece of fruit. And there is indeed some truth to that notion. Perhaps the best way to explain what an act is in Mead's theory is to consider the "insides," so to speak, of the creature. An act, according to Mead, consists of "stages": impulse, perception, manipulation, and consummation. "Impulse" remains rather vague in Mead's account of the act, but it seems to be meant to refer to the purely sensuous moment in, say, the seeing of an object. Mead places particular emphasis on the "distant" object which may be brought into perceptual awareness not only by vision but also by touch. "Perception," Mead writes, "is a relation between a highly developed physiological organism and an object, or an environment in which selection emphasizes certain elements." There is a strong influence of Darwin on Mead's conception of reality. Mead insists that "The object in perception is a distant object." To bring the object closer is to bring it into the "manipulatory area," and that is the sense of the third stage of the act: touching, caressing, handling. The final stage of "consummation" involves, in Schutz's model, eating the apple. And Mead supports this example directly: "The full completion of the act which the distance stimulus initiates is found in some such consummation as that of eating."[283] Obviously, the matter cannot rest there.

For Mead, the act is a process whose stages cannot be separated out ontologically. There are distinctions to be made within a temporal span but not units which can be removed and replaced. Thus, the biological features of a stimulus-response arc do not fully explain what Mead means by perception. But we have enough of Mead now to understand what he intends by the statement, "The percept is a collapsed act." Clearly, "collapsed" has nothing to do with "breaking down"; it refers to a telescoping or condensation of action. The collapsed percept contains what has been or what will be experienced in the stages of the act involving impulse, manipulation, and consummation. The percept is collapsed in the sense that the pleated parts of a camera or a bellows may contract: the accordion at rest. To say, then, that the percept is a collapsed act is to recognize in vision, say, the elements of immediate apprehension, touch, and finality. Such recognition is not basically a theoretical notion but an experiential phenomenon. Sight is virtual touch. And what is so remarkable about Mead's finding is that it is the kernel of a theory of human action—not only an epistemic consideration but a rather passionate view, I would say, of the social world. Seeing is more than believing; seeing is more than seeing. Seeing is subjunctive touching. In turn, touch as the condensed center of perception is the pioneer of the other stages. Of course, consummation is the completion of the act, but it is much more than that. Or, to express the matter in different terms, "completion" is more complex than the devouring of a piece of fruit suggests. No one understood that better than Alfred Schutz.

When does an act begin and when does it end? These are questions which Schutz posed. They are also questions with which Mead was concerned. We may also ask when manipulation begins and ends. He writes: "We approach the distant stimulus with the manipulatory processes already excited. We are ready to grasp the hammer before we reach it, and the attitude of manipulatory response directs the approach."[284] Analogies with the Heidegger of *Being and Time* are obvious. The essential point is that, in the case of consummation, we have to do with an especially complex concept. Included in *The Philosophy of the Act* is part of an article Mead wrote on "The Nature of Aesthetic Experience," a part given the title, "The Aesthetic and the Consummatory."[285] Consummation has a decisive role to play in the realm of value. It should be pointed out that all of Mead's books were posthumously published, edited in most cases by his students. Although Mead published a number of important and substantial articles during his lifetime, his forte was in spoken rather than written language. By all accounts, he was a most brilliant lecturer in class. In fact, most of his books were created out of stenographic notes taken in class by his students. In a way, Mead's writing is composed out of spoken fragments of tremendous power, carrying an internal logic of great force. His *presence* as a teacher, as a lecturer, and as a conversationalist must have been intense. I have met, talked with, known at least half a dozen students of Mead (and the talk was all of Mead) who attested without qualification to his power as a philosopher and thinker whose intellectual originality expressed itself in spoken language. We are fortunate to have those notes, but whatever he did write bears the stamp of his character. Unfortunately, Mead is the most neglected figure of the great pragmatic tradition in the United States.

The central term of Mead's discourse is action; in the full meaning of that term lies the core of our inheritance from him. To say that the percept is a collapsed act is to say that action is the field in which the vital metaphors of our thought are to be discovered. It is important to note, however, that just as Darwin was a significant intellectual influence on Mead's development, so were Whitehead and Bergson. Indeed, Mead's conception of the act is decisively affected by Whitehead's treatment of time. Given the significance of the stimulus-response arc for Mead's theory of perception, it is even more important to understand the temporal suffusion of the elements of that arc to grasp Mead's concept of action. "The response," Mead writes, "is functionally the reality of the stimulation; the end of the act the reality of its beginning. The stimulation implies the response."[286] Although the comparison may seem to be strained at first glance, we are in the neighborhood of existential phenomenology, Sartrean thought in particular.[287] The edges of temporal consciousness flow out; the sense of what is "past" invades a present which is already the anticipated future glancing back at what "went on." Sartre's ecstasies of time are central to the meaning of consciousness as a projective flight, a recouping of what has been in the raking-in of futurity. Of course, the analogy between Mead and Sartre is deeply flawed if we consider the ontological dimension of Sartre's work—a decisive consideration with respect to *Being and Nothingness*. Nevertheless, there *is* an analogy regarding time. Perhaps, if the matter were to be examined in detail, some case might be made for comparing Mead and Sartre by settling on Bergson as a point of connection. Our present way lies in another direction. We are interested in understanding Mead's theory of action—action taken as a dynamic, a unity, which is what Mead envisioned. In *Mind, Self and Society*, a book much more frequently read than *The Philosophy of the Act* (and just as important, certainly, for the understanding of Mead's thought), the philosopher writes: "The social act is not explained by building it up out of stimulus plus response; it must be taken as a dynamic whole—as something going on—no part of which can be considered or understood by itself—a complex organic process implied by each individual stimulus and response involved in it."[288] There is no repudiation of the stimulus-response arc phenomenon in Mead's statement. Rather, to understand the stimulus-response "mechanism" in his terms, we must recognize that in speaking of "stimulus" and "response" we are using a somewhat unreliable, if not treacherous, shorthand regarding what "happens" to the individual. For, in Mead's terms, the "self" is not yet constituted. There is a long distance from the percept to the social self. The measure of "action" is the movement from what Mead calls "gesture" to what he understands by "meaning": "Meaning can be described, accounted for, or stated in terms of symbols or language at its highest and most complex stage of development (the stage it reaches in human experience), but language simply lifts out of the social process a situation which is logically or implicitly there already. The language symbol is simply a significant or conscious gesture."[289] Mead's theory of action shares common ground with phenomenology. The genius of mediation in this instance is Schutz. The phenomenological theory of action is presented in Schutz's essay on "Common-Sense and Scientific Interpretation of Human Action." He writes:

the meaning of an action is necessarily a different one (a) for the actor; (b) for his partner involved with him in interaction and having, thus, with him a set of relevances and purposes in common; and (c) for the observer not involved in such relationship. This fact leads to two important consequences: First, that in common-sense thinking we have merely a *chance* to understand the Other's action sufficiently for our purpose at hand; secondly that to increase this chance we have to search for the meaning the action has for the actor. Thus, the postulate of the "subjective interpretation of meaning," as the unfortunate term goes, is not a particularity of Max Weber's sociology or of the methodology of the social sciences in general but a principle of constructing course-of-action types in common-sense experience.[290]

The first thing to notice is that we have returned directly to action as part of the structure of the life-world. Before we go into that, a smaller point requires clarification. Though that clarification is important, we will limit ourselves in explanation. Why does Schutz say that the "subjective interpretation of meaning" is an "unfortunate term"? Most simply, because "subjective" in Weber's usage refers to "subject-related" and not to subjectivity as some relativistic notion. The subjective interpretation of meaning refers to what the actor ascribes to his action, what he understands by his action, how he interprets his action, how, in fine, he intends his action to be taken or understood. The wretchedness to which Schutz alludes is the seemingly interminable misunderstanding the word "subjective" has generated in the discussion of Weber's views. To return to the life-world: Has a shift in meaning occurred in going from the discussion of Mead to the discussion of Schutz? Are both thinkers concerned with "action" in the same sense of the term? The answer is simply: "Yes." And the "yes" points to the *social* aspect of action. The meaning of action for both men consists in action being embedded in the context of the social. Gesture, symbol—meaning altogether—are constituted in and help to constitute *our* world, the intersubjective reality we are.

Inevitably, the question arises: Is there not a paradox, if not a contradiction, in the relationship of phenomenology to what is egological and what is social? Is there not at least a disparity in the emphasis given by the phenomenologist to the ego and sociality? Is not a reconciliation necessary between what is mine and what is ours? There may be paradox but I find no contradiction between the egological and the social. Apart from the primal ground which Fink spoke of, it has long been maintained by a number of phenomenologists that transcendental subjectivity is intersubjectivity. The formulation may be different but the sentiment is the same. Merleau-Ponty writes:

The true *Cogito* does not define the subject's existence in terms of the thought he has of existing, and furthermore does not convert the indubitability of the world into the indubitability of thought about the world, nor finally does it replace the world itself by the world as meaning. On the contrary it recognizes my thought itself as an inalienable fact, and does away with any kind of idealism in revealing me as "being-in-the-world."[291]

And Merleau-Ponty also writes that "When I return to myself from an excursion into the realm of dogmatic common sense or of science, I find, not a source of intrinsic truth, but a subject destined to be in the world."[292] In *The Crisis of European Sciences and Transcendental Phenomenology*, Husserl has a great deal to say about "the paradox of human subjectivity."[293] And whether or not these were the manuscripts to which Eugen Fink made reference in his discussion of the "primal," Husserl does speak in *The Crisis* of a primal ego. In a passage fundamentally relevant to our present discussion, Husserl writes:

> The "I" that I attain in the epoché, which would be the same as the "ego" within a critical reinterpretation and correction of the Cartesian conception, is actually called "I" only by equivocation—though it is an essential equivocation since, when I name it in reflection, I can say nothing other than: it is I who practice the epoché, I who interrogate, as phenomenon, the world which is now valid for me according to its being and being-such, with all its human beings, of whom I am so fully conscious; it is I who stand above all natural existence that has meaning for me, who am the ego-pole of this transcendental life, in which, at first, the world has meaning for me purely as world; it is I who, taken in full concreteness, encompass all that. This does not mean that our earlier insights, already expressed as transcendental ones, were illusions and that it is not justifiable to speak, in spite of the above, of a transcendental intersubjectivity constituting the world as "world for all," in which I again appear, this time as "one" transcendental "I" among others, whereby "we all" are taken as functioning transcendentally.[294]

We may have succeeded, for present purposes, in abstaining from a serious discussion of the meaning of reduction in Husserlian phenomenology but the cost of that success has come back to haunt us. There is little point at this stage in examining the full significance of epoché, bracketing, and the entire apparatus of phenomenological method. Let us say simply that what is given to the phenomenologist's scrutiny in transcendental reduction may itself be taken as an exemplar of a more primordial stratum of transcendental consciousness, that just as there is an eidetic of the life-world so there may be an *Ur-Welt*, an originary world, of the Lebenswelt. Beyond the distinction between form and content it may be said that there is a distinction to be drawn between the transcendental seen from the standpoint of the phenomenologist and the transcendental understood from the vantage point of the "phenomenological observer." Husserl was concerned for years about the divisibility of the "I"—the I as transcendental subject, the I as transcendental observer, the I as the a priori of consciousness in its intentional history and unfolding. A plethora of "I"-elements, developed in the final period of Husserl's thought, leads to a bewildering image of the ego. Paradox prevails. But what emerges is an enlivened, philosophically refreshed solipsism. Here too paradox prevails.

We are now ready to reassess the claim that "I am the world." From the standpoint of common sense, that claim is absurd. From the standpoint of descriptive phenomenology (or phenomenology as descriptive psychology), the claim is misleading. From the standpoint of transcendental phenomenology, the position of solipsism must be distinguished from the central theses of philosophical idealism. The world and Others in the world are not to be understood as constructions of consciousness. Rather transcendental subjectivity has a primal aspect in which ego and world are polarities which together transcend both methodological and metaphysical solipsism. There may be a "good" and a "bad" solipsism but there is also solipsism as the integrity of an intentional subjectivity which is "in-the-world." The philosophically productive questions to ask now are perplexing. Let it simply be asserted: trapped by language and imprisoned by experience, we simply *are*. And no mockery such as "are what?" will move us, persuade us of another view, another perspective, or another world. It is not a view but a vision of our lives which is called up by solipsism. Visions are made of darkness and light; their substance is Manichean. In Christian terms, the chiaroscuro is quite different.[295]

We are compelled to ask: What does solipsism have to do with action? Is the solipsist-ego an acting agent? If the percept is a collapsed act, then the moment of perception includes, in hidden form, consummation understood as final action. But phenomenology is quite clear regarding action. Let us recall Schutz's distinction between "conduct" and "behavior." The former need not involve outward movement, or action in the public sense. There is action which never comes to the surface. Plans we have not followed up, for example, form an extremely important part of action. There is, indeed, a vast domain of "negative action," that is, the undone, the yet-to-be-done, the abandoned, the phlogiston of imagination. "If an intention to realization is lacking," Schutz writes, "the projected covert action remains a phantasm, such as a day-dream; if it subsists, we may speak of a purposive action or a *performance*. An example of a covert action which is a performance is the process of projected thinking such as the attempt to solve a scientific problem mentally."[296] The action of the solipsistic-ego, in these terms, may be thought of as a negative earthquake of consciousness. The cry, "I am the world" is a

pounding vibration of language, but it is also a return to the formative elements of consciousness: intention understood as conduct, not
behavior.

If the percept is a collapsed act, the present is an abbreviation for the
temporal experience of the individual. An earlier generation in American
philosophy had much to say about "the specious present." The phrase
was taken up by William James in the best textbook ever written: *The
Principles of Psychology*. But James was careful to point out in the body
of his *Principles* that it was Mr. E. R. Clay who was responsible for the
formulation of "the specious present."[297] More recently, the British philosopher C. W. K. Mundle takes up the question of the status of "the
specious present" as a conceptual and experiential notion and finds that
"our problem is also phenomenological":

> The specious present doctrine dissolves into a platitude unless we draw a dis-
> tinction between what is "sensed" (or "immediately experienced" or "directly
> perceived") and what is "perceived" (or "perceptually accepted, recognized
> or judged"). No one doubts that we perceive things changing, that it is cor-
> rect to speak of "seeing" a thing move, and so on. The phenomenological
> question is whether, in such cases, the very recent positions or states of things
> are still being sensed.[298]

The problem of the "specious present" brings us back to the phenomenology of time, to Husserl's doctrine of intentionality, to the distinction between noesis and noema, to the status of Evidenz. At the
same moment, we are reminded of the ego, the transcendental ego, the
metaphor of the "I" as a modality of action. And action brings us back
to the *conduct* which remains hidden but no less consequential in the
economy of life. Finally, we are compelled to confront the paradox
which phenomenology appears to present: the stress on egology and the
recognition of the facticity of the social—the gravity and opaqueness of
the Other. At the eschatalogical last stands the metaphor of solipsism.

What is glimpsed in common-sense fashion regarding solipsism
should not be lastingly ignored. There *is* a foolishness in asserting that
the individual is the sole reality or that the ego's consciousness contains
the entirety of the world. We know such claims to be false in our everyday experience—in the subjectivity of the life-world. The truth is that I
am *not* the Other, cannot ever be the Other, and am myself alone, meta-
physically forsaken, if the truth be told. Yet there remains the distinction
between good and bad solipsism: the philosophical effort to penetrate
transcendental consciousness, to recognize at least the savage limit of
the primal, and to remember the wisdom of common sense while refus-
ing epistemically to accept its precepts. The fundamental situation of
the philosopher is the obverse side of the placement of Schutz's

"wide-awake adult"—that citizen of the Lebenswelt. It is also the case that to be a philosopher is to be strong in metaphors. Perhaps the moral of our study of phenomenology in literature is that philosophy cannot survive without significant metaphors. In this spirit, "I am the world" is a metaphor of union between the transcendental and the inner horizon of the life-world: not the empirical world but the inwardness—the temporality—of mundane existence is the truth of our lives. The fictive does not replace the real but strikes the anvil of possibility in such a way that "pieces" of fire illuminate reality. The tremor of the anvil is action, and action is the metaphor through which it may legitimately be said: I am the world and the world is *ours*.

Notes

Full citations for all references are given in the bibliography.

Chapter 1
Phenomenology in Literature I

1. Reprinted in *Literature and the Question of Philosophy.*
2. Ibid., p. 8. Quoted (with slight corrections) from Daniel Cory, *Santayana: The Later Years*, p. 195.
3. George Santayana, *The Realm of Truth*, pp. 39–40. See Irving Singer, "An Introduction to *The Last Puritan.*"
4. Wallace Stevens, "A Collect of Philosophy," pp. 183–202.
5. Ibid., p. 183.
6. "Monad by monad, then, by way of the course of an immense unity, he achieved God. The concept of this monadic creation seems to be the disappointing production of a poet *manqué*. Leibniz had a poet's manner of thinking but there was something a little too methodical about it. He had none of the enthusiasm of Bruno. There are those who regard a world of monads as poetic. Certainly the idea transforms reality. Moreover, in a system of monads, we come, in the end, to a man who is not only a man but sea and mountain, too, and to a God who is not only all these: man and sea and mountain but a God as well. Yet the idea seems to be completely lacking in anything securely lofty. Leibniz was a poet without flash" (ibid., p. 185).
7. Wallace Stevens, *Letters of Wallace Stevens*; see, for example, letter 796, p. 725.
8. Wallace Stevens, "A Collect of Philosophy," p. 194.
9. "As Gregor Samsa awoke one morning from uneasy dreams he found himself transformed in his bed into a gigantic insect." Franz Kafka, *The Metamorphosis*, p. 67.
10. Ibid., p. 200.
11. Simone de Beauvoir, *La Force de l'âge*, p. 141. I have used the translation by Herbert Spiegelberg in his *The Phenomenological Movement*, p. 485. Note: "my little comrade" is the traditional way in which one "Normalien" greets another.
12. Edward J. Kempf, *Psychopathology*, p. 25.
13. See Erwin W. Straus, *On Obsession.*
14. Cf. Jean-Paul Sartre, who writes: "in emotion, consciousness is degraded and abruptly transforms the determined world in which we live into a magical world. But there is a reciprocal action: this world itself sometimes reveals itself to consciousness as magical instead of determined, as was expected of it. Indeed, we need not believe that the magical is an ephemeral quality which we impose upon the world as our moods dictate. Here is an existential structure of the world which is magical." Jean-Paul Sartre, *The Emotions*, p. 83.

15. Leo Tolstoy, *The Death of Ivan Ilych and Other Stories*, p. 132.

16. Alfred Schutz, *Collected Papers*, Vol. 1: *The Problem of Social Reality*, p. 224.

17. Ibid., p. 146.

18. Ibid., p. 229.

19. Eric Voegelin, *Anamnesis*, p. 33.

20. Edmund Husserl, "Philosophy as Rigorous Science," pp. 110–11.

21. Ibid., p. 115.

Chapter Two
Phenomenology in Literature II

22. Edmund Husserl, *Cartesian Meditations: An Introduction to Phenomenology*, p. 12.

23. Ibid., pp. 15–16.

24. Edmund Husserl, *Ideas Pertaining to a Pure Phenomenology and to a Phenomenological Philosophy*, First Book: *General Introduction to a Pure Phenomenology*, translated by F. Kersten, p. 202.

25. Ibid., p. xx.

26. Wallace Stevens, *Letters*, p. 361.

27. Edmund Husserl, *Ideas* (Kersten translation), pp. 347–48.

28. Edmund Husserl, "Author's Preface to the English Edition" of *Ideas: General Introduction to Pure Phenomenology*, translated by W. R. Boyce Gibson, p. 21.

29. Ibid.

30. Ibid., p. 311.

31. Samuel Beckett, *Waiting for Godot: A Tragicomedy in 2 Acts*, pp. 11 (right), 35 (left).

32. Edmund Husserl, "Philosophy as Rigorous Science," pp. 91–92.

33. Mark DeWolfe Howe, ed., *Holmes-Laski Letters*, Vol. 1, pp. 364, 13.

34. Alfred Schutz, *Collected Papers*, Vol. 1: *The Problem of Social Reality*, p. 75.

35. Camus has expressed this best: "however bitter their distress and however heavy their hearts, for all their emptiness, it can be truly said of these exiles that in the early period of the plague they could account themselves privileged. For at the precise moment when the residents of the town began to panic, their thoughts were wholly fixed on the person whom they longed to meet again. The egoism of love made them immune to the general distress and, if they thought of the plague, it was only in so far as it might threaten to make their separation eternal. Thus in the very heart of the epidemic they maintained a saving indifference, which one was tempted to take for composure. Their despair saved them from panic, thus their misfortune had a good side. For instance, if it happened that one of them was carried off by the disease, it was almost always without his having had time to realize it. Snatched suddenly from his long, silent communion with a wraith of memory, he was plunged straightway into the densest

silence of all. He'd had no time for anything." Albert Camus, *The Plague*, p. 70.

36. Aharon Appelfeld, in a conversation with Philip Roth, in Appelfeld, *Beyond Despair*, p. 64.

37. Leo Tolstoy, *The Death of Ivan Ilych*, p. 116.

38. Edmund Husserl, "Philosophy as Rigorous Science," p. 85.

39. Edmund Husserl, *Ideas* (Boyce Gibson translation), p. 107.

Chapter Three
Phenomenology in Literature III

40. Alfred Schutz, *Collected Papers*, Vol. 1: *The Problem of Social Reality*, pp. 115–16.

41. Aron Gurwitsch, "Problems of the Life-World," p. 35.

42. Edmund Husserl, *The Crisis of European Sciences and Transcendental Phenomenology*, p. 131.

43. Ibid., p. 142.

44. Jean-Paul Sartre, *Anti-Semite and Jew*, p. 60.

45. Alfred Schutz, *Collected Papers*, Vol. 1: *The Problem of Social Reality*, p. 112.

46. Alfred Schutz, *Collected Papers*, Vol. 2: *Studies in Social Theory*, pp. 24, 41.

47. Jean-Paul Sartre, "Intentionality: A Fundamental Idea of Husserl's Phenomenology," p. 5.

48. Ibid.

49. Jean-Paul Sartre, *The Transcendence of the Ego: An Existentialist Theory of Consciousness*, pp. 40, 42. Note: the subtitle of the original French edition is: "Esquisse d'une description phénoménologique."

50. Ibid., p. 39.

51. Aron Gurwitsch, *The Field of Consciousness*, p. 171.

52. Edmund Husserl, *Experience and Judgment: Investigations in a Genealogy of Logic*, p. 50.

53. E. Cobham Brewer, *Dictionary of Phraše and Fable*, p. 393.

54. Sigmund Freud, "The 'Uncanny,'" p. 379.

55. Ibid., p. 397.

56. *Butterworths Medical Dictionary*, p. 181.

57. W. Mayer-Gross, Eliot Slater, and Martin Roth, *Clinical Psychiatry*, p. 459.

58. Thomas Mann, *The Magic Mountain*, p. 9.

59. Ibid., p. 128.

60. Ibid., pp. 266–67. Note: "folderol" is "ete-pe-tete" in the German original.

61. See Friedrich Ueberweg, *History of Philosophy: From Thales to the Present Time*, Vol. 1, p. 117.

62. Jean-Paul Sartre, *L'Imagination*, published in English as *Imagination: A Psychological Critique*; and *L'Imaginaire: Psychologie phénoménolgique de*

l'imagination, published in English as *The Psychology of Imagination*. Note: the bibliographies—Lapointe, for example—cite Bernard Frechtman as the translator of the latter. My own copy merely states: "Translated from the French."

63. Jean Paul Sartre, *The Psychology of Imagination*, p. 270.

Chapter Four
Waiting for Godot

64. Dr. Straus includes his essay on that subject in a part of his book on *Phenomenological Psychology* —a part labeled "Anthropological Studies" (here is a psychiatrist interested in philosophical anthropology). Straus writes: "A breakdown of physical well-being is alarming; it turns our attention to functions that, on good days, we take for granted. A healthy person does not ponder about breathing, seeing, or walking. Infirmities of breath, sight, or gait startle us. Among the patients consulting a psychiatrist, there are some who can no longer master the seemingly banal arts of standing and walking. They are not paralyzed, but, under certain conditions, they cannot, or feel as if they cannot, keep themselves upright. They tremble and quiver. Incomprehensible terror takes away their strength. Sometimes, a minute change in the physiognomy of the frightful situation may restore their strength. Obviously, upright posture is not confined to the technical problems of locomotion. It contains a psychological element. It is pregnant with a meaning not exhausted by the physiological tasks of meeting the forces of gravity and maintaining equilibrium." Erwin W. Straus, *Phenomenological Psychology: Selected Papers*, pp. 137, 148.

65. I read John Lahr's biography of his father after I wrote this line, but I was delighted to see Herbert Berghof's statement that "in Brueghel and Bosch, you have actions pertinent to Beckett. They are doing something very strange and often very silly"; John Lahr, *Notes on a Cowardly Lion: The Biography of Bert Lahr*, p. 276. Note: I almost forgot: the previous line about "stinking breath and feet" is to be found on p. 31 left.

66. Günther Anders, "Being without Time: On Beckett's Play *Waiting for Godot*," p. 146. Note: although my own approach to Beckett's play is different from that of Günther Anders, I would be remiss if I did not express my admiration for his essay.

67. Samuel Beckett, *Waiting for Godot*, p. 37 left and right.

68. Ibid., p. 30 right.

69. Ibid., pp. 25 left, 32 right.

70. Ibid., pp. 56 right–57 left.

71. Ibid., p. 19 left.

72. "Ask him." Samuel Beckett, *En attendant Godot: Pièce en deux actes*, p. 44.

73. Samuel Beckett, *Waiting for Godot*, p. 41 right.

74. "In order to imagine, consciousness must be free from all specific reality and this freedom must be able to define itself by a 'being-in-the-world' which is at once the constitution and the negation of the world; the concrete situation of the consciousness in the world must at each moment serve as the singular motivation for the constitution of the unreal. Thus the unreal—which is always a

two-fold nothingness: nothingness of itself in relation to the world, nothingness of the world in relation to itself—must always be constituted on the foundation of the world which it denies, it being well understood, moreover, that the world does not present itself only to a representative intuition and that this synthetic foundation simply demands to be lived as a situation." Jean-Paul Sartre, *The Psychology of Imagination*, pp. 269–70.

75. Ludwig Landgrebe, *The Phenomenology of Edmund Husserl: Six Essays*, p. 126. Note: the essay from which this quotation is taken is: "The World as a Phenomenological Problem," translated by Dorion Cairns and Donn Welton.

76. Samuel Beckett, *Waiting for Godot*, p. 44 right.

77. Ibid., p. 24 right.

78. Ibid., p. 10 right.

79. Ibid., p. 14 left.

80. Ibid., p. 24 left and right.

81. Ibid., p. 25 right. Note: the French gives the parenthetical direction (*accent anglais*).

82. Ibid., p. 9 left. Note: the French gives "il faut me renvoyer la balle de temps en temps" (p. 18). Is "once in a way" a misprint for "once in a while"?

83. Ibid., p. 34 left.

84. Ibid., p. 51 right.

85. Ibid., p. 9 left and right.

86. Ibid., p. 8 right.

87. Ibid., p. 59 right.

88. I recall reading an interview with Beckett in which the author is asked why his character was named "Lucky." "Because he is," was the reply. Lucky returns but gone is his thinking—at least his speech. If he continues to think, it is in silence. Is that his "luck"? Or is the character "lucky" in the first visit, when Estragon tries to wipe Lucky's tears away with a handkerchief and Lucky kicks him violently? Is the luck in the kick? None of these interpretations is satisfactory. I would say that to the extent Beckett is "answering," he is saying that Lucky has a name. When Vladimir says that they have kept their appointment, he adds: "How many people can boast as much?" and Estragon answers: "Billions" (ibid., p. 51 right). And the names of those billions are unknown, or, like the Unknown Soldier, known but to God. Lucky is lucky, then, in being Lucky. I don't find this an altogether satisfactory explanation of what Beckett might have meant; neither is it an altogether unsatisfactory explanation. On balance—in a world in which unbalance holds sway—it will have to do.

89. Ibid., p. 49 right.

90. As to Lucky's speech, it is evident, if we pick it apart, that there is a message, a counter-gospel regarding human existence. I recall doing that elegant picking about twenty years ago. After the lecture, I was asked whether I had done the picking and found the treasure by myself. "No," I answered, "it's in the secondary literature." My answer was true and also false. I *had* found it on my own, by dint of very hard work and considerable initiative. Having found it, though, I realized that if I could find it so could others. I checked the secondary literature: three or four explorers had gotten there before me. Why bother to explain? Why amend? Who cares for mitigation? I just said "No." That answer

was unjust to myself and it has bothered me for years. Have others been in similar situations and been similarly bothered? Billions. We shall let Lucky's speech go then and consider rather my early labors "crowned by the Acacaca-cademy of Anthropopopometry" (ibid., p. 28 right).

91. Ibid., p. 47 left.

92. Ibid., p. 48 right.

93. Ibid., p. 45 left. Note: in French: "Do do do do," p. 118.

94. Ibid., p. 45 right.

95. Ibid., p. 11 left and right.

96. Ibid., p. 24 right.

97. John Lahr, *Notes on a Cowardly Lion*, p. 262.

98. Ibid., p. 269.

99. Ibid., p. 263.

100. Ibid., p. 281. Note: alas, I missed the New York City production as well.

101. Samuel Beckett, *Waiting for Godot*, p. 35 left.

102. Ibid.

103. Ibid., p. 12 left.

104. Ibid., p. 7 right.

105. Ibid., p. 35 left.

106. Ibid., p. 8 left.

107. *The New Oxford Annotated Bible*, p. 817, annotations.

108. Samuel Beckett, *Waiting for Godot*, p. 8 right.

109. *The Columbia Encyclopedia*, fifth edition, entry for the Dead Sea.

110. Samuel Beckett, *Waiting for Godot*, p. 15 right.

111. Ibid., p. 17 right.

112. Ibid., p. 40 right.

113. Ibid., p. 37 right.

114. Ibid., p. 23 left and right.

115. Ibid., p. 7 left.

116. Ibid., p. 51 right.

117. Ibid., p. 12 right.

118. Ibid., p. 13 left.

119. Ibid., p. 58 left and right.

120. Ibid., p. 60 right.

121. Ibid., p. 31 left.

122. Paul Tillich, *Systematic Theology*, Vol. 2, *Existence and the Christ*, p. 91.

123. *The Encyclopedia of Philosophy*, Vol. 2, p. 307, entry on "Death" by Robert G. Olson.

124. Samuel Beckett, *Waiting for Godot*, p. 41 right.

125. Ibid., p. 59 left and right.

126. Ibid., p. 9 left.

127. Ibid. Note: at one time in the course of the play, the tramps "do the tree," i.e., assume the "shape" of the tree (see p. 49 left and right).

128. Ibid., p. 34 right.

129. Ibid., p. 57 right.

130. Ibid., p. 58 left and right.

131. Ibid., p. 58 left.
132. John Lahr, *Notes on A Cowardly Lion*, p. 253.

Chapter Five
The Magic Mountain

133. Thomas Mann, *The Magic Mountain*, p. 601. Note: there are references to "life's delicate child" throughout the novel.
134. Ibid., p. 596.
135. Ibid., p. 29.
136. Ibid., p. 23.
137. Fritz Kaufmann, *Thomas Mann: The World as Will and Representation*, p. 99.
138. Ibid., p. 16.
139. Fritz Kaufmann, "Art and Phenomenology," p. 191.
140. Thomas Mann, *The Magic Mountain*, p. 86.
141. Ibid., p. 708.
142. Ibid., p. 698.
143. Ibid., pp. 677–78.
144. Ibid., p. 118.
145. Ibid., p. 418.
146. *The Work of Stephen Crane*, edited by Wilson Follett, Vol. 6, *The Black Riders and Other Lines*, p. 56.
147. Edmund Husserl, *Ideas* (Kersten translation), p. 51.
148. Ibid., p. 157.
149. Edmund Husserl, *Ideas* (Boyce Gibson translation), p. 237.
150. Thomas Mann, *The Magic Mountain*, p. 321.
151. Edmund Husserl, *On the Phenomenology of the Consciousness of Internal Time (1893–1917)*, p. 29.
152. Thomas Mann, *The Magic Mountain*, p. 267.
153. This lecture is published together with *The Magic Mountain*, p. 725. Note: I recall (but have not checked) that Samuel Beckett says about *Finnegans Wake* (then "Work in Progress") what Mann says about *The Magic Mountain*: "The book itself is the substance of that which it relates." See Samuel Beckett et al., *Our Exagmination Round His Factification for Incarnation of Work in Progress*.
154. Thomas Mann, *The Magic Mountain*, p. 128.
155. Ibid., p. 9.
156. "But now Joachim had made another discovery, he had fathomed the duplicity of his cousin—without, be it said, any faintest intention of so doing, without having bent his military honour to the office of spy. It happened quite simply that he had been summoned, one Wednesday, from the first rest period, to go down to the basement and be weighed by the bathing-master. He came down the clean linoleum-covered steps that faced the consulting-room door, with the x-ray cabinets on either side: on the left the organic, on the right, round the corner and one step lower down, the analytic, with Dr. Krokowski's visiting-card tacked on the door. Joachim paused halfway down the stair, as he

saw his cousin coming from the consulting-room, where he had just had an injection. He stepped hastily through the door, closed it with both hands, and without looking round, turned toward the door which had the card fastened on it with drawing-pins. He reached it with a few noiseless, crouching steps, knocked, bent to listen, with his head close to the tapping finger. And as the "Come in" in an exotic baritone sounded on the other side, Joachim saw his cousin disappear into the half-darkness of Dr. Krokowski's analytic lair." Ibid., p. 367.

157. Ibid., p. 182.

158. Ibid., p. 100.

159. Ibid., p. 355.

160. Ibid., p. 407. Note: for the discussion that follows regarding Naphta, Lukacs, and Mann, see Judith Marcus, *Georg Lukacs and Thomas Mann: A Study in the Sociology of Literature.*

161. Ibid., p. 118.

162. Ibid.

163. Ibid., p. 486.

164. Ibid., p. 419.

165. Ibid., p. 418.

166. Ibid., p. 409.

167. Ibid., p. 411.

168. Ibid., p. 393.

169. Ibid., p. 405.

170. Ibid., p. 495.

171. Ibid., p. 496.

172. Helmut Kuhn, "The Phenomenological Concept of 'Horizon,'" pp. 107–8.

173. See Thomas Mann, *The Magic Mountain,* p. 596.

174. Ibid., p. 123.

175. See Otto Rank, *The Double: A Psychoanalytic Study.*

176. Thomas Mann, *The Magic Mountain,* p. 654.

177. Ibid., p. 666.

178. Ibid., p. 680.

179. Ibid., p. 681.

180. Ibid.

181. Ibid., p. 105.

182. Ibid., p. 596.

183. Ibid., p. 540.

184. Alfred Schutz, *Collected Papers,* Vol. 2: *Studies in Social Theory,* p. 199.

185. Thomas Mann, *The Magic Mountain,* p. 651.

186. Ibid.

187. Ibid., pp. 91–92.

188. Ibid., p. 114.

189. Ibid., p. 71.

190. Thomas Mann, "The Making of *The Magic Mountain,*" in Thomas Mann, *The Magic Mountain,* p. 726.

191. Thomas Mann, *The Magic Mountain*, pp. 342–43.
192. Edmund Husserl, *On the Phenomenology of the Consciousness of Internal Time (1893–1917)*, p. 375.
193. Thomas Mann, *The Magic Mountain*, p. 267; also see n. 63.
194. Ibid., p. 708.
195. Ibid., p. 706.
196. Ibid., p. 712.
197. Ibid., p. 662.

Chapter Six
The Metamorphosis

198. For a sample see the bibilography in *The Metamorphosis by Franz Kafka*, translated and edited by Stanley Corngold.
199. Vladimir Nabokov, *Lectures on Literature*, pp. 250–83.
200. Franz Kafka, *The Metamorphosis, The Penal Colony, and Other Stories*, pp. 79–80.
201. Max Brod, *Franz Kafka: A Biography*, p. 171.
202. Flannery O'Connor, *The Habit of Being: Letters*, p. 33.
203. John [Johannes] Urzidil, "Recollections" in *The Kafka Problem*, p. 22. Note: this was also pointed out by Stanley Corngold in *Franz Kafka: The Necessity of Form*, p. 51.
204. Franz Kafka, *The Metamorphosis*, p. 67.
205. Ibid., p. 76.
206. Ibid., p. 105.
207. Heinz Politzer, *Franz Kafka: Parable and Paradox*, p. 72.
208. See Stanley Corngold, *Franz Kafka: The Necessity of Form*, pp. 58–59.
209. Hugo Bergmann, *Untersuchungen zum Problem der Evidenz der inneren Wahrnehmung*.
210. E. G. Husserl, *Philosophie der Arithmetik: Psychologische und Logische Untersuchungen*, Vol. 1. Note: this was the only volume published.
211. Evelyn Torton Beck, *Kafka and the Yiddish Theater: Its Impact on His Work*.
212. Franz Kafka, *The Metamorphosis*, p. 82.
213. Ibid., p. 131.
214. Ibid.
215. Alfred Schutz, *Collected Papers*, Vol. 1: *The Problem of Social Reality*, p. 207.
216. William James, *The Principles of Psychology*, Vol. 2, p. 291.
217. Ibid, pp. 292–93.
218. Alfred Schutz, *Collected Papers*, Vol. 1: *The Problem of Social Reality*, pp. 229–30.
219. Ibid., pp. 226–27.
220. Franz Kafka, *The Metamorphosis*, p. 68.
221. Ibid., pp. 68–69.
222. Vladimir Nabokov, *Lectures on Literature*, p. 260.

223. Alfred Schutz, *Collected Papers*, Vol. 1: *The Problem of Social Reality*, p. 233, note.

224. Ibid.

225. Ibid., p. 231.

226. John N. Rosen, *Selected Papers on Direct Psychoanalysis*, 2: 29. Note: he is citing *An Outline of Psychoanalysis* (1940).

227. William James, *The Principles of Psychology*, Vol. 2, p. 294 note.

228. Alfred Schutz, *Collected Papers*, Vol. 1: *The Problem of Social Reality*, p. 241.

229. Joseph Conrad, *Heart of Darkness and The Secret Sharer*, p. 44.

230. Alfred Schutz, *Collected Papers*, Vol. 1: *The Problem of Social Reality*, pp. 243–44.

231. Franz Kafka, *The Metamorphosis*, p. 70.

232. Ibid., pp. 125–26.

233. Ibid., p. 127.

234. Alfred Schutz, *Collected Papers*, Vol. 1: *The Problem of Social Reality*, pp. 228.

235. Isaac Bashevis Singer, "Neighbors," p. 319.

236. Franz Kafka, *The Metamorphosis*, p. 71.

237. Alfred Schutz, *Collected Papers*, Vol. 1: *The Problem of Social Reality*, p. 307.

238. Franz Kafka, *The Metamorphosis*, p. 67.

239. Paul L. Landsberg, "The Metamorphosis," pp. 125–26.

240. Franz Kafka, *The Metamorphosis*, p. 127.

241. Alfred Schutz, *Collected Papers*, Vol. 1: *The Problem of Social Reality*, p. 221.

242. Ibid., p. 220 (italics in the original).

243. Henri Bergson, *An Introduction to Metaphysics*, p. 7.

244. Ibid., p. 36.

245. Ibid., p. 9 (italics in the original).

246. Charles Neider, *The Frozen Sea: A Study of Franz Kafka*, p. 77.

247. Franz Kafka, *The Metamorphosis*, p. 100.

248. Ibid., p. 112. The character and rhythm of these lines might lead a reckless critic to think that the Samsas are assimilated Jews.

249. Ibid., p. 117.

250. Paul L. Landsberg, "The Metamorphosis," p. 129.

251. Edmund Husserl, *Formal and Transcendental Logic*, p. 159.

252. Ibid., p. 160. Note: Dorion Cairns, a student of Husserl and an expert phenomenologist, chooses not to retain the original in this translation.

253. Walter Sokel states: "More than most writers, Kafka favors the subjunctive. The only bridge between the protagonist and his environment is surmise. Kafka's subjunctive acts as the grammatical correlative of the structural device called *anagnorisis*—'discovery'—in Aristotle's *Poetics*." Walter H. Sokel, *Franz Kafka*, p. 11.

254. Franz Kafka, *The Metamorphosis*, p. 125.

255. Ibid., pp. 126–27.

256. Ibid., p. 132.

Chapter Seven
Action

257. "*Pure* phenomenology represents a field of neutral researches, in which several sciences have their roots. It is, on the one hand, an ancillary to *psychology* conceived as an *empirical science.* Proceeding in purely intuitive fashion, it analyses and describes in their essential generality—in the specific guise of a phenomenology of thought and knowledge—the experiences of presentation, judgment and knowledge, experiences which, treated as classes of real events in the natural context of zoological reality, receive a scientific probing at the hands of empirical psychology. Phenomenology, on the other hand, lays bare the "sources" from which the basic concepts and ideal laws of pure logic "flow," and back to which they must once more be traced, so as to give them all the "clearness and distinctness" needed for an understanding, and for an epistemological critique, of pure logic." Edmund Husserl, *Logical Investigations*, Vol. 1: *Prolegomena to Pure Logic*, pp. 249–50.

258. "We must distinguish '*straightforwardly' executed* grasping, perceiving, remembering, predicating, valuing, purposing, etc., from the *reflections* by means of which alone, as grasping acts belonging to a new level, the straightforward acts become accessible to us. Perceiving straightforwardly, we grasp, for example, the house and not the perceiving. Only in reflection do we 'direct' ourselves to the perceiving itself and to its perceptual directedness to the house. In the '*natural reflection*' of everyday life, also however in that of psychological science (that is, in psychological experience of our own psychic processes), we stand on the footing of the world already given as existing." Edmund Husserl, *Cartesian Meditations*, pp. 33–34.

259. For a sympathetic statement of Wernicke's views, see Norman Geschwind, "Aphasia - Clinical Experience and Interpretation." For a critical approach to Wernicke's ideas, see Erwin W. Straus, *Phenomenological Psychology*, ch. 10, "Human Action: Response or Project," pp. 195–216.

260. Leo Tolstoy, *The Death of Ivan Ilych*, pp. 125–26.

261. Alfred Schutz, *Reflections on the Problem of Relevance*, p. 1.

262. Immanuel Kant, *Critique of Pure Reason*, p. 11.

263. Norman Kemp Smith, *A Commentary to Kant's "Critique of Pure Reason,"* p. xxxiii. H. J. Paton comments: "Kant's main ground for attempting a revolution in philosophy is the fact that we possess *a priori* knowledge. Either our ideas must conform to things, or things (as known) must conform to our ideas. If the former hypothesis be adopted, *a priori* knowledge is impossible. Only on the latter hypothesis can the possibility of such knowledge be understood. This is the central and revolutionary doctrine of the *Kritik.*" H. J. Paton, *Kant's Metaphysic of Experience: A Commentary on the First Half of the "Kritik der reinen Vernunft,"* Vol. 1, p. 76.

264. See W. H. Werkmeister, *Kant: The Architectonic and Development of His Philosophy*, pp. 66–68. Note: for a historical survey of the a priori see Rudolf Eisler, *Wörterbuch der philosophischen Begriffe.*

265. See Edmund Husserl, *Ideas* (Kersten translation), pp. 31–32.

266. Edmund Husserl, *Cartesian Meditations*, p. 71.

267. "'Noli feras ire,' says Augustine, '*in te redi, in interiore homine habitat veritas.*'" Ibid., p. 157. Note: the translation I have used is given in a footnote.

268. Edmund Husserl, *On the Phenomenology of the Consciousness of Internal Time*, p. 3.

269. "The world is a spatiotemporal world; spatiotemporality (as 'living,' not as logicomathematical) belongs to its own ontic meaning as life-world. Our focus on the world of perception . . . gives us, as far as the world is concerned, only the temporal mode of the present; this mode itself points to its horizons, the temporal modes of past and future. Recollection, above all, exercises the intentional function of forming the meaning of the past—apart from the fact that perception itself, as the "flowing-static" present, is constituted only through the fact that the static "now" . . . has a horizon with two differently structured sides, known in intentional language as a continuum of retentions and protentions. These first prefigurations of temporalization and time, however, remain in the background. In the recollection founded upon them we have before us, in original intuition, a past—a present which has passed. It too has "being": it has its multiplicities of manners of givenness, its manners of coming to original self-givenness (to immediate self-evidence) as what has passed. Likewise, in expectation or anticipatory recollection, again understood as an intentional modification of perception (the future is a present-to-come), is found the meaning-formation from which arises the ontic meaning of that which is in the future." Edmund Husserl, *The Crisis of European Sciences and Transcendental Phenomenology*, pp. 168–69.

270. Sigmund Freud, "The 'Uncanny'," pp. 390–91.

271. Ibid., pp. 391–92.

272. Alfred Schutz, *Collected Papers*, Vol. 1: *The Problem of Social Reality*, pp. 57–58.

273. Ibid., p. 57.

274. Ibid.

275. Ibid., p. 120.

276. Alfred Schutz, *Collected Papers*, Vol. 3: *Studies in Phenomenological Philosophy*, pp. 51–84.

277. Ibid., pp. 83–84.

278. Ibid., p. 87.

279. Ibid., p. 86.

280. Ibid.

281. George Herbert Mead, *The Philosophy of the Act*, p. 128.

282. Ibid., p. 65.

283. Ibid., pp. 8, 12, 23.

284. Ibid., p. 24.

285. Ibid., pp. 454–59.

286. Ibid., p. 365.

287. "The present of the For-itself [consciousness] is presence to being, and as such it *is* not. But it is a revelation of being. The being which appears to Presence is given as being in the Present. That is why the present is given paradoxically as not being at the moment when it is experienced and as being the unique measure of Being in so far as it is revealed as being what it is in the

Present. Not that being does not extend beyond the present, but this super-abundance of being can be grasped only through the instrument of apprehension which is the Past—that is, as that which is no longer. Jean-Paul Sartre, *Being and Nothingness: An Essay on Phenomenological Ontology*, p. 208.

288. George H. Mead, *Mind, Self and Society: From the Standpoint of a Social Behaviorist*, p. 7.

289. Ibid., p. 79.

290. See Alfred Schutz, *Collected Papers*, Vol. 1: *The Problem of Social Reality*, pp. 24–25.

291. Maurice Merleau-Ponty, *Phenomenology of Pereception*, p. xiii.

292. Ibid., p. xi.

293. Edmund Husserl, *The Crisis of European Sciences and Transcendental Phenomenology*, p. 178 ff.

294. Ibid., p. 184.

295. In *The Last Puritan*, Santayana recounts an especially clever conversation:

> "But if your mother was an Italian, you must be a Cah-tholic?"
>
> "Yes: but I'm afraid I've lost my faith."
>
> "I'm sorry to hear that," said the poor young man gasping, pressing his joined hands between his knees, and gazing upwards in prayer. "And you have become a Protestant?" he ventured less in hope than in fear.
>
> "Sir," I replied, looking at him severely and trying to be as crushing as Dr. Johnson, "I said I had lost my faith, not my reason." George Santayana, *The Last Puritan*, p. 521.

296. Alfred Schutz, *Collected Papers*, Vol. 1: *The Problem of Social Reality*, p. 211.

297. Clay wrote: "The relation of experience to time has not been profoundly studied. Its objects are given as being of the present, but the part of time referred to by the datum is a very different thing from the conterminous of the past and future which philosophy denotes by the name Present. The present to which the datum refers is really part of the past—a recent past—delusively given as being a time that intervenes between the past and the future. Let it be named the specious present, and let the past, that is given as being the past, be known as the obvious past." Quoted in William James, *The Principles of Psychology*, Vol. 1, p. 609. Note: James cites the source of the quotation as "The Alternative," p. 167.

298. C. W. K. Mundle, "Consciousness of Time," p. 135.

Bibliography

Anders, Günther. "Being without Time: On Beckett's Play *Waiting for Godot*," translated from the German by Martin Esslin and revised by the author, in *Samuel Beckett, a Collection of Critical Essays*, edited by Martin Esslin, pp. 140–51. Englewood Cliffs: Prentice-Hall, 1965.

Appelfeld, Aharon. *Beyond Despair: Three Lectures and a Conversation with Philip Roth*, translated by Jeffrey M. Green. New York: Fromm International, 1994.

Beauvoir, Simone de. *La Force de l'âge*. Paris: Gallimard, 1960.

Beck, Evelyn Torton. *Kafka and the Yiddish Theater: Its Impact on His Work*. Madison: University of Wisconsin Press, 1971.

Beckett, Samuel. *En attendant Godot: Pièce en deux actes*. Paris: Editions de Minuit, 1952.

———. *Waiting for Godot: A Tragicomedy in 2 Acts*. New York: Grove Press, 1954.

———. et al. *Our Exagmination Round His Factification for Incarnation of Work in Progress*. London: Faber and Faber, 1929.

Bergmann, Hugo. *Untersuchungen zum Problem der Evidenz der inneren Wahrnehmung*. Halle: Max Niemeyer, 1908.

Bergson, Henri. *An Introduction to Metaphysics*, translated by by T. E. Hulme. New York: G.P. Putnam's Sons, 1912.

Brewer, E. Cobham. *Dictionary of Phrase and Fable*. London: Cassell, 1895.

Brod, Max. *Franz Kafka: A Biography*, translated by by G. Humphreys Roberts and Richard Winston. Second, enlarged Edition. New York: Schocken Books, 1960.

Butterworths Medical Dictionary. Second edition: Macdonald Critchley, editor-in-chief. London: Butterworth, 1978.

Camus, Albert. *The Plague*, translated by Stuart Gilbert. New York: Alfred A. Knopf, 1952.

The Columbia Encyclopedia, edited by Barbara A. Chernow and George A. Vallasi. Fifth edition. New York: Columbia University Press, 1993.

Conrad, Joseph. *Heart of Darkness and The Secret Sharer*, with an introduction by Franklin Walker. New York: Bantam Books, 1981.

Corngold, Stanley. *Franz Kafka: The Necessity of Form*. Ithaca: Cornell University Press, 1988.

———, ed. and trans. *The Metamorphosis by Franz Kafka*. New York: Bantam Books, 1981.

Cory, Daniel. *Santayana: The Later Years, a Portrait*. New York: George Braziller, 1963.

Crane, Stephen. *The Work of Stephen Crane*, edited by Wilson Follett. Vol. 6: *The Black Riders and Other Lines*. Introduction by Amy Lowell. New York: Alfred A. Knopf, 1926.

Danto, Arthur C. "Philosophy as/and/of Literature," in *Literature and the Question of Philosophy*, edited and introduced by Anthony J. Cascardi, pp. 3–23. Baltimore: Johns Hopkins University Press, 1987.

Eisler, Rudolf. *Wörterbuch der philosophischen Begriffe*. Book 1, dritte Auflage. Berlin: Ernst Siegfried Mittler, 1910.

The Encyclopedia of Philosophy. Vol. 2: Paul Edwards, editor-in-chief. New York: Macmillan and Free Press, 1967.

Farber, Marvin, ed. *Philosophical Essays in Memory of Edmund Husserl*. Cambridge: Harvard University Press, 1940.

Flores, Angel, ed. *The Kafka Problem*. New York: New Directions, 1946.

Freud, Sigmund. "The 'Uncanny,' " in *Collected Papers*. Vol. 4 translated by Joan Riviere, pp. 368–407. New York: Basic Books, 1959.

Geschwind, Norman. "Aphasia—Clinical Experience and Interpretation," in *Language and Language Disturbance: The Fifth Lexington Conference on Pure and Applied Phenomenology*, edited by Erwin W. Straus, pp. 195–216. Pittsburgh: Duquesne University Press, 1974.

Gurwitsch, Aron. *The Field of Consciousness*. Pittsburgh: Duquesne University Press, 1964.

———. "Problems of the Life-World," in *Phenomenology and Social Reality: Essays in Memory of Alfred Schutz*, edited with an introduction by Maurice Natanson, pp. 35–61. The Hague: Martinus Nijhoff, 1970. Reprinted in Gurwitsch, *Phenomenology and the Theory of Science*, edited by Lester Embree, pp. 3–32. Evanston: Northwestern University Press, 1974.

Howe, Mark DeWolfe, ed. *Holmes-Laski Letters*. Vol. 1. Cambridge, Mass.: Harvard University Press, 1953.

Husserl, Edmund. *Cartesian Meditations: An Introduction to Phenomenology*, translated by Dorion Cairns. The Hague: Martinus Nijhoff, 1960.

———. *The Crisis of European Sciences and Transcendental Phenomenology: An Introduction to Phenomenological Philosophy*, translated with an introduction by David Carr. Evanston: Northwestern University Press, 1970.

———. *Experience and Judgment: Investigations in a Genealogy of Logic*, revised and edited by Ludwig Landgrebe and translated by James S. Churchill and Karl Ameriks, with an introduction by James S. Churchill and an afterword by Lothar Eley. Evanston: Northwestern University Press, 1973.

———. *Formal and Transcendental Logic*, translated by Dorion Cairns. The Hague: Martinus Nijhoff, 1969.

———. *Ideas: General Introduction to Pure Phenomenology*, translated by W. R. Boyce Gibson. New York: Macmillan, 1931.

———. *Ideas Pertaining to a Pure Phenomenology and to a Phenomenological Philosophy*. First Book: *General Introduction to a Pure Phenomenology*, translated by F. Kersten. The Hague: Martinus Nifhoff, 1982.

———. *Logical Investigations*. Vol. 1: *Prolegomena to Pure Logic*, translated by J. N. Findlay. New York: Humanities Press, 1970.

———. *On the Phenomenology of the Consciousness of Internal Time (1893–1917)*, translated by John Barnett Brough. Dordrecht: Kluwer Academic Publishers, 1991.

————. *Philosophie der Arithmetik: Psychologische und Logische Untersuchungen*. Vol. 1. Halle: C.E.M. Pferrer (Robert Stricker), 1891.

————. "Philosophy as Rigorous Science," in Edmund Husserl, *Phenomenology and the Crisis of Philosophy*, translated with notes and an introduction by Quentin Lauer, pp. 71–148. New York: Harper Torchbooks, 1965.

James, William. *The Principles of Psychology*. 2 vols. New York: Henry Holt, 1893; reprint New York: Dover, 1950.

Kafka, Franz. *The Metamorphosis, The Penal Colony, and Other Stories*, translated by Willa and Edwin Muir. New York: Schocken Books, 1975.

Kant, Immanuel. *Critique of Pure Reason*, translated by Norman Kemp Smith. London: Macmillan, 1950.

Kaufmann, Fritz. "Art and Phenomenology," in *Philosophical Essays in Memory of Edmund Husserl*, edited by Marvin Farber, pp. 187–202. Cambridge: Harvard University Press, 1940.

————. *Thomas Mann: The World as Will and Representation*. Boston: Beacon Press, 1957.

Kempf, Edward J. *Psychopathology*. St. Louis: C. V. Mosby, 1920.

Kuhn, Helmut. "The Phenomenological Concept of 'Horizon,'" in *Philosophical Essays in Memory of Edmund Husserl*, edited by Marvin Farber, pp. 106–23. Cambridge: Harvard University Press, 1940.

Lahr, John. *Notes on a Cowardly Lion: The Biography of Bert Lahr*. New York: Alfred A. Knopf, 1969.

Landgrebe, Ludwig. *The Phenomenology of Edmund Husserl: Six Essays*, edited with an introduction by Donn Welton. Ithaca: Cornell University Press, 1981.

Landsberg, Paul L. "The Metamorphosis," translated by Caroline Muhlenberg, in *The Kafka Problem*, edited by Angel Flores, pp. 122–33. New York: New Directions, 1946.

Mann, Thomas. *The Magic Mountain*, translated by H. T. Lowe-Porter. New York: Alfred A. Knopf, 1955. This edition contains Mann's essay "The Making of *The Magic Mountain*."

Marcus, Judith. *Georg Lukacs and Thomas Mann: A Study in the Sociology of Literature*. Amherst: University of Massachussetts Press, 1987.

Mayer-Gross, W., Eliot Slater, and Martin Roth. *Clinical Psychiatry*. Third edition. London: Bailliére Tindall, 1979.

Mead, George Herbert. *Mind, Self and Society: From the Standpoint of a Social Behaviorist*, edited with an introduction by Charles W. Morris. Chicago: University of Chicago Press, 1934.

————. *The Philosophy of the Act*, edited with an introduction by Charles Morris in collaboration with John M. Brewster, Albert M. Dunham, and David L. Miller. Chicago: University of Chicago Press, 1938.

Merleau-Ponty, Maurice. *Phenomenology of Perception*, translated by Colin Smith. New York: Humanities Press, 1962.

Mundle, C. W. K. "Consciousnes of Time," in *The Encyclopedia of Philosophy*. Vol. 8, edited by Paul Edwards, p. 135. New York: Macmillan and the Free Press, 1967.

Nabokov, Vladimir. *Lectures on Literature*, edited by Fredson Bowers with an introduction by John Updike. New York: Harcourt Brace, 1980.

Neider, Charles. *The Frozen Sea: A Study of Franz Kafka*. New York: Oxford University Press, 1948.

The New Oxford Annotated Bible. New Revised Standard Version, edited by Bruce M. Metzger and Roland E. Murphy. New York: Oxford University Press, 1991.

O'Connor, Flannery. *The Habit of Being: Letters*, edited with an introduction by Sally Fitzgerald. New York: Farrar, Straus, Giroux, 1979.

Paton, H. J. *Kant's Metaphysic of Experience: A Commentary on the First Half of the "Kritik der reinen Vernunft."* Vol. 1. New York: Macmillan, 1936.

Politzer, Heinz. *Franz Kafka: Parable and Paradox*. Ithaca: Cornell University Press, 1966.

Rank, Otto. *The Double: A Psychoanalytic Study*, translated and edited with an introduction by Harry Tucker, Jr. Chapel Hill: University of North Carolina Press, 1971.

Rosen, John N. *Selected Papers on Direct Psychoanalysis*. Vol. 2. New York: Grune and Stratton, 1968.

Santayana, George. *The Realm of Truth*. Triton edition, vol. 15. New York: Charles Scribner's Sons, 1940.

Sartre, Jean-Paul. *Anti-Semite and Jew*, translated by George J. Becker. New York: Schocken Books, 1948.

———. *Being and Nothingness: An Essay on Phenomenological Ontology*, translated with an introduction by Hazel E. Barnes. New York: Philosophical Library, 1956.

———. *The Emotions: Outline of a Theory*, translated by Bernard Frechtman. New York: Philosophical Library, 1948.

———. *L'Imaginaire: Psychologie phénoménolgique de l'imagination*. Paris: Gallimard, 1940. Published in English as *The Psychology of Imagination*, translated by Bernard Frechtman. New York: Philosophical Library, 1948.

———. *L'Imagination*. Paris: Félix Alcan, 1936. Published in English as *Imagination: A Psychological Critique*, translated with an introduction by Forrest Williams. Ann Arbor: University of Michigan Press, 1962.

———. "Intentionality: A Fundamental Idea of Husserl's Phenomenology," translated by Joseph P. Fell. *Journal of the British Society for Phenomenology* 1:2 (May 1970), 4–5.

———. *The Transcendence of the Ego: An Existentialist Theory of Consciousness*, translated and annotated with an introduction by Forrest Williams and Robert Kirkpatrick. New York: Noonday Press, 1957.

Schutz, Alfred. *Collected Papers*. Vol. 1: *The Problem of Social Reality*, edited with an introduction by Maurice Natanson and with a preface by H. L. Van Breda. The Hague: Martinus Nijhoff, 1962. Vol. 2: *Studies in Social Theory*, edited with an introduction by Arvid Brodersen. The Hague: Martinus Nijhoff, 1964. Vol. 3: *Studies in Phenomenological Philosophy*, edited by I. Schutz with an introduction by Aron Gurwitsch. The Hague: Martinus Nijhoff, 1966.

———. *Reflections on the Problem of Relevance*, edited, annotated, and with an introduction by Richard M. Zaner. New Haven: Yale University Press, 1970.

Singer, Irving. "An Introduction to *The Last Puritan*," in the critical edition of *The Last Puritan* by George Santayana, edited by William G. Holzberger and Herman J. Satkamp, Jr. Cambridge: MIT Press, 1994.

Singer, Isaac Bashevis. "Neighbors," in *A Crown of Feathers and Other Stories*, translated by the author and Herbert R. Lottman, pp. 309–320. New York: Farrar, Straus, and Giroux, 1974.

Smith, Norman Kemp. *A Commentary to Kant's "Critique of Pure Reason."* Second edition. Atlantic Highlands: Humanities Press, 1962.

Sokel, Walter H. *Franz Kafka*. New York: Columbia University Press, 1966.

Spiegelberg, Herbert. *The Phenomenological Movement: A Historical Introduction*. Third edition, with the collaboration of Karl Schuhmann. The Hague: Martinus Nijhoff, 1982.

Stevens, Wallace. "A Collect of Philosophy," in his *Opus Posthumous*, edited with an introduction by Samuel French Morse. New York: Alfred A. Knopf, 1966.

(Stevens, Wallace.) *Letters of Wallace Stevens*, selected and edited by Holly Stevens. New York: Alfred A. Knopf, 1966.

Straus, Erwin W. *On Obsession: A Clinical and Methodological Study*. New York: Nervous and Mental Disease Monographs, 1948.

———. *Phenomenological Psychology: Selected Papers*, translated in part by Erling Eng. New York: Basic Books, 1966.

Tillich, Paul. *Systematic Theology*. Vol. 2: *Existence and the Christ*. Chicago: University of Chicago Press, 1957.

Tolstoy, Leo. *The Death of Ivan Ilych and Other Stories*, translated by Alymer Maude with an afterword by David Magarshack. New York: New American Library Signet Classic, 1960.

Ueberweg, Friedrich. *History of Philosophy: From Thales to the Present Time*. Vol. 1, translated by Geo. S. Morris with additions by Noah Porter. New York: Charles Scribner's Sons, 1891.

Urzidil, John [Johannes]. "Recollections," in *The Kafka Problem*, edited by Angel Flores, pp. 20–24. New York: New Directions, 1946.

Voegelin, Eric. *Anamnesis*, translated and edited by Gerhart Niemeyer. Notre Dame: University of Notre Dame Press, 1978.

Werkmeister, W. H. *Kant: The Architectonic and Development of His Philosophy*. La Salle: Open Court, 1980.

Index

About the Author

Maurice Natanson was Professor of Philosophy at Yale University until his retirement in 1995. He is the author of *Anonymity: A Study in the Philosophy of Alfred Schutz*. His book *Edmund Husserl: Philosopher of Infinite Tasks* won the National Book Award in 1974. *The Erotic Bird*, his final book, was completed just before his death in 1996.